EXILES AND EXPATRIATES *in* THE HISTORY *of* KNOWLEDGE, 1500–2000

PETER BURKE

EXILES AND EXPATRIATES *in* THE HISTORY *of* KNOWLEDGE, 1500–2000

THE MENAHEM STERN JERUSALEM LECTURES

BRANDEIS UNIVERSITY PRESS

HISTORICAL SOCIETY OF ISRAEL

BRANDEIS UNIVERSITY PRESS

Waltham, Massachusetts

BRANDEIS UNIVERSITY PRESS / HISTORICAL SOCIETY OF ISRAEL
An imprint of University Press of New England
www.upne.com

Manufactured in the United States of America
Designed by Richard Hendel
Typeset in Arno and Mantinia types by
Passumpsic Publishing

Library of Congress Cataloging-in-Publication Data
available upon request

5 4 3 2 1

In memory of

my grandparents,

immigrants all

For my favorite expatriate,

Maria Lúcia

CONTENTS

FOREWORD

Dror Wahrman

Many years ago in Cambridge I heard an anecdote about Professor Peter Burke, which may well be apocryphal. But as historians we know that stories that are *not* true are often more revealing than those which are. The story was that when Peter came from the University of Sussex, where he taught through the sixties and seventies, for an interview at the University of Cambridge, one of the interviewers asked him, "Dr. Burke, what languages do you know?" Peter's measured response was "Well, I know and use in my work every language from Moscow to Lisbon, but my spoken Norwegian isn't very good." The panel hired him.

In another context, this story could be told about the (surely mistaken) image of the academic hiring process in some old-school university settings back then, which could have been completed without reading the candidate's CV. But I'm invoking this anecdote to introduce Peter Burke because his linguistic skills are truly extraordinary, even unique. They afford him broad access to scholarship and sources in all European languages, allowing him to write books that really take the whole of Europe as their topic, something many claim to do but few actually can.

Another layer was added to this anecdote when I learned years later about Peter's family history, which in itself encompassed the whole of Europe, the same territory spanned by his works. On one side, Peter Burke's father's parents came from the westernmost part of Europe, from Ireland; on the other side were his mother's parents, Jews from Vilnius. (His mother then converted to Catholicism to marry the Irish father.) So Peter's vision of Europe might be taken to a certain degree as genetically determined.

The other formative moment I would like to mention is his military service in Asia — in Singapore, I believe. He was a clerk — therefore by definition bored — and thus he started exploring people quite different from any he'd ever seen before. After developing a considerable appreciation for cultural difference, he came upon a book by the famous anthropologist E. E. Evans-Pritchard. As a consequence, Peter suddenly realized that what he was engaged in was actually what in certain circles is called fieldwork, and that those circles fell under the rubric of anthropology. When he eventually became a historian, he remained one of the main champions of the use of social science methodologies in the writing of history.

So what is Peter Burke a historian *of*? That's a question rather difficult to answer, since there are few topics Peter has *not* written about. Indeed, every time I take a different turn in my own intellectual interests, once I learn the terrain a bit, I find Peter's unmistakable footprints there before me. Writing and teaching recently about the uses of art as historical evidence brought me to Peter's *Eyewitnessing: The Uses of Images as Historical Evidence* (2001). When I took what for me was a surprising step and taught a course about Venice as a unique laboratory of European culture, sure enough: I discovered an early book of Peter's of which I was unaware, *Venice and Amsterdam: A Study of Seventeenth-Century Elites* (1974). And since my current work is about the self-image of an early modern wannabe absolutist ruler, August the Strong of Saxony, and his cultural politics centered on precious objects, I must first contend with Peter's *The Fabrication of Louis XIV* (1992). And so on . . .

So let me conclude with just a few words about three significant directions in Peter Burke's work, including in the book I just mentioned.

In 1978 Peter's *Popular Culture in Early Modern Europe* was published. This was a book with a unique achievement: it provided a major sweeping synthesis of that new and exciting field before—not after!—the field had actually matured in its development. How did he do it? By reading every study and numerous sources from every part of Europe, including Scandinavia and the Balkans, and then putting together a narrative that traced three hundred years of history. The book manifested a profound belief in the unity of Europe during the period before the rise of nationalism: the key variables were not England versus Germany versus

Russia, but highland versus lowland, town versus country, shepherd versus weaver—and also, crucially, elite versus popular culture: how the elites first were enamored of popular culture in the Renaissance, then wagged a finger at it during the Reformation and Counter-Reformation, and finally simply moved away from it completely during the eighteenth-century Enlightenment. The influence of this seminal work is hard to overstate.

The second direction I wish to mention is again one in which Peter, more or less, founded a whole new field: the social history of language. It is hardly surprising that at some point languages became for him not only a powerful tool of research but an object of research in their own right. Several of Peter's books, from *The Art of Conversation* (1993) to *Languages and Communities in Early Modern Europe* (2004), explore the social historian's history of language. How was language used in specific circumstances? How, in a concrete example, did it come to be linked to identities in the period from the fifteenth to the eighteenth centuries? And so on. One could say that Peter brought history into the field of sociolinguistics. (It is also worth mentioning in this context that every one of Peter's major works was translated in turn into a mind-boggling variety of different languages. For *Popular Culture in Early Modern Europe,* for instance, the list includes Albanian, Belarusian, Bulgarian, Chinese, Croat, Czech, Dutch, German, Hungarian, Italian, Japanese, Korean, Polish, Portuguese, Spanish, Swedish, Turkish, Ukrainian—again, a cultural and linguistic reach almost certainly unparalleled among modern historians.)

The last book I'd like to mention for a second time is *The Fabrication of Louis XIV*. This is a book that reconfigured our understanding of the zenith of European absolutism, by treating Louis XIV as the first major modern media event and the king himself as a media mogul—again, long before such formulations became fashionable.

I will stop here, though there are some twenty-five more books to go. But if I may, I would like to end on a more personal note. Peter would surely not remember this, but my standing here now, as a historian of Europe, owes something significant to him. He visited Tel Aviv University in the mid-eighties: I was then a physics PhD student hanging around the history department and trying to figure out whether what they were doing was more interesting than my potential future career in science. We met in the cafeteria of the humanities building and talked at some length about the future in history, as it were. Generously giving of his time, he made the field sound very exciting and accessible (I didn't know about all these languages then . . .). So here I am now, having switched careers as he suspected I would, grateful for the opportunity to offer a few introductory words to the readers of this book, based on Peter Burke's stimulating Jerusalem lectures.

PREFACE

Like my parents, I have been lucky enough not to have the experience of exile, but all four of my grandparents were born outside Britain. My mother's family were exiles in the sense that they were refugees, or to use the dichotomy so frequently employed in studies of migration, "pushed" out of the Russian Empire by fear of pogroms. My father's family, on the other hand, were expatriates, "pulled" from the west of Ireland to the north of England by the hope of a better life, choosing to move to a place that offered new opportunities.

As a British university student and teacher from 1957 onward, I found it impossible not to have known many exiles and expatriates as academic colleagues, to have made friends with some, and to have engaged in discussions with others over the years. At Oxford, I learned much from the seminars as well as the lectures of Edgar Wind, while at St Antony's College, János Bak initiated me into Hungarian history and Juan Maiguashca into Latin American history and much more. Outside Oxford, I learned much from dialogues with Arnaldo Momigliano in a sort of extended conversation that was conducted in three countries and spread over twenty years, as well as from less frequent encounters with Ernst Gombrich and Eric Hobsbawm. In similar fashion, thirty years of conversation with David Lowenthal and Mark Phillips have taught me a good deal about distance—and also about proximity.

At the University of Sussex in its early days, I became a close friend of the sociologist Zev Barbu, a Romanian who opposed the postwar Communist regime, and the art historian Hans Hess, who left Germany in 1933, as well as enjoying frequent conversations with the Indian historian Ranajit Guha, the Anglo-Italian John Rosselli (son of Carlo, an exile murdered by Fascists in France), the philosopher István Mészáros (a former student of Georg Lukács), and Eduard Goldstuecker, who became professor of comparative literature at Sussex when he was forced to leave Czechoslovakia in 1968. In Cambridge, I came to know other exiles, including two more Czechs, Ernest Gellner and Dalibor Vesely, the Slovak Mikuláš Teich, and the Hungarian István Hont, as well as the expatriate Japanese Toshio Kusamitsu.

Other debts are more closely connected with the making of this book. The catalyst was the invitation to deliver the Menahem Stern Lectures to the Historical Society of Israel in spring 2015. I am extremely grateful for the invitation and for the impeccable organization of my visit by Maayan Avineri-Rebhun, as well as for the warm response from the audience, for comments by Elihu Katz, and for hospitality and conversation in Jerusalem with Albert I. Baumgarten, Yaacov Deutsch, Aaron L. Katchen, and especially with Yosef Kaplan.

Pepe González, Tanya Tribe, and Ulf Hannerz all invited me to present papers on the role of exiles in the history of sociology and art history in England, papers that I did not yet know would lead to a book. Pepe's advice and references have helped me improve what I had written about the Spanish exiles of the 1930s in Mexico and elsewhere. Joanna Kostylo, an expatriate Pole, allowed me to read her draft chapters on Italian Protestant physicians in sixteenth-century Poland. Eamon O'Flaherty contributed valuable information about Irish exiles and exiles in Ireland. David Maxwell encouraged me to study Africa and missionaries, and Peter Burschel to focus on what was lost, especially by Germany in the twentieth century. For references, books, suggestions, and e-conversation, I should also like to thank Antoon de Baets, Alan Baker, Ângela Barreto Xavier, Melissa Calaresu, Luke Clossey, Natalie Davis, Simon Franklin, Elihu Katz, David Lane, David Lehmann, Jennifer Platt, Felipe Soza, and Nicholas Terpstra. Audiences for papers on this topic in Ankara, Cambridge, Graz, Madrid, Medellín, Rio de Janeiro, Vienna, and Zurich all gave me ideas. Portions of the manuscript were read by Yosef Kaplan, Mikuláš Teich, and Joan-Pau Rubiés, and the whole book was read by my wife Maria Lúcia García Pallares-Burke, who made her usual valuable suggestions.

EXILES AND EXPATRIATES *in* THE HISTORY *of* KNOWLEDGE, 1500–2000

INTRODUCTION

In 1891, at a time when this observation was not yet commonplace, the great historian of the frontier Frederick Jackson Turner remarked, "Each age writes the history of the past anew with reference to the conditions uppermost in its own time."[1] As we move into the future, we tend to look at the past from new angles. For example, the rise of historical demography in the 1950s was a response to contemporary debates about the population explosion, while the events of May 1968 in Paris stimulated the studies of early modern popular revolt published in the 1970s in France and elsewhere. Today, it is obvious enough that the rise of environmental history responds to current debates about the future of the planet, global history to discussions of globalization, the history of diasporas to concern about migration, and the history of knowledge to debates about our "knowledge society."

Some scholars took up these topics in earlier generations. Immigrants, for instance, were studied by historians who were themselves immigrants (like Piotr Kovalevsky, who wrote about the Russian diaspora), or their children, as in the case of Oscar Handlin, born in Brooklyn to Russian Jewish parents and the author of *Boston's Immigrants* (1941) and *The Uprooted* (1951), or more recently by Marc Raeff, born in Moscow, educated in Berlin and Paris, a professor in New York and the author of *Russia Abroad: A Cultural History of the Russian Emigration, 1919–1939* (1990). All the same, the rise of interest in both the history of diasporas and the history of knowledge since the beginning of the twenty-first century is a remarkable one.

Beginning from present concerns is not a reason for embarrassment, either individual or collective. Professional historians reject what they sometimes call "presentism," but it is necessary to distinguish questions and answers. We are surely right to ask present-minded questions, although we need to avoid present-minded answers, obliterating the otherness or foreignness of the past. In this way historians can contribute to understanding the present through the past, viewing the present from the perspective of the long term.

This book is located at the crossroads of two of the trends just mentioned, the history of knowledge and the history of diasporas, concerned as it is with exiles and expatriates and what might be called their "displaced," "transplanted," or "translated" knowledges. It might be described, like two earlier volumes of mine, as an essay in the social history, the historical sociology, or the historical anthropology of knowledge, inspired by the work of Pierre Bourdieu, Michel Foucault, and Karl Mannheim. Mannheim, who was twice an exile, transplanted from Hungary to Germany and later from Germany to England, argued that knowledge was socially situated. His argument was intended to apply to everyone, but his point is particularly obvious in the case of exiles, who have to respond to major changes in their situation.[2]

The Vocabulary of Exile

To describe more or less forced migration, the Hebrew word is *galut,* while "exiles" is an old term in many European languages.[3] In Italian, *esìlio* is a term used by Dante to describe the state of exile, which he knew all too well, while *èsule,* referring to an individual exile, is used by the sixteenth-century historian Francesco Guicciardini. Ariosto refers to a *prófugo* in the sense of someone who has fled, while Machiavelli uses the more neutral term *fuoruscito,* someone who has gone out. In Spain, the word *exilio* only came into use in the twentieth century. The traditional Spanish term, *destierro,* "uprooting," is vividly concrete in its reference to the loss of one's native land. One relatively optimistic exile, the Spanish philosopher José Gaos, who took refuge in Mexico after the civil war, preferred the neologism *transtierro,* declaring that he "felt not uprooted in Mexico but . . . transplanted" (*no me sentia en México desterrado, sino . . . transterrado*). However, his fellow exile Adolfo Sánchez Vázquez vehemently contradicted Gaos on this point.[4]

Gaos may have been exceptionally fortunate in his new environment, but his concept is a valuable one, like the idea of "transculturation" (*transculturación*) coined by the Cuban sociologist Fernando Ortiz to replace the term "acculturation" used by anthropologists at the time (the 1940s).[5] Unlike "one-sided concepts" such as acculturation or assimilation, *transculturación* and *transtierro* imply that change takes place for both parties in the encounter, as many examples in what follows will suggest.[6]

"Refugees" is a noun first recorded in both French and English, appropriately enough, in 1685, the year of the expulsion of Protestants from France following the Revocation of the Edict of Nantes. Examples of the new word include the *Histoire de l'établissement des François réfugies dans . . . Brandebourg,* published in Berlin by Charles Ancillon, himself a refugee, in 1690, and the anonymous *Avis important aux réfugiés sur leur prochain retour en France,* published in the Netherlands in the same year. The German term *Flüchtling,* someone who has fled, also dates from the seventeenth century, while *Verfolgte,* to refer to someone who is pursued or persecuted, is more recent. "Displaced persons" is a relatively new coinage, first recorded toward the end of World War II, though a *List of Displaced German Scholars* was published in London in 1936.[7]

As for "expatriates," in the sense of voluntary migrants, the term appears in English in the early nineteenth century. Expatriates are sometimes described as having been "pulled" toward a new country rather than "pushed" from their homeland. This mechanistic language obscures the choices that refugees had to make, even if those choices were both hard and limited. In other words, the distinction between voluntary and forced migration is not always a clear one, a difference of degree rather than a difference of kind.[8] To take examples that will be discussed later, in the 1930s some German Jewish scholars in Turkey and some Spanish Republican scholars in Mexico may be described both as exiles (because they were virtually forced to leave their homelands) and as expatriates (because they were invited elsewhere). Again, in the 1970s, some Latin American intellectuals were neither expelled from their homelands nor in serious danger, but left because they rejected undemocratic regimes. In doubtful cases, I shall have recourse to the neutral term "emigrant" or *émigré*, which will also be employed when discussing exiles and expatriates together.

Personal Problems

From a subjective point of view, the label of "refugee" or "exile" is sometimes difficult to accept. The Chilean writer Ariel Dorfman rejected the term "refugee," preferring to speak of himself as an "exile." Again, the German philosopher Hannah Arendt declared in 1943 that "we don't like to be called 'refugees.' We ourselves call each other 'newcomers' or 'immigrants.'" In similar fashion, John Herz (originally Hans Hermann Herz), a leading political scientist who moved from Germany to the United States in the 1930s, spoke not of exile but of his "emigration."[9]

Some individuals accepted none of these labels. They were in denial for some time after their arrival, thinking of themselves as only temporarily absent from their homeland. The sociologist Nina Rubinstein, the daughter of refugees from Russia and later a refugee from Germany herself after 1933, described this initial stage of denial or disbelief as a recurrent one in the history of displacement. Denial is clear enough in the case of some of the Huguenots who left France in the 1680s, like the pastor Pierre Jurieu, expecting an early return. Again, in 1935, two years after his arrival in Britain, the art historian Nikolaus Pevsner "did not see himself as an emigrant or a refugee."[10]

Denial is one story to tell about exiles. There are many others, many of which involve the loss to which the title of this book refers. Transplanting from homeland to what it is convenient to call the "hostland" involves the trauma of displacement and a broken career, feelings of insecurity, isolation and nostalgia for the homeland, along with practical problems such as unemployment, poverty, the struggle with a foreign language, and conflicts with other exiles and with some locals (because the fear or hatred of immigrants is nothing new).[11] Loss of professional status following immigration must not be forgotten, as a number of cases from the "Great Exodus" of Jewish scholars in the 1930s remind us (Karl Mannheim, for instance, Victor Ehrenberg, and Eugen Täubler, all of them discussed in Chapter 5).

The shock of exile also includes the loss of an individual's former identity. It was surely significant that when the refugee art historian Kate Steinitz wrote under a pseudonym, she chose "Annette C. Nobody." The struggle to construct a new identity has often been symbolized by a change of name. Thus the Austrian critic and journalist Otto Karpfen became Otto Maria Carpeaux in his new life in Brazil, while the Polish sociologist Stanisłas Andrzejewski, finding that the English were unable to pronounce his name, changed it to Stanislav Andreski.[12]

In short, for many individuals exile proved to be a traumatic experience, which sometimes led to suicide, as it did for the writer Stefan Zweig and for Edgar Zilsel, a philosopher-historian of science described by a colleague as an "outstandingly brilliant" mind. Both men were Austrian Jews who fled in 1938, when Nazi Germany invaded their country. Zweig ended up in Brazil, Zilsel in the United States. Zweig is still well known, while Zilsel is almost forgotten. He obtained a Rockefeller research grant and a teaching post at Mills College in California, but killed himself with an overdose of sleeping pills in 1944. The broken career of this pioneer in the historical sociology of science has been called a "tragic case of failed transfer of knowledge."[13] Zilsel was not the only exiled intellectual to commit suicide. Other examples include the romance scholar Wilhelm Friedmann, the medievalist Theodor Mommsen, the Spanish historian Ramón Iglesia, the German historian Hedwig Hintze, and the German art historian Aenne Liebreich (the last two killed themselves, like Walter Benjamin, when their escape was blocked).

A major problem for early twentieth-century exiles in particular was the need to become fluent in a new language. The situation of many early modern exiles was easier in this respect, because Latin was the scholarly *lingua franca* in the age of the *Respublica literarum*, while French was spoken and understood in many parts of Europe. The loss of opportunities to use one's native language abroad is probably felt most acutely by imaginative writers like Zweig. Think, for example, of the tragic destiny of the Hungarian novelist Sándor Márai, one of the most successful writers in Hungary in the 1930s and 1940s. Opposing the new Communist regime, Márai left the country in 1948. The regime responded by banning his books in Hungary. Outside the country, the books were free to circulate, but they could be read only by the relatively few people who knew Hungarian. It is scarcely surprising that Márai wrote very little in the forty years of life that remained to him before he too killed himself.

Academic exiles also suffered in this way, although to a lesser degree. One scholar who bore vivid witness to this problem was the Austrian art historian Hans Tietze, who was fifty-eight when he went into exile, "comparing his new language to the enforced use of a sieve which caused all subtle shadings and inflections to drain away." Another was the Italian literary scholar Leonardo Olschki, who took refuge in the United States in 1939, and wrote with black humor that in his circle of fellow exiles, they referred to the sort of English that they were learning to speak as "Desperanto."[14]

Yet another witness was the German art historian Erwin Panofsky, noting that a scholar in the humanities who lives abroad "finds himself in a real quandary. With him the stylistic formulation is an intrinsic part of the meaning he tries to convey. Consequently, when he writes himself in a language other than his own, he will hurt the reader's ear by unfamiliar words, rhythms and constructions; when he has his text translated, he will address his audience wearing a wig and a false nose" (as this passage suggests, Panofsky himself, here writing in English, had himself escaped from the quandary, but some of his colleagues never did). As the exiled art historian Nikolaus Pevsner noted when reviewing the English version of Paul Frankl's classic study of Gothic, the result was "sense lost in transit."[15]

W. G. Sebald, himself living as an expatriate in England (but writing in his native German), distilled many stories about survival and death, adaptation and refusal to adapt in his novels, including the four vividly imagined life histories in *The Emigrants* (*Die Ausgewanderten*, 1992). These stories illustrate the point that Theodor Adorno made, in his usual dogmatic way, after his own return from exile in the United States: "every intellectual in emigration is, without exception, damaged (*beschädigt*)."[16] Exiles are both intellectually and emotionally dislocated.

For a sixteenth-century example, one might cite the scholar-printer Henri Estienne, a Protestant who fled from Paris to Geneva. Estienne was described by his son-in-law, the learned Isaac Casaubon, as "neither able to return home nor to find a place that is right for him elsewhere." This description may remind some readers of the Austrian writer Stefan Zweig's description of himself as "homeless in all countries," or that of the critic Edward Said as "out of place" everywhere.[17]

Thinking of the insecurity of exiles, we might take the case of two Hungarians, both of them Jewish, who fled their country in 1919 when the Soviet-style regime of Béla Kun was displaced by Admiral Horthy and a White Terror began. The philosopher-critic Georg Lukács, living in Vienna, carried a pistol in his pocket to guard against possible attempts to kidnap him and take him back to Hungary. The physicist Leó Szílárd, who was living in Berlin in 1933, kept his most important belongings packed in two suitcases, so that he would be ready to move at any time at a moment's notice.[18]

Expatriates too face serious problems on occasion. They too suffer from nostalgia, even if they can usually return home if they want to. As Malinowski's posthumously published diaries suggest, anthropologists sometimes suffer from a sense of isolation when they do fieldwork among a people with very different habits from their own. Again, expatriates, even able ones, may find it difficult to make a career in the country they have chosen.

Take the case of Rüdiger Bilden, a pioneer in Brazilian and Latin American studies. Bilden was a German who decided to emigrate to the United States as a young man of twenty-one, arriving there just before the outbreak of the World War I. He studied at Columbia University, where scholars of the caliber of Franz Boas believed that he had a brilliant future ahead of him. That future never materialized. Bilden never obtained a permanent academic post, and although he was full of ideas, he published very little. He was in part a victim of his own perfectionism, never finishing his PhD thesis, but he also had the misfortune to be in the wrong place at the wrong time, a German in the United States during two world wars as well as the Great Depression. He died unknown and in poverty, while his younger friend, the Brazilian scholar Gilberto Freyre, made his reputation by developing ideas that Bilden had put forward years earlier.[19] In the history of exiles and expatriates, as in history in general, there are losers as well as winners.[20]

Once heard, the stories of the losers are difficult to forget, like the everyday problems of exile even in the lives of successful individuals. Soon after Pevsner arrived in England, he wrote to his wife, "Swimming in these waters isn't going to be easy. Each sentence, each lecture, each book, each conversation here means something completely different from what it would mean back home."[21] The fact that some émigrés moved from one hostland to another, or to more than one, suggests that settling down was not a simple process. "New niches have new requirements for survival."[22] To succeed abroad, it is often necessary to reinvent oneself, to enter a new field, or to master a new discipline.

The Silver Lining

This book concentrates on some of the positive consequences of exile, the silver lining of the dark cloud, viewing it as one of the "blessings of adversity," as the Dutch anthropologist Anton Blok calls them. Blok argues that individuals who become famous as innovators have usually experienced unusual difficulties in their lives and careers, challenges to which they responded in a creative manner.[23] However, I do not assume that everything happened for the best. The central theme of this study, the distinctive contributions made by exiles and expatriates to the creation and dissemination of knowledge, necessarily privileges the positive aspects. All the same, the broken careers, the books that might have been written, and the contributions to knowledge that might have been made if exile had not happened must not be forgotten, even if such losses can never be calculated. Even the gains are often "unmeasurable," as in the case of German refugee historians of the 1930s, whose "main influence" in Britain and the United States is said to have been in their teaching, in personal encounters rather than publications.[24]

Many exiles succeeded to some extent in transplanting themselves by following one of three strategies, as one of them, the lawyer Franz Neumann, noted in the 1950s: assimilation to the culture of the hostland, resistance to it, or, most fruitful of the three, the integration or synthesis of items from the two cultures.[25] The second strategy for exiles was resistance, by means of self-segregation, an attempt to rebuild their former community on foreign soil, living near fellow exiles, speaking their native language, attending their own schools, reading their own newspapers, worshipping in their own churches, synagogues, or mosques, and so creating a Little Italy, Germany, or Russia with its own patterns of sociability. Nina Rubinstein's dissertation on refugees from the French Revolution emphasized their desire to keep together rather than to adjust to the culture of their hostland.[26] As Neumann suggested, it was also possible to follow some sort of middle way. This book suggests that contributions to knowledge came in particular from the scholars who stationed themselves somewhere between these two extremes.

The experience of exile also varied with different generations. For the first generation of adult migrants, it was usually difficult to adapt to the culture of the hostland. Assimilation was easier for the younger generation, and as a result, role reversal sometimes took place, with the son becoming the "guardian and provider" of his parents — as in the case of the publisher George Weidenfeld, who arrived in London with his family in 1938.[27] As for the third generation, that of the grandchildren, they may not have thought of themselves as exiles at all, although they were still marked by the experience of growing up in a more or less foreign family.

Individuals from all three generations played an important role in both the movement and the creation of knowledge.

The reception of the ideas of the exiles in their new home also varied according to generations in the hostland. The most important part of what the newcomers had to contribute was not information but a way of thinking, a mentality or habitus that differed from the one dominant in the country in which they had settled. As a result, the refugees were not always well understood or appreciated in the hostland by members of their own generation or an older one. The next generation, on the other hand, including students taught by the exiles, was often more open to their ideas. Although many of them did not live to see it, the arrival of the exiles made a difference to their hostlands over the long term.

Focusing

This book presents select case studies in the history of knowledge in Europe and the Americas over the last 500 years or so, more exactly from 1453, when the Ottomans took Constantinople, to 1976, when a military regime was established in Argentina. In order to make this huge subject manageable, it needs to be limited. Despite the importance of "know-how" and of "skill migration," what follows concentrates on scholars and scientists and their contributions to the "commonwealth of learning" and the "republic of science."

Within the academic world, I shall say relatively little about the natural sciences, although brief references to various sciences will recur at regular intervals for comparative purposes. This omission is partly due to what the Catholic Church calls or used to call "invincible ignorance" on my part. In any case, the production of knowledge by scientists depends less on where they are living than is the case in the humanities, even if they discover new plants when living abroad, or produce new hypotheses after discussions with foreign colleagues. In the humanities and social sciences, on the other hand, the effects of displacement on the production of knowledge are more pervasive. In discussing these effects, I shall sometimes privilege examples from my own profession, appropriately enough in a study that has grown out of lectures delivered to the Historical Society of Israel.

Because it is concerned with the dissemination as well as with the production of knowledge, a special place in the book is reserved for a few nonacademic groups, especially translators, printers, journalists, and publishers, who will frequently figure in the following pages, together with some librarians, from Walter Gottschalk at the University of Istanbul to Willi Gutsmann at the University of East Anglia. Indeed, some of the printer-publishers of early modern Europe, for instance, notably the exiles Prosper Marchand and Jean-Frédéric Bernard, viewed their principal role as the propagation of certain kinds of knowledge, and the same point might be made about Russian publishers in Berlin in the 1920s or Spanish publishers in Mexico City and Buenos Aires in the 1940s.

Narrowing the topic down a little more, travelers, students, and diplomats will all be excluded from the expatriates to be discussed here, on the grounds that they tended to live abroad for a relatively short period. So will internal exiles, who oppose the dominant political or religious system and attempt to live in their own country as if they were abroad. Early modern Europe provides numerous examples of individuals who did not accept the official religion in their part of the world but kept their heads down—Jews and Muslims in Christian countries, Catholics in Protestant countries (and vice versa), and groups whose views were unorthodox everywhere, such as the Family of Love, whose members probably included the printer Christophe Plantin, the geographer Abraham Ortelius, and the biblical scholar Benito Arias Montano. In the twentieth century, political dissidents ranged from the Jewish linguist Victor Klemperer, who survived in Hitler's Germany and confided his subversive thoughts to his diary, to the Russian nuclear physicist Andrei Sakharov, who campaigned for human rights and suffered internal exile in the sense of banishment from Moscow to Gorky.

Exiled and expatriate novelists and poets—Camões and Cervantes, for instance, Conrad and Mickiewicz, Joyce and Nabokov —will also be excluded from this study, because one has to stop somewhere, and to put it mildly, the subject of this book remains rather extended. It would not be difficult to write a study of imaginative writers in exile on the same scale as this one. For example, the detachment with which Henry James observed both Britain and the United States fits in very well with one of the central themes of the book.[28] Again, the novels of Ruth Prawer Jhabvala, who was born in Germany, grew up in England, and lived for decades in both India and the United States, reveal the acute vision of the outsider. Turning that sharp eye on her own predicament, Jhabvala declared in a public address in 1979, "I stand before you as a writer without any ground of being out of which to write: really blown about from country to country, culture to culture till I feel, till I am, nothing. As it happens, I like it that way." She returned to this theme on other occasions. "Once a refugee, always a refugee. I can't ever remember not being all right wherever I was, but you don't give your whole allegiance to a place or want to be entirely identified with the society you're living in."[29]

What this book will try to reveal is the extraordinary, disproportionate contribution of both exiles and expatriates not only to the dissemination of knowledge but also to its creation. Living in Britain today, it is difficult to escape awareness of the contribution of exiles and other immigrants to the country's intellectual life (even if some people, including government ministers, manage to do so). All the same, until I began to work on this book, I did not know quite how much so many exiles had contributed, not only in Britain (and still more in the United States, land of immigrants), but in other parts of the world as well.

Method

To measure the importance of the contribution of exiles to knowledge, it would be necessary to compare the achievements of the group with that of a control group of non-exiles, matched with the exiles in all other respects—conditions that are virtually impossible for historians to meet. Instead, what follows concentrates on a few case studies. It will focus on the relation between the contributions to knowledge made by exiles and the situation of the individuals and groups who made them.

Although my approach to the subject will not be truly global, it will at least be comparative. One aim is to combine a panorama, an account of the major movements of exiled scholars in the West over more than five centuries, with case studies presented in more detail and, it is hoped, depth. Another is to keep a balance between an emphasis on recurrent processes and a stress on specific contexts, by means of explicit comparisons and contrasts.

Comparative historians are usually concerned with different places rather than different periods. In my view, however, systematic comparisons and contrasts between different periods of history are also needed, in order to establish what was specific to each. What, for example, are the crucial differences between early and late modernity? As part of a long-term attempt to promote dialogue between early modern and late modern historians, this book is concerned with both periods. For example, the case studies of expatriates compare and contrast the German scholars who worked in eighteenth-century Russia with the French intellectuals who studied and taught in Brazil in the 1930s.

The central comparison—and contrast—offered here will be the one between seventeenth-century Protestant exiles and twentieth-century Jewish ones. The parallel between the two diasporas is obvious enough, and it is no accident that several Israeli historians, among them Myriam Yardeni (who left Romania as a child after World War II), have written on the earlier period while thinking of the later one. Irene Scouloudi, the daughter of a Greek immigrant and the long-serving secretary of the Huguenot Society of London, was also inspired by the parallel between past and present.

Some differences between the two diasporas are equally apparent: the importance of the clergy in the first case, for instance, in an age of confessional migration, versus the importance of professors in the second diaspora, at a time when the role of universities in the dominant culture of knowledge was more important than ever before—or indeed than it has been since the 1930s. Within the second case study there will also be comparisons and contrasts between the effects of the arrival of the refugee scholars on two cultures, British and American, and their influence on two disciplines, sociology and art history.

The analyses offered in this book are based on collective biography or "prosopography," a method that was employed by German historians of ancient Rome and introduced to Britain by the émigré historian Lewis Namier. The main problem raised by this approach to the study of exiled or expatriate scholars might be described as the "iceberg problem." That is, the exiles who are well documented, the "illustrious immigrants," are only the more visible tip of a much larger group.[30] For the early modern period, we often have little more than the names of individual scholars, though it is likely that significant contributions to knowledge were made by many more people whose names have been lost. Only in the case of the great Jewish diaspora of the 1930s is there sufficient information about a sufficient number of scholars to allow analyses of percentages. Even then, as in the case of some of the female scholars named in the appendix, crucial details are missing, even from standard works of reference.

Despite these gaps, collective biography provides significant details, undermines rash generalizations, and allows more of the iceberg than usual to come into view. It reminds us of the importance of contributions made by scholars of the second rank and prevents us from succumbing to what the sociologist Robert Merton famously called the "Matthew Effect" (referring to the passage in the New Testament stating that "to him who hath shall be given"), noting how often the discoveries and the ideas of lesser-known scientists have come to be attributed to a few famous ones.[31]

The individual stories of twentieth-century refugee intellectuals are of course much better known, thanks to their letters and memoirs, than the stories of their early modern colleagues. The secondary literature is also very much richer. For this reason I shall try to practice a form of what Marc Bloch called the "regressive method," asking some of the questions that scholars have asked about the 1930s about the early modern period, the 1680s in particular, but trying to answer them in ways that are appropriate to a more remote time.

1 : THE VIEW FROM THE EDGE

This book is concerned with the special contributions to knowledge made by exiles. For this reason it risks what may be called "triumphalism," dwelling on successes and forgetting failures. Hence it is important to emphasize, right from the start, that outsiders suffer from limitations, especially the lack of local or insider knowledge. Conversely, insiders as well as outsiders enjoy what are known as "cognitive privileges," although their contributions to knowledge are not the subject of this book. It has also been observed that "not every work of history written in exile is significant and innovative [. . .] emigrants tend to have their own prejudices, defences and resentments."[1] This observation is surely valid for other disciplines as well as for history. All the same, the open conflict between different prejudices may lead to new insights.

The reason for writing this study is not simply to list the various contributions that exiles have made to knowledge but also to ask what made those contributions distinctive. It will examine "process" as well as "product," attempting to discover how the various contributions to knowledge by *émigrés* were made.[2] This question might be answered in a word, "deprovincialization." More exactly, the encounter between the exiles and their hosts led to a process of double deprovincialization. The exiles were deprovincialized by their movement from one culture to another. They also helped to deprovincialize their hosts by presenting them not only with different knowledges but also, still more important, with alternative ways of thinking. In short, exile, and to a lesser extent, expatriation, was an education for both sides of this encounter.

Exile as Education

The fundamental question that this book attempts to answer is whether a distinctive contribution to knowledge has been made by exiles and expatriates in different places and times. This section offers a preview of the conclusions of this study, which the following chapters will attempt to justify. It suggests that exile is a form of education, a tough form of education for the exiles themselves and a gentler one for some of the individuals who encountered them in the hostland.

Presenting exile as education — even as what might be called an unsentimental education — runs the obvious risk of underestimating the negative side of these events. Emigrants who segregate themselves may learn nothing as well as forgetting nothing, as Talleyrand said of the royal family when they returned to France after 1815. Conversely, hosts often fail to learn from the newcomers, and misunderstandings often occur.

All the same, in many cases, something valuable is learned by both parties to the encounter. Exiles gain new insights, a kind of reward for the struggle to survive in an alien culture. Expatriates also learn from their experiences abroad, although the pressures to learn are not so strong in their case, because they have an exit strategy. They have, in a manner of speaking, a return ticket in their pocket, together with the expectation of returning home at some point. As for citizens of the hostland, students who encountered exiled scholars often discovered something that they could not have learned from other teachers, as I can testify from personal experience, in Oxford in the 1950s. The same can be said about students in the former homeland in cases in which exiles returned.

The Return of the Native

Most of this study is concerned with the interaction between exiles or expatriates and the culture of the country to which they have moved, but there is also something to say about the consequences for knowledge in the original homelands of the emigrants. The negative consequences of the "brain drain" are obvious enough, but there are sometimes positive consequences as well, at least when some exiles return or "remigrate." As we shall see in a later chapter, a number of returned exiles brought new ideas and new methods back with them to Germany after 1945.

Another striking example of "the return of the native" is that of the Brazilian historian and sociologist Gilberto Freyre, who was sent by his family to study in the United States for almost five years from the age of eighteen onward. Two intense months in England, mainly in Oxford, convinced him that he should have been born an Englishman. When he visited Lisbon, he viewed it "with English eyes rather than Brazilian ones." It might be argued that he saw Brazil in a similar way after his return to his native province of Pernambuco in 1923. The great strength of the book that made him famous, *Casa Grande e Senzala* (1933), which views colonial Brazil through the prism of its sugar plantations, was described by one of Freyre's most perceptive critics, the anthropologist Darcy Ribeiro, as its combination of the perspectives of insider and outsider, thanks to the author's two identities, "the Pernambucan and the Englishman."[3]

Deprovincialization

The kind of education just described may be summed up as a widening of horizons or a process of deprovincialization. The German theologian Paul Tillich remarked that it was only when he was living in the United States that he "became aware" of his "formerly unconscious provincialism" and that it gradually "began to recede," so that he no longer viewed Germany as the center of theological studies. According to a community study by two anthropologists, the inhabitants of the village of Átány used to joke that "Hungary is in the center of the world, Átány is in the center of Hungary."[4] Joking apart, one possible definition of provincialism is to believe that one's community is at the center of the world (the American sociologist William G. Sumner defined ethnocentrism as "the view of things in which one's own group is the center of everything").[5] Tillich's testimony is not the only firsthand account of this process. The German historian Hajo Holborn, for instance, who moved to the United States in 1934 and became a professor at Yale, declared, "My transformation into an American has given me a much broader perspective on all things German."[6]

Similarly, the Peruvian journalist and theorist José Maria Mariátegui, who lived in Italy in the 1920s, declared that his years abroad had widened his horizons and described himself as "departing for a foreign country not in search of the secret of others but in search of our own secret." As the English writer G. K. Chesterton once wrote, "the object of travel is not to set foot on a foreign land; it is at last to set foot on one's own country as a foreign land." The Brazilian journalist (and later, historian) Sergio Buarque, who spent the years 1929–30 in Berlin, declared in later life, "It is only when you get far away that you begin to see your own country whole."[7] As the German historian Ernst Kantorowicz once wrote, "An advantage is in-dwelling in every disadvantage."[8]

Deprovincialization is what has been called an "umbrella term," erected over different processes. It may be useful to distinguish three such processes. The first is mediation, the second is detachment, and the third is hybridization.

Mediation

Writing about what he called the "function" of refugees, Karl Mannheim emphasized their opportunities for mediation between the culture of their homeland and that of the country to which they had fled.[9] Mediation includes dissemination, and for this reason a number of printers and publishers will make their appearance in this study. Attempts at dissemination face obvious linguistic obstacles. All the same, the native language of exiles is sometimes an asset as well as a liability in their new home. It is a form of intellectual capital, allowing them to make a living by giving language lessons or by producing grammars and dictionaries. Some of the Greek refugees from the Ottoman conquest of Byzantium gave lessons in ancient Greek, while a number of the French Protestants in exile in Amsterdam, London, and Berlin made their living as language teachers. Their displacement turned many exiles into translators, appropriately enough, perhaps, because they themselves had been "translated" in the archaic sense of that English verb, in other words transferred from one place to another.

Mediation between languages easily extends to mediation between cultures. Greek scholars in Renaissance Italy introduced some of their hosts to the world of ancient Greece. Huguenot refugees spread the knowledge of French culture. Russian exiles in Britain and the United States, among them Isaiah Berlin, George Florovsky, and George Vernadsky, spread the knowledge of Russian culture. German Jewish scholars who came to the United States and Britain from the 1930s onward taught German history and published books about it. Whether they are prompted by nostalgia or the need for employment, some scholars in exile switch from their former speciality to the study of their home culture, like Konstantin Mochulsky, a former specialist in Romance literature who took refuge from the Bolshevik Revolution in Paris and proceeded to publish books in Russian about Russian writers, notably Dostoyevsky.

Conversely, some exiles become specialists in the culture of their new home. The Huguenot Paul de Rapin-Thoyras became famous for his history of England, written in French and read in many parts of Europe. Other Huguenot refugees spread the knowledge of English and German culture in France and elsewhere by translating texts and publishing articles in journals. Eduard Bernstein, a German socialist exile who lived in London between 1888 and 1901, carried out research on seventeenth-century English radical thinkers, and was the first to draw attention to the writings of one of them, Gerard Winstanley. Israel Gollancz, a second-generation refugee, became a professor of English at King's College London from 1903 to 1930 and a noted Shakespeare scholar.

One Russian historian in exile in Italy, Nikolay Ottokar, became a specialist in the history of Florence. Two Russian exiles who came to Britain, Paul Vinogradoff in the early 1900s and Michael Postan in the 1920s, became authorities on medieval English society, like the Pole Lewis Namier in the case of eighteenth-century England. Among the refugees who arrived in the 1930s, Geoffrey Elton became an authority on England under the Tudors and Nikolaus Pevsner an authority on English architecture.

Peter Hennock (originally Ernst Peter Henoch), who chose England in the nineteenth century as his field of research, has noted how immigrants are often "preoccupied with the country of their adoption" and that "as historians they have sometimes felt that they could recognize the crucial elements in their adopted country more clearly than native historians." As an immigrant, Hennock explained, he could never take English history for granted (illustrating, once again, the uses of detachment).[10]

It was not only in England that immigrants helped the natives understand their own culture. Otto Maria Carpeaux, a Viennese who fled to Brazil after 1938, became a leading critic of Brazilian literature, as well as introducing Brazilian readers to a number of major European writers, notably Franz Kafka and Robert Musil.

Like interpreters, anthropologists offer an example of professional mediators, translators between the culture in which they do their fieldwork (a temporary exile) and their home culture. The very idea of "cultural translation" came from a British anthropologist, Edward Evans-Pritchard. Hence we should not be surprised to find that exiles and expatriates have played a major role in the history of anthropology, especially in Britain and the United States. In the case of Britain, the Pole Bronisław Malinowski virtually founded the discipline. In America, the role of founder was played by the German immigrant Franz Boas. Among his students, Robert Lowie (formerly Löwe) came from Vienna and Paul Radin from Russian Poland, while Alfred Kroeber, born in the United States, was the son of immigrants who spoke German at home.

Stay-at-home scholars can also be mediators, sitting in their studies in what have been called "centers of calculation," especially major cities, collecting the information provided by the exiles and expatriates and making syntheses.[11] An obvious example is that of the German Jesuit Athanasius Kircher, who was based in Rome but was able to make use of the information provided by Jesuit colleagues. Some of them wrote to him sending their observations (on the comet of 1652, for instance) and answering his questions. Others conversed with Kircher on their return after years of working as missionaries in China, India, and elsewhere.[12] Thanks to this Jesuit network, Kircher was able to publish books on a variety of subjects — on China, geology, medicine, and so on. His contribution to knowledge from his study depended on the work of missionaries in the field, just as they depended in turn on face-to-face encounters with informants.

Distanciation

Like deprovincialization, the concept of "distanciation" is an umbrella covering a number of the consequences of distance. One of most important of these is the ability to see what is often called the "big picture." Alexis de Tocqueville once compared the theorist to a traveler who climbs a hill to view a city as a whole for the first time: "pour la première fois, il en saisit la forme." The point had already been made with the same image by the historian August Schlözer: "one can know every single street of a big city, but without a plan or a view from an elevated point, one will not have a feeling for the whole."[13]

In similar fashion, the distance imposed by exile has allowed some scholars to take a bird's eye view and see the big picture more clearly than before. Erich Auerbach, for instance, who left the University of Marburg for Istanbul in 1935, after being dismissed from his chair, turned his loss of access to German libraries from a disadvantage into an asset by producing *Mimesis* (1946), his famous panorama of Western literature from the Bible and Homer to Virginia Woolf.

Again, the most famous book by the Brazilian historian-sociologist Gilberto Freyre, *The Masters and the Slaves* (*Casa Grande e Senzala*, 1933) was written in exile, first in Lisbon and then in Stanford, following the revolution of 1930 in which Getúlio Vargas came to power. Indeed, Freyre's friend Rodrigo Mello Franco de Andrade called *Casa Grande* one of the few positive consequences of that revolution.[14] The Spaniard Américo Castro worked mainly as a medieval philologist as long as he lived in his native country, but in exile in the United States, he became more ambitious and wrote the book for which he is best remembered, a highly original—and controversial—interpretation of Spanish history, attempting to explain the rise of intolerance and emphasizing what made Spain different from other countries.[15]

Not all scholars in exile responded to the challenge of distance in the manner exemplified by Auerbach, Freyre, and Castro. The Austrian philologist Leo Spitzer, for instance, Auerbach's fellow exile in Istanbul, continued to prefer micro-analysis to macro-analysis, the search for significant detail to painting the big picture. All the same, the concern with the big picture recurs in the intellectual history of exiles and expatriates.

Fernand Braudel offers a famous example of an expatriate whose major works were marked by his years abroad. Braudel was also an exile, in two prison camps in Germany, but before that time he had lived for more than a decade in Algeria, teaching in a *lycée* (where he met his future wife), and he had also spent two years in Brazil, lecturing at the newly founded University of São Paulo (1935–37). Braudel once described distance and distanciation (*le dépaysement, l'éloignement*) as important instruments of knowledge (*grands moyens de connaissance*): it is intriguing, to say the least, that he had nothing to say about the value of proximity. His book on the Mediterranean, with its Olympian viewpoint, offers a vivid illustration of his desire and his need to see the big picture, *mon désir et mon besoin de voir grand,* as he put it. His choice of the distant view was linked to his concern with the *longue durée,* a period of time far longer than any human experience can stretch.[16]

The experience of exile encourages this detached approach. The German sociologist Georg Simmel wrote about what he called "the objectivity of the stranger," describing it not as "mere detachment" but as a composite of "indifference and involvement." For his part, Mannheim emphasized "the acquisition of perspective," in other words, an awareness of alternatives and a distance from the conventional wisdom in both homeland and hostland that encourages innovation.[17] Literally detached from their homeland and not yet attached to their hostland, it is no surprise to find exiles speaking and writing about both cultures from the point of view of outsiders. An obvious example is Pierre Bayle, who fled to the Dutch Republic following the persecution of French Protestants in the 1680s (to be discussed in the following chapter). Bayle might be described as a seventeenth-century Mannheim, a cool observer of humanity who was fascinated by differences in opinions and prejudices. He once confessed that he hardly ever read historians to learn what happened in the past, but simply to discover "what is said in each nation and in each party."[18]

Another striking example of detachment is that of Lewis Namier, who came from Russian Poland and was originally known as Ludwik Bernsztajn Niemirowski. Namier came to England in 1907, studying at Balliol College Oxford, becoming a British subject—and changing his name—just before the outbreak of World War I. His identity is not easy to define. Namier was an outsider in England because he was a Polish immigrant. He was an outsider in Poland because he was Jewish. He was an outsider among the Jews because he was the son of a landowner and because he had been brought up a Catholic. Namier came to identify with England, at least in some respects, and his work on the history of Parliament expressed this identification. However, it might also be said of him that his detachment from English culture and his lack of emotional investment in English myths about themselves, including the conventional wisdom of historians, allowed him to take a fresh look at English history, and especially to demystify the eighteenth-century party system. It is only fair to add that this demystification provoked criticisms, some of them palpable hits. Namier was accused of leaving out ideas and ideals such as the devotion to liberty, and so of reducing political history to the struggle for power.[19] On the positive side, Namier's awareness of what was happening in historical studies elsewhere in Europe allowed him to introduce the English to prosopography, a technique that had been pioneered by German scholars working on ancient Rome, although the method of collective biography was sometimes criticized as "mechanically scientific."[20]

Another vivid example of detachment is offered by the cosmopolitan Eric Hobsbawm, who was born in Alexandria and lived in Vienna and Berlin before he moved with his aunt and uncle to England in 1933 at the age of sixteen and completed his education in London and Cambridge. Hobsbawm, who lived for the last eighty years of his long life in England, always maintained a certain distance from his adopted country. For example, he described Cambridge in his student days as "isolated and parochial," and commented on what he called the "extraordinary provincialism of the British in the 1930s."[21]

Ernst Gellner, who came from Czechoslovakia and, like Hobsbawm, attended an English grammar school just before World War II, published a famous critique of the dominant English tradition of philosophy in *Words and Things* (1959), making a contribution to the sociology of knowledge at the same time as observing the English with a distant, anthropological eye, asking why "Linguistic Philosophy" became "so very acceptable" in a particular time and place and describing it as a philosophy "eminently suitable for gentlemen," and above all for "the Narodniks of North Oxford." As his biographer remarks, "Gellner was an outsider looking in on a world made strange to him by his background and experience."[22] As a critic of the dominant philosophy, Gellner had little chance of academic employment in Britain, so he moved into another intellectual field, social anthropology. Always the outsider, however, Gellner was regarded by philosophers as an anthropologist and by some anthropologists at least as a philosopher, while he began his career at the London School of Economics (LSE) in the department of sociology.

Anthropology is a discipline marked by distanciation as well as mediation, practicing what Claude Lévi-Strauss called "the distant view" (*le regard éloigné*).[23] All the same, some anthropologists are more detached than others. Some probably grew up this way. A substantial group of anglophone anthropologists came from Jewish families from South Africa, belonging neither to the white minority nor the black majority.[24] Others learned to be detached after leaving their homeland. Like Fernand Braudel,

Pierre Bourdieu spent a number of years in Algeria, which helped distance him from French culture, especially bourgeois culture, which he observed from outside in *La distinction* (1979). The American sociologist Thorstein Veblen had done something similar to Bourdieu in the case of the American bourgeoisie of the Gilded Age in his *Theory of the Leisure Class* (1899). Veblen was the son of immigrant Norwegian farmers, while Bourdieu was the son of a village postman, so both of them were detached from, if not in open rebellion against, the social class that they were studying.

Again, an economist whose practice was close to anthropology, Albert Hirschman, was born in Berlin and ended up in the United States in what he called his "fourth—or is it the fifth?—emigration." Hirschman has been described as trebly detached: from the universities in which he worked, from the conventional wisdom of his colleagues, and from political groups, declaring both that "I part company with radicals" and that "I part company with liberals."[25]

Effective comparison depends on detachment from the objects compared. It is no wonder, then, that exiles and expatriates have played a role disproportionate to their numbers in this form of analysis: in comparative religion, for instance (the German Max Müller in Oxford, the Romanian Mircea Eliade in Chicago); comparative history (the Pole Joachim Lelewel in Belgium, the German Fritz Redlich in the United States); and comparative sociology (the German Reinhart Bendix in the United States, the Pole Shmuel Eisenstadt in Israel).

In the case of history, Helmut Koenigsberger, who went to school in England on his arrival from Germany, was impressed by the emphasis on the history of Parliament in his lessons and asked his history master why German historians did not place the same emphasis on their parliaments. In later life, both he and his fellow refugee Francis Carsten turned to the comparative history of parliaments.[26] The field of comparative literature offers still more examples of the role of exiles, including the Austrian Leo Spitzer in Istanbul and Baltimore, the German New Zealander

Peter Dronke in Cambridge, the Czech René Wellek at Harvard, and two Italians, Renato Poggioli at Harvard and Franco Moretti in New York and Stanford. Because generalizations depend on comparisons, exiles have also made a disproportionate contribution to social and cultural theory.

In a sense, the exile (and to a lesser degree the expatriate) is the intellectual par excellence because he or she is "extraterritorial," as the German critic and historian Siegfried Kracauer described himself, an outsider belonging neither to hostland nor homeland.[27] Not all exiles reveal this awareness, but the experience of exile surely encourages it. Hence exiles, like children, tend to see the world around them with fresh eyes. For example, Pevsner devoted a book to a topic that local scholars had simply taken for granted, the Englishness of English art.

Karl Mannheim described detachment in a somewhat exaggerated way when, following his senior colleague Alfred Weber, he described intellectuals as "free-floating" (*freischwebende*), an "unanchored, relatively classless stratum."[28] We might therefore speak of "Mannheim's paradox," in other words, of the apparent contradiction or conflict between the idea of "situated" knowledge on which he placed so much emphasis and the idea of "floating" free, a metaphor that is both attractive and dangerous. The danger is that of encouraging what the Neapolitan historian Giambattista Vico might have called the arrogance (*boria*) of intellectuals, in other words, their sense of superiority to others, whom they often consider to be stuck in the mud of locality and the prejudices that go with it. Qualifying Mannheim's description, we might say that exiled intellectuals were and are relatively detached. They do not float free from all ties, but they are located on the edge of two cultures. This location is often uncomfortable but it leads to insights, notably an acute awareness of alternative ways of thinking, an insight denied to individuals who are comfortably rooted in their native soil and so risk provincialism or even parochialism.

Mannheim's former assistant Norbert Elias, a refugee in England from 1933 onward, not only wrote with detachment but also wrote about it. He stressed the danger of "involved forms of thinking," associating them with "wishful thinking," "short-term feelings," and "the inability to distance oneself from traditional attitudes." On the other side, he associated the rise of modern science with "the breakthrough from the dominance of involvement to the dominance of detachment in human knowledge."[29] Like Braudel, he had virtually nothing to say about the negative side of detachment or the possible intellectual advantages of involvement with a given topic. A number of Elias's publications may be viewed as responses to his experience of exile, beginning with a brief essay on the expulsion of the Huguenots from France and including not only the essay on detachment but also a book-length study of outsiders.[30]

Hybridization

Exiles and expatriates illustrate what a study of the Belgian historian of science George Sarton, who spent most of his career in the United States, called "the role of the émigré or outsider in catalyzing intellectual and social development."[31] The American sociologist Robert Park noted that one result of immigration was the appearance of "a new type of personality" that he called the "cultural hybrid," "living and sharing intimately in the cultural life and traditions of two distinct peoples." Park's example was the "emancipated Jew," linking his article with an earlier essay on "The Intellectual Pre-Eminence of Jews in Modern Europe" by another American sociologist, Thorsten Veblen (himself the son of immigrants, as we have seen). Veblen suggested that the Jews were most creative at the moment when they had escaped from their own tradition without yet having assimilated that of their Gentile neighbors. In other words, they were between worlds. They would find themselves between worlds once again in the 1930s, at least if they had sufficient foresight or luck to leave their homeland in time.[32]

Some of the exiles developed an acute awareness of the strengths and weaknesses of both homeland and hostland. Of Adorno, for instance, it has been said that "as an American, he was obviously a displaced European, while as a European, he was deeply affected by his years in America. As a result he was able to remain in permanent exile from both contexts."[33] Again, Bernhard Groethuysen, who was born in Berlin but lived in Paris and published his famous *Origines de l'esprit bourgeois* (1927) and other works in French, was described by a reviewer as a "wanderer between two worlds," Germany and France.[34]

Bifocal Vision

The historian Fritz Stern, a child when he left Germany for the United States, may be described as another wanderer. In his autobiography, Stern suggests that he "gradually acquired something like bifocal views [. . .] I tend to see things German with American eyes, and things American also with German eyes." In similar fashion, making use of a different metaphor, the historian and philosopher of science Yehuda Elkanah, who was born in Yugoslavia but lived in Israel, Germany, and Hungary, remarked in an interview, "In Europe I find myself talking with an American voice but in the USA with a European one."[35] Less comfortable with the situation, a third exile, Henry Pachter, reminisced, "I found myself constantly caught between two camps—explaining Europe to Americans and explaining America to Europeans."[36]

Such exiles were well qualified for the task of what yet another exile, Franz Neumann, called the "integration" of two traditions, hybridization. The task is of course a collective one in which both exiles and "natives" take part, as in the case, to be discussed in more detail later, of the encounter between German theory and Anglo-American empiricism. Perceived analogies between items in different traditions lead to convergence between them, as in the famous case of the analogy between the Virgin Mary in Catholic tradition and the Goddess of Mercy (Kuan Yin, Kwannon) in Buddhism.

Expatriates too contribute to the hybridization of knowledges, whether they teach in or learn from their new environment, or indeed do both. For example, a recent essay on knowledge and colonialism discussed the encounter between British medics and indigenous healers in India and Africa under the vivid title "pidgin-knowledge."[37] Similarly, though looking at small groups in the present rather than large groups over the long term, in his book *The Difference*, the American psychologist Scott Page has argued that when problems need to be solved, even more important than ability is what he calls "cognitive diversity." In other words, two or three points of view are better than one, and a group including individuals from different cultures is especially likely to exhibit this kind of diversity.[38]

The dissemination of knowledge often depends on the movement of texts and also that of other objects, as the impact of a long series of international exhibitions from 1851 onward demonstrates. All the same, dissemination is more effective when it results from face-to-face encounters, a point memorably made by the Hungarian philosopher Michael Polanyi—another exile—in his account of personal knowledge. In short, "ideas move around inside people."[39] "Non-routine information," as a Swedish geographer emphasizes, "requires direct personal contacts."[40] Implicit knowledge in particular is difficult to communicate in other ways. The crafts offer obvious examples, because apprentices learn by observing the master and then by trying to imitate his work while the master observes and corrects the imitation.

Face-to-face encounters assist innovation as well as the transmission of traditions. As we shall see, new ideas are frequently the result of encounters between people who think in different ways and so view the same problem from different angles. What has been called "the displacement of concepts" is important in the process of innovation, and it often turns out that the individuals who treat concepts in this creative manner are themselves displaced people, moving from one network if not from one country to another.[41]

It is often the case that the insights that historians believe to be their discoveries were anticipated by the people they are writing about, and it is worth noting that some central ideas presented here were originally formulated by twentieth-century exiles such as Karl Mannheim, Franz Neumann, and Norbert Elias. Mannheim and Elias both analyzed the insights associated with detachment, while Neumann, as we have seen, distinguished between possible strategies for exiled scientists or scholars. All three have their place in a tradition that might be described as the theory of exile, a tradition that goes back more than a century.

Theory

Georg Simmel, a sociologist who failed to be appointed to a chair in Germany because he was Jewish, in other words not quite German, published a famous essay in 1908 about "the stranger" (*der Fremde*), focusing on the innovative contributions made by people who, like himself, were at once inside and outside a given social group. Eighty years later, another sociologist, Zygmunt Bauman, himself a Polish Jew exiled in England, described the Jews as "the very epitome of Simmel's strangers — always on the outside even when inside, examining the familiar as if it was a foreign object of study, asking questions no one else asked, questioning the unquestionable and challenging the unchallengeable."[42]

A similar point was made by Robert Park, a leading figure in the so-called Chicago School of sociology, which focused on the city and its inhabitants, including immigrants. In 1928 Park published an article suggesting that migration produced a "changed type of personality" that he called the "marginal man," an "emancipated individual" who "learns to look upon the world in which he was born and bred with something of the detachment of a stranger."[43]

Later writers offered further variations on this theme, noting that exiles sometimes deprovincialize their hosts, or at least some of their hosts, by confronting them with unfamiliar points of view, as two Polish exiles of the 1960s and 1970s, the philosopher Leszek Kołakowski and the sociologist Zygmunt Bauman, have described in memorable fashion. The philosopher Leszek Kołakowski, who was exiled from Poland after criticizing the regime in the 1960s, titled one of his provocative essays "in praise of exile," beginning from the proposition "that the position of an outsider offers a cognitive privilege is well known and unquestionable" and going on to suggest that exile is less a misfortune than a challenge, especially the challenge to confront different perspectives.[44]

Asked in an interview whether he had adjusted to English culture, Kołakowski's compatriot Zygmunt Bauman replied that "adjustment was never a priority." The real challenge was "to reveal the meaning of my differences to my English colleagues and students and perhaps persuade them to find some interest or use in what was originally alien to them." Expanding on what he had just said, Bauman remarked that "the only way to repay the hospitality of my English hosts was to offer them something they did not yet have and could not acquire without a face-to-face encounter with an alternative way of thinking and acting," one that would "enrich them in the same way that I was enriched by my encounter with everyday life in Britain." He concluded that gains from being "out of place" are much greater than the losses. "To be 'inside' but partly 'outside' is [. . .] a means of preserving the freshness, innocence and the blessed ingenuousness of vision."[45]

More ambivalent was Edward Said, an expatriate in the United States but also before this a refugee from Palestine. Said called exile a "terrible experience," but he also found compensations for this "disorienting loss," notably what he called, in a favorite adjective of his, a "contrapuntal" vision, a "double perspective" in which "an idea or experience is always counterposed with another [. . .] making them both appear in a sometimes new and unpredictable light." In short, exiles, "unsettled" themselves, have the power to unsettle others.[46]

Receptivity

Exile and expatriation are forms of cultural encounter, which obviously need to be examined from both sides. Just as individual emigrants or whole diasporic communities have been more or less open to the cultures of their hostlands, so these hostlands have been more or less receptive to foreigners, or to different kinds of foreigner. The Greek scholars who fled to Italy were fortunate enough, relatively speaking, to find Italians who wanted to learn what they had to teach. The Huguenot scholars who arrived in Amsterdam, London, or Berlin found a similar situation. Again, to take examples from the 1930s, adaptation to the new culture was easier for Spaniards in Mexico, for instance, than it was for Germans in Britain, because the Spaniards spoke the same language as their hosts (or more or less the same language, as one of them wryly commented). Thanks to its tradition of hosting exiles, Britain was relatively open to foreigners in the 1930s, while the United States was still more open at that time. At the microlevel of academic departments, expanding universities, from Istanbul to Mexico City, accepted foreign scholars more easily than universities that lacked the funds for more appointments.

The testimony of two exiled scholars of the 1930s is worth noting at this point. Erwin Panofsky wrote about what he called the "providential synchronism" between the need to escape from Germany on the part of Jewish art historians and the rise of the discipline of art history in the United States. And the social psychologist Marie Jahoda has noted what she called the "intricate interplay" between what the immigrants bring and "what they find in the new host culture."[47]

The question of receptivity on the part of the host countries, or more exactly of individuals and groups in those host countries, will recur in these pages. Indeed, the whole book may be described as a study in the history of reception, in a double sense that includes the warm or cool reception of the exiles by individuals in the host countries as well as the active or creative reception of their ideas and the knowledges that they brought with them. What follows concentrates on cases from Europe and the Americas, North and South. However, the topic is a global one, so it may be illuminating to frame the Western cases with a brief account of contributions to knowledge made by exiles in the ancient, East Asian, and modern Arab worlds.

2 : A GLOBAL TOPIC

The contribution of exiles to knowledge is of course a global topic, as a few ancient, medieval, and modern examples — so many snapshots — may suggest.

In classical antiquity, discussions of exile range from positive to negative, from Ovid's lapidary statement "Exile is death" (*exilium mors est*) to Plutarch, consoling a friend by telling him that in a sense, all humans are exiles.[1] The expatriate Galen and the exile Polybius are outstanding members of a group of Greek scholars in Rome, at a time when Greek origins gave scholars prestige, as Italian origins would do during the Renaissance. Galen of Pergamon, whose many medical treatises made him famous, settled in Rome in the year 162 and served three emperors as a court physician. Galen's location in a metropolis is likely to have helped in both the formulation and the spread of his ideas.[2]

Two of the most famous historians of the ancient world, Polybius and Josephus, were exiles. Polybius, who came from the Greek city of Megalopolis in Arcadia, was taken to Rome as a hostage, together with many other patricians, in the year 167 and remained there for seventeen years. His experiences as a Greek living in Rome and moving in the circle of the aristocracy were a good preparation for his *Histories*, in which the rise of Rome was the central theme. Polybius wrote "with both a Greek and a Roman public in mind," but especially as a mediator, explaining Rome to his fellow Greeks.[3]

The diaspora of Jewish scholars after the destruction of the Temple of Jerusalem by the Romans in the year 70 offers another famous instance of the intellectual consequences of exile, even though "the dispersal of Jews had begun long before the Temple fell" (the Babylonian exile lasted from 597 to 538 BCE). The Jewish equivalent of Polybius was Titus Flavius Josephus, who fought against the Jews and then served two emperors as an interpreter, taking a Roman name, before writing (in Greek) his history of *The Jewish War*.[4] An intellectual strength of both historians, obviously linked to their situation, was their ability to view the Romans not only from outside but also from within.

Byzantines, Persians, and Arabs

In what Western historians call either late antiquity or the early Middle Ages, contacts between Byzantines, Persians, and Arabs furthered the dissemination of knowledge and ideas. Following the closure of the Nestorian academy in Edessa (now in Turkey) by the Byzantine emperor, who regarded Nestorian Christians as heretics, in the year 489, the functions of the academy as a center of medical and philosophical learning were taken over by similar institutions, notably one in Gundeshapur (Jundisabur, now in Iran). This school became a meeting place between Greek, Persian, and also Indian knowledges. Again, after the year 529, when the Byzantine emperor closed the famous Platonic Academy in Athens, a number of Greek philosophers migrated to the rival and enemy Sasanian Empire centered in what is now Iran. The Sasanian ruler, Khusrau I (otherwise known as Chosroes), was a patron of learning and himself a translator from Sanskrit and Greek. Khusrau invited Indian and Chinese scholars to his court, gave refuge to Nestorian Christians from the Byzantine Empire, and commissioned translations from Greek and Syriac (a language close to Aramaic) into Pahlavi (Old Persian). In this way, personal encounters between scholars from different cultures encouraged the dissemination of different knowledges.

For example, Aristotle's *Organon* (a study of logic) and Ptolemy's *Almagest* (a study of astronomy) were translated from Greek into Pahlavi at this time, together with a number of medical texts. Later on, these texts were translated once more, this time from Pahlavi into Arabic following the Arabic conquest of Persia. Via the Arabs, the texts were transmitted to the medieval West, where they were translated once again, this time into Latin. Thus Persia, and Khusrau in particular—alongside, ironically enough, the Byzantine emperors—played a crucial role in this collective enterprise of the transmission of ancient Greek knowledge. Given the number of retranslations, it is hardly necessary to say that the process of transmission included hybridization, the conscious or unconscious adaptation of the texts to the cultures that received them.[5]

Itinerant Monks, Christian and Buddhist

In the history of the spread of both Christianity and Buddhism, and of some secular knowledge as well, itinerant monks played a major role. In sixth-century Europe, the Irish missionary Columbanus and his disciples founded monasteries that became important not only in the establishment of Christianity but also in the preservation and transmission of classical learning. Columbanus founded Bobbio in Northern Italy and Luxeuil in Burgundy, a follower of his founded St. Gallen in Switzerland, and monks from Luxeuil established Corbie in Picardy. All four abbeys became major centers of knowledge in early medieval Europe.

The reception of Buddhism in China, Korea, and Japan also owed a great deal to expatriates seeking knowledge or seeking to transmit it over the centuries. Among the leading figures in this transmission, between the fourth and the fourteenth century, were the monks Kumarajiva, Xuanzhang, Ganjin, Ennin, and Dhyanabhadra. In the fourth century, Kumarajiva, an Indian monk, moved to the Chinese city of Chang'an, where he translated sacred texts from Sanskrit into Chinese. In the seventh century, Xuanzhang, a Chinese monk, made an epic seventeen-year journey to India and back, returning with many sacred texts in Sanskrit that he spent the rest of his life translating. In the eighth century, another Chinese monk, Jianzhen, traveled to Japan, where he spent the last ten years of his life. Known by the Japanese as Ganjin, he founded a temple and a school and introduced the Japanese aristocracy to the doctrines of the Buddha. In the ninth century, Ennin, a Japanese monk, traveled to China, where he spent nine years studying with monks and copying the Buddhist scriptures, before returning to Japan to spread the knowledge of the tantric tradition of meditation. In the fourteenth century, the Indian monk Dhyanabhadra arrived in Korea and established a monastery on the model of the famous college of Nalanda.

This process of reception continued into the early modern period, shifting from early Indian Buddhism to the Zen movement that developed in China and was brought to Japan. In the seventeenth century, for instance, the Chinese monk Yinyuan Longqi traveled to Japan with his disciples to establish a Zen temple there. Like Ganjin, he remained in Japan for the rest of his life.[6]

Journalism

In the Islamic world in what Westerners call the Middle Ages, exiles and expatriates played an important role in creating and transmitting knowledge. As in the case of the ancient world, this was a time when frontiers mattered much less than they would later, while both classical Arabic and what linguists call "New Persian" were commonly known by the learned. All the same, differences in culture were still significant, as some scholars knew from experience. The Persian astronomer Abu Ma'shar (known in the West as Albumasar) studied in Benares and worked in Baghdad. The Persian philosopher (or better, the polymath) Al-Farabi, known in his day as the second Aristotle, on whom he commented, came from a town in what is now Kazakhstan and lived in Baghdad and Damascus. The geographer Al-Idrisi came from Morocco but worked in Palermo. The grammarian Abu Hayyan came from Granada but lived in Cairo. The historian Ibn Khaldun came from Tunis and later lived in Fez, Granada, and Cairo.

Turning to the modern world, a few exiles stand out for the impact that their ideas have made on Western intellectuals, on fellow Muslims, or on both. One is Edward Said, who could scarcely have been more conscious of his position as an exile, for worse and for better. Another, earlier example is Jamal al-Din al-Afghani, who was born in Iran and lived in India and in Egypt, developing his critique of Western imperialism.

A key collective example of the significance of exiles for the dissemination of knowledge comes from the history of journalism. A number of important newspapers and periodicals were founded by Arabs from Syria who had moved to Egypt because censorship was less strict there in the age of Khedive Ismail and British Consul-General Lord Cromer. These Arab journalists included the brothers Salim and Bishara Taqla, who founded *Al-Ahram* (1875); Farah Antun, who wrote for *Al-Ahram*; Faris Nimr, who founded several journals, including *al-Muqattam*; and the Muslim reformer Muhammad Rashid Rida, who wrote for the journal *al-Manar*. These writers were based in Alexandria or Cairo, but their writings were addressed to the whole Arab world, which, thanks to a common written language, was not difficult to reach.[7]

Journalism is a common occupation for political exiles in various places and periods. Famous examples include the South American Andrés Bello, who published the *Repertorio Americano* (1826) when he was living in London; the Russian Alexander Herzen, whose periodical *Kolokol* ("The Bell") was also produced in London (1857–65); and the Chinese reformer Liang Qichao, who fled to Japan and there produced a journal in Chinese, *Xinmin Congbao* ("New Citizen," 1902–7). Further examples, notably those of Protestant exiles in Berlin, London, and the Dutch Republic, will appear in a later section.

Examples such as these offer important reminders that the contribution of exiles and expatriates to knowledge is not confined to the West in the last 500 years or so, like the case studies offered in the remainder of this book. To those case studies we now turn, beginning with exiles in early modern Europe.

3 : EARLY MODERN EXILES

This chapter is concerned with what the German historian Heinz Schilling has called "confessional migration" at a time, the sixteenth and seventeenth centuries, when "the religious refugee became a mass phenomenon," perhaps for the first time in history.[1] It considers the consequences for knowledge of the exile of five religious groups: Jews; Muslims; and Orthodox, Catholic, and Protestant Christians.

The Greeks

From the point of view of displacement, the early modern period may be said to begin in 1453 with the fall of Constantinople, the capital of the shrunken remains of Byzantium, to the forces of the Ottoman sultan Mehmet II, "the conqueror." The fall of the city was followed by the flight of many Greeks, including some famous scholars, to Italy. In fact, this flight had begun earlier, in the course of the Ottoman advance. After all, since 1422, Constantinople had been "under virtually constant siege."[2] The movement of refugees also continued much later than 1453, from Greek islands such as Corfu and especially Crete.

As for the consequences of this movement, it was traditionally claimed that the year 1453 marked the beginning of the Renaissance, or at least of Renaissance humanism. The claim might be described as "the myth of 1453," in the sense of dramatizing a process by presenting it as a single event with a precise date, thus making it more memorable. The story goes back to the fifteenth century itself. By the 1460s, the humanist Pier Candido Decembrio was claiming that "since the city of Constantine has been destroyed by the barbarous infidels [. . .] it is hardly credible, but many Italians have become Greek themselves." The idea was still being taken seriously 300 years later, by Voltaire for example, although by that time it had been criticized by some scholars.[3]

After all, it is obvious enough that the revival of the classical tradition in literature and learning as well as in the visual arts began in Italy long before the year 1453, whether in the age of Petrarch (1304–74), Lovato Lovati (1241–1309), or still earlier. Some Italian humanists spent years in Greece before 1453, among them Giovanni Aurispa, who settled in Chios and built up a collection of manuscripts of Sophocles, Thucydides, and other ancient writers; Guarino of Verona, who studied with Manuel Chrysoloras in Constantinople; and Francesco Filelfo, who studied with Manuel's nephew Janos.

It might be argued that the exodus of Greek scholars was relatively fortunate in its timing. The scholars arrived, contrary to the myth, when the early Renaissance was already in progress, resulting in a growing demand for knowledge of the Greek language and Greek philosophy at just the moment that the exiles were able to supply it, spreading that knowledge first in Italy and then in other parts of Europe. The increased availability of Greek scholars was matched by the increased receptivity of their Italian colleagues.

It is not difficult to compile a list of about fifty Greeks who contributed to this dissemination. One of the first important figures was Manuel Chrysoloras, who was invited to Florence by Coluccio Salutati, arrived in 1397, taught Greek to leading humanists such as Leonardo Bruni, Ambrogio Traversari, and Guarino of Verona, and published a Greek grammar. A second was Theodorus Gaza, who came from Thessalonika (now Salonika) and fled to Italy after the city was captured by the Turks in 1430. He taught Greek in Ferrara before moving to Rome, where he was active as a translator and interpreter of Greek philosophy, and then to Naples. A third was Demetrios Chalcondyles, who came from Athens and arrived in Italy in 1447, becoming the first professor of Greek at the University of Padua as well as teaching in Perugia, Florence, and Milan. A fourth was Ioannis Argyropoulos, who was indeed a refugee from Constantinople, where he had been captured in 1453. Like Chrysoloras before him, he taught in Florence.

Thanks to teachers such as these, a number of Italian humanists learned to read Aristotle and Plato in the original Greek, thus escaping from the misunderstandings that had stemmed from reading a Latin translation of an Arabic translation of the original text (because it was the Arabs who transmitted ancient Greek knowledge to the West in the Middle Ages). The humanist slogan *ad fontes*, "Back to the Sources," could not have been put into practice without the help of exiles such as these, or their fellow exile the Jew Yohanan Alemanno, who was born in Constantinople, moved to Italy, probably around 1453, wrote on philosophy, and gave Hebrew lessons to the humanist Giovanni Pico della Mirandola.

For a less learned section of the public, some of the exiles translated books from Greek into Latin. Theodore Gaza, for instance, translated Aristotle. Demetrios Chalcondyles helped Ficino with his translation of Plato. George of Trebizond (Trapezuntius) translated both Aristotle and Plato (though his translations were criticized at the time for inaccuracy). In a later generation, Maximos Margounios, a Cretan who became the bishop of the Greek island of Cythera (Kythira), lived in Venice, wrote poetry, and translated into Latin works by Greek-speaking theologians such as Gregory of Nyssa and John of Damascus. Himself of mixed origin (his father was Greek, his mother Venetian), Margounios mediated not only between languages but also between beliefs, attempting to reconcile Catholics, Lutherans, and Greek Orthodox. His attempts were unsuccessful.

It was not only to Italians that exiled scholars passed on the knowledge of the language and culture of ancient Greece, but to other Europeans as well. Chalcondyles, for instance, taught the German scholar Johann Reuchlin and the Englishmen William Grocyn and Thomas Linacre; and a cousin of Theodorus Gaza, Andronicus Callistus, taught the Spanish humanist Antonio Nebrija. These foreigners came to Italy to study, but later on, some Greek scholars moved to France and elsewhere. Georgios Hermonymos, who came from Sparta, moved to Paris, where his students included Erasmus and Guillaume Budé. Janos Laskaris, who fled from Constantinople in 1453, also moved to Paris after teaching Greek in Italy. Demetrios Doukas, a Cretan who moved to Venice, was invited to Spain, where he taught Greek at the University of Alcalà and joined the team that was working on a multilingual edition of the Bible, the so-called Complutensian Polyglot.

Lesser-known scholars also taught Greek in Italy and elsewhere, while other exiles made a contribution to knowledge in other ways. Some were physicians, a profession that (unlike law for example) can easily be practiced by immigrants. Thomas Frank, who was Greek despite his name, became personal physician to Cardinal Beaufort in England and then to King Charles VII of France. Other exiles made a living by copying Greek manuscripts, for which the demand was increasing. Janos Bessarion, a Greek bishop who moved to Italy and became a cardinal, was the patron of a number of scribes and by the end of his life owned nearly 800 Greek manuscripts, which he left to the church of San Marco in Venice.

From working as a scribe, it was only a short step to working as a printer of Greek texts or a corrector for the press. Printers did not move from Constantinople—the new invention had not yet reached Byzantium by 1453—but some refugees became printers. Demetrios Damilas, for instance, who came from Crete, was active as a scribe and a printer in Milan and elsewhere. The books he printed included a Greek grammar. Zacharias Calliergis, another Cretan, moved to Venice, and became famous for his fine calligraphy before he turned printer in 1515, designing a font of Greek type and hiring fellow Cretans to work in his establishment as compositors and correctors. In the late fifteenth century, there were about 4,000 Greeks living in Venice, most of them Cretans, so Calliergis had a wide choice of potential recruits. The famous scholar-printer Aldus Manutius, who came from the Papal States, moved to Venice to set up his press in 1494. Because he specialized in Greek texts, it is likely that Aldus located his enterprise in Venice in order to be close to a Greek-reading workforce (including scholars such as Marcus Musurus) and also to his raw material, the manuscripts that Bessarion had bequeathed to the city.

These teachers, translators, copyists, printers, and correctors for the press may all be described as mediators, in this case, unusually, not so much between the hostlands and their own Byzantine, Eastern Christian culture as between the hostlands and the language and culture of ancient Greece. However, the exiles and their students in Italy and elsewhere were also interested in Greek-speaking "Fathers of the Church." The Cretan exile George of Trebizond translated the treatise by the early Christian Eusebius, *The Preparation for the Gospel*, while the humanist Leonardo Bruni, who learned Greek from the exile Manuel Chrysoloras, translated a work by the fourth-century theologian Basil of Caesarea.

The Jewish Diaspora

The next important date in the history of European exiles is 1492, with the flight of Jews from Spain to escape forced conversion, following the Christian conquest of Granada. The flight was (as in other cases discussed in this book, from 1453 to 1933) not only an event but part of a process, so that the date needs to be placed in a wider context, "the long shadow of 1391," an earlier moment of pogroms and forced conversions.[4] The Jewish exiles who fled in order to avoid conversion in 1492 probably numbered 100,000 or more (though older estimates were as high as 200,000). More than half of them fled to Portugal, where in 1497 they once more faced the alternatives of conversion or flight.

Abraham Zacuto, for instance, formerly professor of astronomy at the University of Salamanca, fled to Portugal in 1492 and later moved to Tunis. He was not the only scholar to take refuge in North Africa: Jacob Beirav fled from Spain to Fez (moving on to Egypt, Jerusalem, Damascus, and finally Safed), while Abraham ben Salomon of Torrutiel, best known as a chronicler, was taken from Spain to Fez as a child. Other refugees went to Italy, like the Abravanels, Isaac the rabbi and his son Judah Leon the philosopher, who left Spain for Naples; or Jacob Mantino ben Samuel, who moved to Italy, studied at the University of Padua, and spent much of his career translating Hebrew books into Latin.[5]

Yet others fled to the Ottoman Empire, especially to Istanbul, Salonika, and Safed.[6] They included scholars such as the lawyer and mystic Joseph Caro; the Talmudist and Kabbalist Joseph Taitatzak, who fled to Salonika; and the doctor Moshe Hamon, from Granada, who was taken to Istanbul as a child, became physician to the sultan Suleiman the Magnificent, collected books, wrote treatises, and was active as a patron of learning.[7] Knowledge of the Kabbalah spread from Spain to the Ottoman Empire, to Safed in particular.

Other scholars, from Spanish or Portuguese families who had converted to Christianity, came out as Jewish following their emigration. Famous examples include two humanist physicians: Amatus Lusitanus, who moved to Salonika in the middle of the sixteenth century, and Didacus Pyrrhus Lusitanus, who did the same in Ragusa. By the seventeenth century, Safed and Salonika (which came to be called a "second Jerusalem") had become centers of rabbinic and kabbalistic studies. Istanbul, Salonika, and Safed "replaced Toledo, Cordova and Barcelona as major centers of Jewish scholarship and intellectual life."[8]

Reading accounts of the achievements of scholars in this diaspora, it is difficult to resist the impression that the exiled scholars maintained the traditions of studying the Bible, the Torah, and the Kabbalah rather than either learning from or contributing to the cultures of the places where they settled. In this respect they were quite unlike their equivalents in the Great Diaspora of the 1930s. Perhaps the view expressed by Rabbi Yosef Yavetz, who had left Spain for Italy, that Spanish Jews had been too much interested in secular knowledge, was widely shared.

All the same, the treatise by Yavetz itself illustrates one major exception to this traditionalism: the writing of history. History had not played a major role in Jewish cultural traditions in the Middle Ages. After 1492, however, a few scholars made a turn in this direction. The trauma of 1492 provoked a number of individuals to record and interpret what had happened: Isaac Abravanel, for instance, Moses Almosnino, Abraham Ardutiel, Joseph ha Cohen, Shem Tov ibn Jamil, Gedaliah ibn Yahya, and Abraham Zacuto. The expulsion of 1492 was viewed as a reenactment of Jewish history, a new Exodus. It was also interpreted as divine punishment for the sins of the Jews. Yet another response, by Isaac Abravanel for instance, was to trust in Providence and to expect the coming of the Messiah before very long, responding in this way to the Christian polemics that accompanied the expulsion. In short, as Yosef Yerushalmi puts it, "the primary stimulus to the rise of Jewish historiography in the sixteenth century was the great catastrophe."[9] In similar fashion, the French invasion of Italy in 1494 and the consequent psychological need to explain the disaster inspired a number of histories of this event and its consequences, including Francesco Guicciardini's masterpiece, the *History of Italy*.

A second wave of exiles left Spain, Portugal, and the Spanish Netherlands in the seventeenth century, most of them bound for Amsterdam, known at the time as "the Jerusalem of the North."[10] Among the most famous Jewish scholars who were active there were Menasseh ben Israel, a preacher and theologian who corresponded with some of the most famous European scholars, such as Hugo Grotius and Claudius Salmasius; Uriel da Costa, whose critique of traditional Judaism—revealing the detachment typical of some exiles—led to his excommunication and finally suicide; and of course the philosopher Baruch Spinoza, who, thanks to his unorthodox beliefs, was expelled from the Jewish community in Amsterdam in 1656.

Spinoza's family had been expelled from Spain in 1492 and had migrated to Portugal and more recently to France and the Dutch Republic, where Baruch was born. However, Portuguese was his mother tongue. Whether or not he saw Dutch culture through Sephardic eyes and Sephardic culture through Dutch eyes, his life between cultures is likely to have freed him from any kind of orthodoxy and encouraged him to develop original ideas.

These migrations deprived the homelands of some valuable skills. A French diplomatic agent in Istanbul noted that the Jewish refugees in the city included artisans who were teaching the Turks how to manufacture firearms and ammunition.[11] Physicians in both Spain and Portugal were often Jewish, and many of them left after 1492. On the other hand, unlike their Greek colleagues in Italy, exiled Jewish scholars taught and mainly wrote their books for other Jews, with exceptions such as Elia del Medigo, the son of refugees from Germany, who lived in Perugia and taught the famous humanist Pico della Mirandola some Hebrew and Arabic.

Jewish printers, who were already well established in Spain by 1492, took part in the general exodus and set up their presses in new places. Two families of printers were particularly important in this respect, the Soncino and the Ibn Namias families, who founded presses in Istanbul, Salonika, and Manastýr in the late fifteenth and early sixteenth centuries. Because they printed books in Hebrew for Jewish readers, they were exempt from the sultan's general prohibition of printing. Similarly, Jewish printers in seventeenth-century Amsterdam (Joseph Athias, for instance, Immanuel Benveniste, David de Castro Tartas, and Menasseh ben Israel, who has already been mentioned as a scholar) specialized in books in Hebrew, as well as publishing Jewish texts in Spanish translation.

However, Athias did not restrict his activities to this kind of book. He claimed to have produced over a million English Bibles, and he also printed Catholic liturgical books.[12] Tartas published books in Yiddish, including a romance about King Arthur, testifying to the wide appeal of romances of chivalry at this time. He was far from alone: 318 Jewish printers are known to have worked in Amsterdam between 1600 and 1732, producing books in Yiddish for export to Poland and in Hebrew for the local Jewish community as well as for export elsewhere.[13]

As for secular knowledge, a remarkable book was published in Spanish in Amsterdam in 1688 by a cultivated Sephardic merchant, Joseph Penso de la Vega, under the intriguing title *The Confusion of Confusions*. Taking the form of a lively dialogue between "a subtle philosopher, a prudent merchant and a learned broker," it describes the stock exchange. The author dwells on the stratagems of the speculators and includes the first references in print to bulls (whom he calls *amantes*) and bears (*contramino-*

res). He describes the stock market as an "intricate labyrinth" and also as the theater where the best human comedy takes place. It is not difficult to imagine how he would have written about later confusions such as the South Sea Bubble of 1720, which affected Amsterdam as well as London, or indeed about the international bubble of 2008.[14]

It was in Amsterdam in the seventeenth century that the Ashkenazi Jews from Eastern Europe, fleeing the Thirty Years' War and the pogroms that took place in the wake of the revolt of Bohdan Khmelnytsky in the Ukraine, encountered the Sephardic Jews from Iberia.[15] Whether this encounter had significant intellectual consequences is difficult to say, but some evidence suggests a positive answer to the question.

For example, Uri Phoebus Halevi, who was born in Amsterdam and was active as a printer there and for a time in Poland, worshipped in both Ashkenazi and Sephardi congregations at different periods and employed compositors from both groups. David de Castro Tartas, the son of "new christians" from Portugal who was financed by Ashkenazi merchants, published books and newspapers for both publics, the Spanish *Gazeta de Amsterdam* for one group and the Yiddish *Dinstagishe un Freytagishe Kuranten* for the other.[16] Saul Levi Mortera, an authority on the Talmud whose pupils included Spinoza, was an Ashkenazi from Venice who, unusually, became a rabbi the Sephardic community in Amsterdam. Another Ashkenazi who was active among the Sephardim was Shabetai Bass, most famous for compiling the first printed bibliography of Hebrew books, under the poetic title "The Lips of the Sleeping" (*Sifte yeshenim*, 1680). Some Ashkenazi compositors and correctors for the press worked in Sephardic printing houses, again in Amsterdam.[17]

In short, the contribution to knowledge made by the Jewish exiles was not so much mediation between two cultures as an attempt to maintain their religious traditions in adverse circumstances. The most obvious examples of mediation are those of Jewish interpreters (known as *linguas*, "tongues") working for the Portuguese who had expelled them in India and elsewhere in the Portuguese Empire. Jewish interpreters were employed by Vasco da Gama, for instance, and also by the discoverer of Brazil, Pedro Alvares Cabral.[18]

The best example of a Jewish exile as mediator is probably Garcia de Orta, physician to King João III of Portugal, who was a "new christian," the son of Spanish refugees. In his early thirties, Garcia de Orta moved to Goa, perhaps to avoid the investigations of the Inquisition. He studied the indigenous medicinal plants and published a dialogue about them, *Colóquios dos simples,* which became well known in Europe in Latin translation. One of the participants in the dialogue is an Indian physician, suggesting that Garcia learned from local practitioners as well as examining local herbs.[19]

Another example is Jacob Castro Sarmento, who fled from Portugal to England in 1720 to escape the attentions of the Inquisition. He published the first book in Portuguese to support the ideas of Isaac Newton, a study of the theory of tides published in London in 1737. Whether this book found many readers is uncertain. It is likely that Castro's English grammar, published in Portuguese in Lisbon in 1751, had better fortune.[20]

The Muslim Diaspora

Like the Jews, the Muslims of Spain and Portugal were forced to choose between conversion and exile. Many left Granada from 1492 onward, Portugal from 1497, Castille from 1502, and Aragon from the 1520s. It is likely that 100,000 Muslims left Spain, mainly for North Africa, followed by smaller numbers of Muslims from Portugal.[21] A second wave followed in 1609–14, when the Spanish government expelled the "Moriscos," in other words the Muslims who had (at least officially) converted to Christianity. Around 300,000 left Spain, of whom a third came from Valencia. Most of them went to Tunisia or Morocco, some to Algeria or Istanbul. This "skill migration" was a major loss to Spain, a loss of market gardeners, silk weavers, workers in ceramics (including the famous tiles or *azulejos*), masons, and carpenters. Less is known about the loss of scholars.

As in the case of the Jews, the Muslim exiles do not seem to have played an important part as mediators, although Sidi Ali, who came from Granada, went to India as interpreter to the Portuguese viceroy Afonso de Albuquerque. However, so little is known (at least to historians who cannot read Arabic) about the impact of these exiles from Spain on their hostlands that any form of conclusion would be unwise.

The best-known example of intellectual mediation was actually an unwilling one. Hasan al-Wazzân, known in the West as Leo Africanus, was born in Granada. He moved to Fez with his parents in 1492, studied there, and followed a career as a diplomat. In his late twenties, he was captured by Christian pirates and taken to Rome, where he was christened "Leo" in honor of his master, Pope Leo X, and taught Arabic in Bologna, writing a grammar of the language. At the pope's request, al-Wazzân wrote his famous *Description of Africa*, first published in Italian in 1550. Translated into French, Latin, and English by the year 1600, this text made an important contribution to Western knowledge of Africa, North Africa in particular.[22] Together with the Italian Jewish scholar Jacob Mantino, al-Wazzân worked on an Arabic-Hebrew-Latin dictionary, thus presenting a good example of a contribution to knowledge via hybridization.

The Catholic Diaspora

After 1492, the next important diasporas follow the European Reformation and they are not very closely associated with precise dates, at least not until the Revocation of the Edict of Nantes in 1685, to be discussed later. Catholics fled from countries that became officially Protestant, such as England, Scotland, Sweden, and the new Dutch Republic, while Protestants fled from countries that remained Catholic, especially Italy and Spain.

One notable feature of the Catholic exile was the foundation of colleges for exiles, including the Collegium Germanicum et Hungaricum (1552), the English College (1579), and the College of St. Isidore (1625: for Irishmen), all in Rome; the English College at Douai in France (1561); the Royal English College,

Valladolid (1589); the College of St. Gregory, Seville (1592); the Royal Irish College, Salamanca (1593); the College of St. Omer (1593); and the Royal Scots College in Madrid (1627).[23]

What kind of contribution to knowledge did the exiles make? Although they offered a general education, the main purpose of the colleges just mentioned was to train priests to go back to their native lands. In other words, as in the case of the Jews, the main intellectual function of the Catholic exiles was to teach other exiles, to maintain religious traditions rather than to mediate between cultures or produce new knowledge. The same point might be made about many of the books written by these exiles. The Irish Franciscan Luke Wadding, for instance, who was rector of the College of St. Isidore, devoted many years to writing the annals of his order. And take the case of the Englishman Richard Smith, professor of divinity at Oxford, who became chancellor of the university founded in Douai by King Philip of Spain. Whether he was defending the Catholic faith or attacking Calvin, Beza, and Melanchthon, Smith was probably writing not so much in order to convince Protestants as to prevent fellow Catholics from wavering. On the other hand, Smith's Latin secretary, the priest Richard Lassels, was active as a mediator. He translated a work by the Catholic historian Cesare Baronio, but he is best known for his *Description of Italy*, an account of Italian culture for an English public that grew out of his experience of guiding members of the upper class on their tour of the country.[24]

Some other exceptions to this rule deserve to be noted. In the first place, exiles spread the knowledge of the new developments in Catholicism often described as the "Counter-Reformation."[25] English Catholics, for instance, learned about new forms of devotion from their compatriots who were living in France, Flanders, Italy, or Spain. In the seventeenth century, Catholics in the Southern Netherlands learned about the theology known as "Jansenism" from French leaders of the movement such as Antoine Arnauld and Pasquier Quesnel, both of whom fled to Brussels.

In this dissemination of new forms of Catholicism, translation was of course important. The English printer John Heigham, for instance, in exile in Douai and St. Omer, translated works by Italian, Spanish, and French devotional writers. Mateo Martinez Waucquier, who came from Middelburg in the Northern Netherlands and moved to Antwerp in the South to escape the Reformation, spent much of his life translating works of Catholic devotion (by Teresa of Avila, for instance, and François de Sales) into Latin, so that they could spread more widely. In similar fashion, Michael ab Isselt, another refugee from the Northern Netherlands (in his case from Amersfort), living in Cologne, translated the Spanish devotional writer Luis de Granada into Latin. Isselt edited the *Mercurius Gallo-Belgicus*, a periodical published in Cologne, between 1592 and his death in 1597. Cologne (where many works of Catholic devotion were published in Latin), together with Rome and Antwerp, became a major center for the circulation of Catholic knowledge at this time.

In a few instances, Catholic exiles played an important role in the dissemination of secular knowledge. Early examples are the brothers Johannes Magnus, archbishop of Uppsala, and his brother Olaus, both of whom left Sweden when King Gustav Vasa imposed Protestantism, and went to live in Venice and then, in 1537, in Rome. As exiles often do, the brothers turned to studying the history of their homeland. Johannes wrote a history of the kings of the Goths (whom the Swedes believed to be their ancestors), while Olaus published a history of Northern Europe, thus disseminating knowledge of Scandinavia. A generation later, the Irishman Richard Stanihurst, an alchemist and historian who moved to the Netherlands, published a history of Ireland (1584) and a life of St. Patrick (1587), both in Antwerp.[26] As in the case of the Magnus brothers, we are entitled to suspect that research was driven by nostalgia.

At least one Catholic exile who turned to translation concentrated on secular works. Aegidius Albertinus came from Deventer in the Northern Netherlands, leaving it for Spain and then for Munich, where he became court librarian, as well as translating the Spanish moralist Antonio de Guevara into Latin and the picaresque romance *Guzmán de Alfarache* into German.

Some Catholic exiles, such as the Englishman Thomas Stephens, became Jesuits and were sent on missions, to India in the case of Stephens. The Jesuits will appear in Chapter 4 in the role of expatriates rather than exiles, with a significant collective exception that deserves to be mentioned here. When King Carlos III of Spain ordered the Jesuits out of his dominions in 1767, over 2,000 left Spain and Spanish America, mainly for Italy.[27]

Among the Spaniards were some scholars, the linguist Lorenzo Hervás for instance, who has been described as "the great forgotten figure of the Spanish Enlightenment." Although it is sometimes said that he was a former missionary in the New World, Hervás did not leave Europe. It was in Rome, still a center of knowledge where he, like Athanasius Kircher before him, acquired information from missionaries who had learned Amerindian languages in the field, information that he passed on in his turn to Wilhelm von Humboldt, who made use of it in his studies of comparative linguistics. Hervás spent much of his time in Italy compiling a catalogue of world languages, assisted in his work by access to libraries in Rome. All the same, he was more than a collector; he was also a theorist, who provided Humboldt not only with information but also with ideas that the German scholar developed.[28]

In similar fashion, another Spanish Jesuit, Juan Andrés, spent part of his exile writing a history of the origin and progress of "every" literature. Not all the Spanish Jesuit scholars shared what have been called the "encyclopedic" aims of Hervás and Andrés, but others seem to have felt more European in Italy than they had felt at home, and contributed to what has been described as the "hybridization" of Spanish and Italian culture (*una compenetración de culturas*).[29]

A few of the exiled Spanish American Jesuits, on the other hand, wrote histories of their native regions. Juan Ignacio Molina, from what is now Chile, published his *Compendio della storia geografica, natural e civili del regno del Cile* in Italian (1776). He has recently been praised for his gifts for observation and precise description. Miguel de Olivares, also from Chile, wrote a history of the Spanish conquest of the region.[30] Juan de Velasco, from what is now Ecuador, wrote the *Historia del Reino de Quito* (1789). Francisco Javer Alegre, from Mexico, wrote a history of the Jesuits in New Spain. Most important of all, Francisco Javier Clavijero produced his *Historia Antigua de México* (1780–81). Clavijero knew Nahuatl, emphasized the significance of indigenous sources for the history of Mexico, and argued that the Mexicans were already civilized peoples before the Spaniards arrived. These scholars, who were all creoles, were reacting against the European critique of the New World as either infantile or degenerate, a critique launched by scholars and writers such as the Comte de Buffon and Cornelis de Pauw.[31]

It remains intriguing that these five Jesuits all produced their most important work abroad, whether they too were driven by nostalgia for the *patria* or simply made good use of their enforced leisure. A recent study of these Jesuits asks whether they would have written the same books if they had not been exiled. Although the author's reply is "probably yes," the subtitle of his essay, "creative sorrow," implies the opposite.[32]

The Elizabethan Exiles

At this point it may be fruitful to focus more sharply on the English Catholic exiles who left their homeland in the reigns of Edward VI and Elizabeth I. Most of them went to the Netherlands, especially Leuven (Louvain) and Antwerp, or to France, especially Rouen, Rheims, and Douai. From about the year 1580, Rouen was "something of a centre for English Catholic printing," with the advantage that it was not far from England, allowing books to be smuggled in by sea.[33]

Two collective enterprises on the part of Catholic exiles are particularly worthy of note. One was the new translation of the Bible into English by Gregory Martin, based in Douai and assisted by other exiles, among them William Allen, Richard Bristow, William Reynolds, and Thomas Worthington. The other was the attack on the Church of England and its defenders (notably John Jewel, bishop of Salisbury and author of an *Apologia* for the Anglicans) on the part of a group of friends who had studied at New College Oxford and moved to Leuven: Thomas Dorman, Thomas Harding, and Thomas Stapleton. These books were printed by another English exile in Leuven, John Fowler, who had also studied at New College. Fowler printed an attack on Jewel by yet another New College man, John Rastell, who had moved to Germany.

It is difficult to avoid the impression that many English exiles resisted assimilation, studying and teaching in English colleges in France, Spain, or Italy and writing books in English, published in Douai or Leuven by English printers such as John Fowler, Henry Jaye, or Laurence Kellam (themselves exiles), to be read by Catholics at home.

There were, however, key exceptions to this rule. Nicholas Sanders, for instance, wrote a Latin history of the English "schism," *De origine ac progressu schismatis Anglicani* (1585), its many editions published in Cologne, Ingolstadt, Rome, and elsewhere attesting to its international success. William Reynolds translated works by his friends Allen and Harding into Latin so that they would reach an international readership. Richard Verstegan, who settled in Antwerp, is remembered today as the author of a study of English antiquities, *The Restitution of Decayed Intelligence* (1605), once again a product of nostalgia for the homeland. However, he was also important, as his biographer points out, as a "cultural intermediary," at ease in French, Flemish, and Spanish and active as a printer, translator, and newswriter for a journal called the *Nieuwe Tijdinghen*; organizer of an information network; and author of the *Theatrum Crudelitatum Haereticorum Nostri Temporis* (*Theatre of the Cruelties of the Heretics of Our Time*, 1586).[34]

In this age of religious conflict, some printers were mercenaries, publishing both Catholic and Protestant works if they thought that they would sell, but others, like the exiles just mentioned, printed in order to serve their cause.

The Protestant Diaspora

The Jewish, Muslim, and Catholic diasporas all made an impact on cultures of knowledge in Europe and elsewhere, but this impact is better documented, more obvious, and probably more important in the case of the Protestants, as what follows will try to show. The arrival of the exiles often made a significant impact on the local order of knowledge, most quickly and most obviously in the domain of the crafts, and later and more gradually in the case of scholars.

Italians

The Protestant diaspora came predominantly but not completely from Northern Europe. In the South, Spain contributed Miguel Servet, for instance, who was burned for heresy in Geneva; Francisco Enzinas, who translated the New Testament into Spanish; and Cipriano de Val, who chose England for his refuge.

However, Italians were much more numerous. Following the establishment of the Roman Inquisition in 1542, Italian Protestants of different kinds (from Calvinist to Unitarian) left the peninsula for a variety of destinations such as Switzerland, England, Germany, Transylvania, and Poland. On arrival, they often acted as mediators, contributing to the spread of knowledge by transmitting to their hosts much of the learned and literary culture of Renaissance Italy.[35] For example, a number of the refugees were physicians, some of them trained at the University of Padua. Niccolò Buccella and Gianbattista Gemma, for instance, became physicians to the king of Poland, Stefan Batory, and it is likely that they disseminated over Central and Eastern Europe the knowledge of new medical discoveries made in Padua and elsewhere in Italy.[36] Another refugee, Jacopo Aconcio, an engineer, was employed in England to drain marshes and inspect fortifications. Aconcio also wrote a book about reading and writing history that was translated, rather freely, into English and published in 1574.

Other refugees were more concerned with the humanities, like the literary critic Ludovico Castelvetro, celebrated for his commentary on Aristotle's *Poetics*, who left Italy for Lyon, Geneva, and Vienna; and his nephew Giacomo, who subsidized the publication in London, in Italian, of two famous pastoral poems, *Aminta* by Torquato Tasso, and the *Pastor Fido* by Giambattista Guarini. Another refugee, the lawyer Scipione Gentili, translated Tasso's epic *Gerusalemme Liberata* into Latin, while his nephew Robert, born in London, was a polyglot who made a living translating books into English from Latin, Italian, Spanish, and French. A more famous translator, John Florio (whose hybrid name suggests a hybrid identity), was also born in London, the son of the refugee Michelangelo Florio. Both father and son published introductions to the Italian language, while John, who taught French as well as Italian, is now remembered for his English version of Montaigne's essays.

The main center for translations from Italian was Basel, where books by Machiavelli, the historians Francesco Guicciardini and Paolo Giovio, and other humanists were turned into Latin by exiles such as Celio Secundo Curione, professor of rhetoric at the university; the physician Giovanni Niccolò Stoppani, another professor in Basel; the ex-Benedictine monk Francesco Negri; and Silvestro Teglio, the translator of Machiavelli's *Prince*. Some of these translations were printed by another Italian Protestant exile, the former Dominican friar Pietro Perna, who settled in Basel and also published a number of Protestant writers.[37] Mediation in the opposite direction was provided by Ortensio Lando, a former Augustinian monk turned Protestant, who worked as corrector of the press in Basel and translated Thomas More's *Utopia* into Italian (1548).[38]

Netherlanders

An early example of a refugee from the Netherlands who made an important contribution to the dissemination of knowledge is that of Daniel Bomberg, a printer who left Antwerp for Venice by 1516 and continued to print books in Hebrew until his death in 1549. Bomberg was a Christian but he employed Jewish scholars as compositors and correctors, just as Aldus had employed Greeks.

The main waves of refugees came later. Between 1567 and 1573, about 60,000 Protestants left in order to avoid persecution by the regime of the Spanish soldier the Duke of Alba, who governed the Netherlands for Philip II of Spain. A second wave of 100,000 to 150,000 Protestants left the South in the 1580s, when Spanish forces reasserted control of Antwerp and other cities. This second wave has been called "one of the four great western European migrations of early modern times," comparable with that of the Jews in 1492 and the Protestants in the 1560s and 1680s.[39]

Many Netherlanders moved to Germany and to England. They included merchants, bankers (like Johann von Bodeck, who fled from Antwerp in 1584 and settled in Frankfurt), and many artisans, bringing their know-how to their hostlands, setting up luxury industries and introducing innovations, "new forms of mass production, of techniques and labour organization." For example, the refugees made the rapidly growing city of Danzig (now Gdańsk) a major center for making glass and furniture.[40] The engraver Théodore de Bry, who came from Liège, moved to Strasbourg, then Antwerp, and finally to Frankfurt, where he became a printer-publisher, specializing in illustrated books about the New World and followed in this career by his son Jean-Théodore.

Other Protestant refugees from the Netherlands moved to England, especially London and East Anglia, at least for a time. Among them were at least five pastors who mediated between the cultures of their homeland and their hostland, learning English (a language understood by very few foreigners at this time) and translating into Dutch works of devotion by writers such as the popular theologian William Perkins. Vincent Meursevoet, who lived for a time in Norwich, translated more than thirty-five books, while Jan Lamoot, who came to England as a child and went to school in London, translated at least eight.

However, the majority of Flemish Protestants left the Southern Netherlands for the North, especially after the Spanish recapture of Antwerp in 1585. They included some distinguished men of learning. The engineer Simon Stevin, for instance, migrated from Bruges to Leiden in 1581. The humanist Caspar Barlaeus, born in

Antwerp in 1584, moved with his family to the North soon afterward, and became a professor first in Leiden and later in Amsterdam. Johannes de Laet, who combined the life of a merchant with that of a scholar, moved from Antwerp to Amsterdam with his family in 1584, when he was three years old. Petrus Plancius, a minister and also an astronomer, fled from Brussels to Amsterdam and was active there in the fields of cartography and navigation. The biblical scholar Johannes Drusius and the theologian-historian Wilhelmus Baudartius both came from the South, and took refuge in England for a time and then in the Northern Netherlands. They both became professors at the University of Leiden before moving to the University of Franeker in Friesland.

Among these refugees there were, once again, a number of printers. Lodewijk Elsevier, for instance, moved from Leuven to Leiden in 1581, while Jan Commelin, the founder of a family of printers and scholars, left Antwerp for Amsterdam. Two printers, Cornelisz Claesz and Joost de Hondt, both specialists in cartography, moved from Antwerp to Amsterdam in the early 1580s. In their new home, they collaborated in the publication of maps, helping to make Amsterdam into the major center of map production and geographical knowledge that it was in the seventeenth century. The printer and instrument-maker Levinus Hulsius, who came from Ghent, transferred his business to Nuremberg and then to Frankfurt.

The English

During the reign of the Catholic Queen Mary (1553–58), English Protestants also fled abroad. Remembered as the "Marian Exiles," they usually went to Strasbourg, Frankfurt, Zurich, and Basel. They did not stay long, but their years abroad were a form of education, whether formal or informal. Thirty-eight English students appear in the matriculation register at the University of Basel between 1554 and 1559, "all of them Protestant refugees." More generally, thanks to their years abroad, "the mental vision of these islanders was to be widened to comprehend new horizons."[41] One exile in Geneva, Stephen Wythers, translated Calvin's critique of relics and the Lutheran scholar Johann Sleidan's history of the four great empires of antiquity. Another exile, in Strasbourg, John Foxe, published the first version, in Latin, of what was to become an English Protestant classic, the *Acts and Monuments*, better known as Foxe's Book of Martyrs.

A still more famous English diaspora was that of the so-called Pilgrim Fathers in the New World. They were Protestants who separated themselves from the Church of England and moved first to the Dutch Republic and then, from 1620 onward, to New England. For the most part, they were concerned to reconstruct their community in a new place rather than to acquire knowledge, although they must have learned something in order to survive in an environment in which many plants and animals were unknown to them on arrival. Similarly, they were mainly unconcerned to transmit knowledge to their Indian neighbors. An exception to the first generalization was Roger Williams, a clergyman who arrived in Boston in 1631 but moved to a new settlement, Providence, in 1636. Williams learned the language of an Indian people, the Narragansetts, publishing a phrase book, *A Key Into the Language of America* (1643), on his return to England. All the same, unlike other clergymen who studied the languages of the Americas, notably the Jesuits, Williams did not try to convert his Indian neighbors. He studied their culture for its own sake, admiring it in many respects, notably the spirit of harmony, as well as using it to criticize Puritan theocracy.[42]

Central Europeans

Czech Protestants and other religious dissidents left Bohemia after their Calvinist king was defeated in the battle of the White Mountain (*Bílá Hora*) in 1621. Jan Amos Komenský, for instance, better known as Comenius, was a pastor of the Moravian Brethren, a pre-Protestant group, and an advocate of what he called *Pansophia*, universal knowledge leading to universal wisdom. In the 1620s he took refuge in Poland and later lived in Sweden, Prussia, England, and Transylvania.[43] Wherever Comenius went, he tried to spread his ideas on education and other matters. In his time in England, together with his associates the Scot John Dury (who had lived in the Dutch Republic, France, and Poland) and Samuel Hartlib (born in Poland, though his mother was English), Comenius made a contribution to the intellectual ferment of the 1640s.

Comenius, Hartlib, and Dury, followers of Francis Bacon with a vision of "universal reformation" (in other words, the reform of society through education), were all invited to England by the anti-court party in 1641. They have been called "the real philosophers, and the only philosophers, of the English Revolution."[44] Of the trio, Comenius was the most original thinker and the leader, and it has sometimes been suggested that his visit to England had something to do with the foundation of the Royal Society. At any rate, some of his followers were among the founders.[45] It was Hartlib, though, who was close to John Pym, leader of the parliamentary opposition to the king in 1641, and also the mediator par excellence, "one of the key intellectual brokers of seventeenth-century Europe."[46] His wide network of friends and correspondents, from France to Bohemia, made him known as "the great intelligencer of Europe."

These "three foreigners," as a well-known study calls them (though Dury was born in Edinburgh) belonged to a larger group of confessional exiles who moved eastward to Poland (like the female astronomer Maria Cunitz) and Transylvania (like the encyclopedist Johann Heinrich Alsted and his former student Johann Heinrich Bisterfeld) as well as westward to the Dutch Republic and England.

A number of these exiles belonged to the Hartlib network. Johannes Moriaen, for instance, was a German minister (the son of a Dutch Calvinist exile) who moved to Amsterdam, became a merchant, and arranged for books by Comenius to be printed there. Henry Oldenburg came from Bremen, an important center of Calvinism in the 1630s, migrated to England and, after a spell as a private tutor in Kent, became the secretary of the Royal Society as well as taking over from Hartlib the management of his international network of colleagues and correspondents. In addition to these forms of mediation, Oldenburg was active as a translator and turned François Bernier's famous description of India into English.

A third member of the Hartlib network was another central European exile, Theodore Haak, who was born in Germany (his mother was a Huguenot refugee) but spent much of his life in England. Haak was another mediator, especially via translation. While he was still living in Germany, he translated a treatise by a Puritan divine, David Dyke, into German, and while he was living in England, he translated *Paradise Lost* into German and the annotations on the new Dutch Bible into English. Working for the Council of State during the English Commonwealth, he translated official publications, again into German. Working for the Royal Society, of which he was a Fellow, Haak translated into English an Italian treatise on dyeing and a German treatise on amber.[47] Collectively, these Central Europeans made a significant contribution to what Bacon called "the advancement of learning."

Although the early modern Protestant diaspora was a movement on a much smaller scale than the Great Exodus of the 1930s, to be discussed in what follows, it is not fanciful to compare the two. In both cases, the refugees showed a commitment to an ideal of international scholarship that transcended political conflicts and might even be a means to end them. The Republic of Letters owed a good deal to their mediation between homelands and hostlands. English scholars such as the chemist Robert Boyle and the bishop John Wilkins, inventor of what he called a "philosophical language" that was intended to facilitate international communication, owed something, however difficult to define, to their association with refugees such as Hartlib, Haak, Oldenburg, and the linguist Cyprian Kinner, a former assistant to Comenius.

Some of the refugees were also committed to the ideal of detachment, or as they called it, impartiality. "*Unparteiisch* was one of Moriaen's highest commendations of a group or an individual," while John Dury presented himself as "a peacemaker without partiality."[48] The theme of impartiality recurs in the case of the Huguenot exiles of the 1680s, to be discussed later in this chapter.

The French

The most famous group of Protestant exiles was surely the French, beginning with Jean Calvin, who fled to Basel and moved to Strasbourg before establishing himself in Geneva in 1541, and including Calvin's disciple Theodore Beza, who arrived in Geneva in 1548. It has been argued that Calvin's ideas were shaped in important respects by his experience as a refugee.[49]

A new wave of refugees followed the pogrom of Protestants in Paris in 1572, known as the "Massacre of St. Bartholomew." French refugees scattered. Franciscus Junius the elder, best known for his work on a new translation of the Bible into Latin, moved to Heidelberg. The scholars François Hotman, Isaac Casaubon, Louis Turquet de Mayerne, and Joseph Justus Scaliger all took refuge in Geneva, like the scholar-printers Robert and Henri Estienne. Another printer, André Wechel, fled to Frankfurt in 1572, like his son-in-law the printer Jean Aubry and Aubry's colleague Claude de Marne. One enterprising Huguenot, François Caron, born in Brussels to a family of French refugees, arrived in Japan in a Dutch ship in 1619, and remained for over twenty years, becoming the head of the Japanese branch of the Dutch East India Company, the VOC, and contributing to European knowledge of East Asia with his description of the kingdoms of Japan and Siam.

French Protestants also fled to England and the Netherlands. A famous example is Théodore Turquet de Mayerne (son of the historian Louis), a distinguished physician who left France after the assassination of Henri IV. Mayerne became physician and secret agent to James I, and remained in England for forty years, even though he "refused [. . .] unless pressed, to speak or write English."[50] Some of the refugees supported themselves by teaching their native language, French being their main form of intellectual capital, while language teaching was and is a domain, like the crafts, where face-to-face contact is crucial, with the pupil, like an apprentice, imitating the master or mistress. A study of the teaching of French in England in the sixteenth and seventeenth centuries mentions eighteen individuals (including two women and two refugees from Antwerp) active before 1685.[51] However, the language teachers who have left traces on the historical record are, once more, just the tip of an iceberg, often known only because they published grammars, phrase books or dictionaries.

Among the exiles in London, Claude de Sainliens (who was known in England by a translation of his name, "Holyband") taught French, Italian, and Latin, and published manuals entitled *The French Schoolmaster* (1573), *The French Littleton* (1576), and *The Italian Schoolmaster* as well as dictionaries. Jacques Bellot wrote another early "teach yourself French," *Familiar Dialogues* (1586). Pierre (or Peter) Erondell published a phrase book entitled *The French Garden* (1605) and intended for women in particular. Both Sainliens and Bellot were published by a fellow exile, Thomas Vautrollier, who also printed Calvin's *Institutes*, an English translation of the Calvinist poet Guillaume Du Bartas, the Latin translation of the Bible by Beza, and works of Protestant apologetics.[52]

In the Dutch Republic, the exile Thomas La Grue published a French grammar (in Latin), as well as translating books from Dutch into French, while the pastor Barthelémy Pielat published what he called an "anti-grammar" (*L'anti-grammaire*, 1673). Nathanael Duez taught French and Italian at the University of Leiden. A Catholic expatriate, Jean-Nicolas de Parival, also taught French there as well as writing a book, *Les délices de la Hollande* (1651), to introduce the inhabitants of his homeland to the culture of his hostland.

As a number of these examples show, the movement of French Protestants abroad continued even after the Edict of Nantes (1598), which gave them the right to practice their religion.

The Exodus of the 1680s

The consequences of exile for knowledge are most obvious and best documented in the case of the diaspora that followed the notorious Revocation of the Edict of Nantes by Louis XIV in 1685, so this diaspora will be examined in greater detail than the cases discussed so far. French Protestants, about 800,000 Calvinists, known as Huguenots, faced the alternatives of conversion to Catholicism or expulsion, the same difficult choice that Spanish Jews had faced nearly 200 years earlier. Calculations of the numbers that chose to leave "Babylon," as they called it, vary. Older figures were high: 300,000 or 15 percent of the Huguenot population. However, they have been revised downward by later scholars to 200,000 or more recently, still further down, to 150,000.[53] The dramatic event of the Revocation was only one moment in a longer story of Protestant exiles, but it was the moment with the greatest consequences for the dissemination of knowledge.

The 150,000 or more exiled Huguenots made their way for the most part to the Netherlands (especially Amsterdam, Rotterdam, and The Hague), to England (especially London), and to Prussia (especially Berlin). In Prussia and some parts of the Netherlands, the exiles were offered privileges to encourage them to settle. In the Netherlands and London they were able to link up, in an unusual example of delayed chain migration, with their sixteenth-century predecessors who had established the Walloon churches in those countries.

This migration became known as the "Refuge" and the exiles as *réfugiés* or refugees. The Netherlands in particular was described by one of these Bible-minded Protestants, Pierre Bayle, as a kind of Noah's Ark, "la grande Arche des fugitifs."[54] These fugitives were helped to adapt to their new environment by members of the earlier wave of Huguenot refugees, as well as by some civic authorities, in Rotterdam for instance, who created teaching posts for scholars such as Jurieu and Bayle. The regular use of French by elites in the United Provinces (and also at the court in Berlin) made life easier for the new arrivals.

Other Huguenot exiles went to Switzerland, Ireland, Sweden, Russia, the Cape of Good Hope, and North America, from Massachusetts to South Carolina. Boston, for example, became the new home of Pierre Daillé, son of the famous scholar Jean Daillé, and also of the merchant Pierre Baudouin, whose family Americanized their name to Bowdoin, the name of a liberal arts college founded by the family in Maine in 1794.[55]

Loss and Gain

For France, the Huguenot emigration was a significant loss of intellectual capital. Besides the relatively few scholars and other knowledge workers on whom this section will concentrate, France was deprived of the skills of many textile workers (especially silk weavers and linen weavers) and also of leather workers, woodworkers, printers, clockmakers, glassmakers, papermakers, soapmakers, hatmakers, ivory carvers and metalworkers, including the silversmiths who moved to London and produced what is still known as "Huguenot silver."

For the United Provinces of the Netherlands, England, Prussia, and elsewhere, the gain in skills was equally significant.[56] In England, the recovery of the silk industry from its decline owed much to the immigrants, while in Ireland the Huguenots helped make linen into a leading product. An interesting case of interaction between craft and academic knowledges is provided by the Dollond family, who took refuge in London. The father was a silk weaver who moved from Normandy to Spitalfields. His son Jean or John turned from weaving to experiments in optics, thanks to which he was elected a Fellow of the Royal Society, while in 1750 John's son Peter founded a firm that made optical instruments (it became Dollond and Aitchison in 1927, and was taken over by Boots in 2009). Not for the first time, or the last, the movement of people was a powerful means of technology transfer.[57] Needless to say, local artisans did not view the immigrants in this positive manner but resented their competition.

The economic consequences of the Revocation were mentioned at the time. Marshal Vauban, an acute commentator on the French economy as well as a master of siegecraft, compared the expulsion of the Huguenots with the expulsion of the Moriscos from Spain earlier in the seventeenth century, noting the negative consequences of both events. The Protestant pastor Pierre Jurieu, himself an exile in Rotterdam, made a similar comparison, lamenting the decline of French industry.[58]

Leaving skill migration on one side, what follows will concentrate on Huguenot scholars and other people involved in the transmission of knowledge, focusing on ninety-six individuals, including the most famous participants in the diaspora of the 1680s.

Doctors and Booksellers

Like the artisans, some lay exiles, such as physicians or booksellers, continued to practice their business or profession in their new home. As the example of Théodore de Mayerne reminds us, physicians, like surgeons and apothecaries, were prominent in earlier waves of Huguenot migration to London and elsewhere. Four French medical men who moved to London were elected Fellows of the Royal Society in the 1690s, among them the surgeon Paul Buissière and Paul Silvestre, physician to King William III.

Seventeen of the ninety-six individuals just mentioned were active in London, Amsterdam, or Rotterdam as printers, publishers, or booksellers (roles that were often combined at this time). One printer-bookseller who moved his business from France to his new home was Henri Desbordes, who moved from La Rochelle to Amsterdam in 1682 after his bookshop was closed and he was briefly imprisoned for printing an attack on a famous French bishop, Jacques Bossuet. Others included the Huguetan brothers in Amsterdam, who owned a dozen presses there and also established a branch in London, and Paul Vaillant, who moved to London, specializing in religious books imported from Amsterdam and Paris. Vaillant's sons published the translation of Bayle's famous *Dictionary* into English in 1734, and they were still operating a bookshop in the Strand in the 1740s. These publishers often employed fellow exiles as correctors of French books for the press, and published works by exiled writers. Abram Acher, for instance, who migrated from Dieppe to Rotterdam, published books by his compatriot Pierre Jurieu. Henri Desbordes both employed and published Pierre Bayle. Pierre Brunel, established in Amsterdam at the sign of "the Golden Bible," did in fact print Bibles as well as books by fellow Huguenots.

New Careers

Other exiles chose, or were forced to choose, a new career. Law, for instance, does not travel very well, as some members of the diaspora of 1933, discussed later, experienced when they moved from Germany or Austria to the United States, changing profession to become political scientists or specialists in international relations. In similar fashion, in the seventeenth century, the jurist Charles Ancillon, for instance, became the official historian of the elector of Brandenburg-Prussia. Another jurist, Jean Barbeyrac, taught *belles-lettres* in Berlin before he was appointed to professorships in law, first at the University of Lausanne and later at the University of Groningen. A third, Jacob Le Duchat, who moved from Metz to Berlin, became an editor of literary texts. Some refugees, unwilling or unable to settle down, moved from one new occupation to another. Abel Boyer, for example, was active as (among other things) a private tutor, a translator, a journalist, and a historian.[59]

The clergy, 680 of them to be exact, were disproportionately represented in the exodus. They moved to Protestant countries where there were already plenty of preachers (405 of them arrived in the United Provinces).[60] Some of them, Jurieu for example, continued to act as ministers, in churches in Amsterdam, London, Berlin, and elsewhere, especially in churches founded for the exiles and using the French language (there were sixty-two such churches in the Netherlands by 1688, and around twenty-five in London).[61]

However, as one might have guessed, even with this rise in their clientele, the supply of Calvinist preachers in the hostlands was now much greater than the demand for them.[62] Many of the exiled clergy faced unemployment. So what did this well-educated and highly articulate group do? Perhaps the most remarkable case of adaptation in a new environment was that of Nicolas Chevalier, a pastor who took refuge in the Dutch Republic and combined the professions of bookseller and medalist, producing a history of the deeds of William III in medals, in competition with the better-known "medallic history" of Louis XIV. Other pastors in exile used their verbal skills in a number of ways, occupying various cultural niches in the host countries, especially as mediators between homeland and hostland. The prestige of the French language abroad, similar to that of Italian during the Renaissance, was another important part of their cultural capital.[63]

Many of these exiles became teachers and professors. Pierre Jurieu, for example, was not only pastor of the French church in Rotterdam but also professor at a new college, the newly founded École Illustre, together with his former protégé Pierre Bayle. Michel Maittaire, who began his new life in England, became a teacher at Westminster School. Etienne Chauvin, who moved to Berlin, combined a post as pastor with another one as professor of philosophy, as well as becoming inspector of the Collège Français (founded in 1689) and also the founder of a learned journal. These recruits to the profession tended to teach theology or philosophy, but Etienne Morin taught oriental languages at the Amsterdam Athenaeum, the nearest equivalent to a university in the city, from 1686 onward.

Some exiles became private tutors. Abel Boyer taught French to the duke of Gloucester, while in the next generation Prince Frederick, later Frederick the Great, had a Huguenot governess, Marthe de Montbail, and a Huguenot tutor, the nobleman and army officer Jacques-Egide Duhan de Jandun. Another nobleman, Solomon de Foubert, former master of a riding academy in Paris, opened an academy in London in the 1680s. At a lower social level, a number of Huguenot refugee teachers of French could be found in London or nearby in the later seventeenth century, many of them located in or near St. Paul's churchyard. Fortunately, the demand for French lessons was increasing, along with the supply. "The ever-growing call for teachers of French was met by the great invasion of Protestant refugees."[64]

Other refugees became librarians. Peter Colomiez became librarian to the archbishop of Canterbury at Lambeth Palace. Élie Bouhéreau, a physician who took refuge in Ireland, became librarian of Marsh's Library in Dublin, in 1701. He was the first public librarian in Ireland. The scholar Henri Justel arrived in England in 1681 and was elected a Fellow of the Royal Society thanks to his activities as a correspondent to that body. The former owner of a library of 7,000 volumes, Justel was appointed keeper of the royal manuscripts and librarian to the king at St. James's Palace.[65] Other exiles became compilers of works of reference, such as Boyer's French-English dictionary or Bayle's famous *Dictionnaire* (to be discussed later), or editors of literary texts. The former lawyer Jacob Le Duchat, for instance, edited books by Villon, Rabelais, and Brantôme.

At least twenty refugees and their children were active as translators, exemplifying this recurrent form of mediation between cultures. The majority of translations were made from English into French, and the most famous of the translators was Pierre Coste, who settled in London and translated three works by John Locke (*On Education, The Reasonableness of Christianity,* and *An Essay Concerning Human Understanding*), as well as Newton's *Optics.*[66] François Michel Janiçon, who fled to Utrecht as a child and worked as a tutor and a journalist, translated Richard Steele's *Ladies' Library*. Steele's periodical *The Tatler* was translated, under the title *Le babillard,* by Armand de la Chapelle. *The Spectator,* which Steele wrote together with Joseph Addison, was turned into French by Élie de Joncourt, a pastor and teacher who also translated works by Alexander Pope and George Berkeley.[67] Pierre-Antoine Motteux, who fled to London in 1685 and was also active as an auctioneer and a playwright, completed the translation of the works of Rabelais into English. Spreading the knowledge of a distant culture, Pierre Des Maizeaux translated the description of Japan written by the German physician Engelbert Kämpfer (the English version was already in print, while the German original remained in manuscript).

In the other direction, Abel Boyer translated Fénelon's political romance *Télémaque* into English, while Motteux translated Cervantes as well as Rabelais. In two typical examples of the internationalism of the Republic of Letters at this time, Jean

Barbeyrac, an exile in Switzerland, translated the German Samuel Pufendorf's treatise on natural law into French and published it in Amsterdam, while Jacques Lenfant, an exile in Berlin, translated a treatise by the French philosopher Nicolas Malebranche into Latin and published it in Geneva. In short, we might say, with only a little exaggeration, that the Revocation of the Edict of Nantes marks an epoch in the history of translation.[68]

Historians and Journalists

Other refugees became historians. Some were appointed official historians, like some sixteenth-century Italian expatriates, to be discussed in the following chapter. They include Charles Ancillon, a refugee in Berlin who was appointed official historian to the elector; Antoine Teissier, another official historian in Berlin; Henri Basnage, historian to the States of Holland; Isaac de Larrey, historiographer to the States-General; and Nicholas Frémont d'Ablancourt, historiographer to William III. Others wrote unofficially. Paul de Rapin-Thoyras, a friend of the Basnage brothers, became interested in English history while fighting for the Protestant cause in Ireland. Rapin wrote, so he explained, "for the instruction of foreigners" in his *Histoire de l'Angleterre* (1723), a work of mediation that was completed by another exile, David Durand.[69] Elie Benoist turned to history for the first time when in exile, and it has been suggested that his history of the Edict of Nantes was part of a collective attempt "to construct a distinct exile identity."[70]

In some cases the link between the topics chosen by these historians and their religious beliefs is obvious enough. "The historical projects of the Huguenots were, of course, mainly responses to Catholic challenges."[71] Stimulated by the desire to defend their faith, a number of exiles turned to history, especially histories of heresy. Jacques Lenfant, for instance, wrote on the history of church councils and heretics such as the Hussites, often regarded as forerunners of Protestants. Isaac de Beausobre wrote on another group of heretics, the Manichees (viewing their leader as a precursor of Luther). Pierre Jurieu wrote about the

Jews, while Jacques Basnage wrote a famous book on the history of the Jews and especially on the "dispersion" of these "refugees," as he called them. One might describe his history as "allegorical" in the sense that he was writing about one diaspora while thinking of another (indeed, his book has been viewed as "an anti-Catholic allegory.") Basnage's comment that "we shall here see a church, that has been hated and persecuted for seventeen hundred years, subsisting and still numerous," must have comforted Huguenot readers.[72] Alternatively, speculating a little, we might think in Freudian terms of Basnage's interest in the Jews as a "displacement" of his concern with his own people, a displacement of which he was not necessarily conscious.

The most important niche of all was what we call journalism. However, it is necessary to distinguish two groups of refugee writers. On one side are the few individuals who wrote for political journals, as in the case of Abel Boyer, editor of the *Post-Boy*, or François Michel Janiçon, who wrote for the gazettes of Rotterdam, Amsterdam, and Utrecht. On the other side are a greater number of exiles who wrote about books, editing scholarly journals or contributing to them.[73] In other words, to take a contemporary analogy, the majority of Huguenot journalists wrote not for the equivalent of the *Times* but for that of the *Times Literary Supplement*. Examples include the *Histoire des Ouvrages des Savants*, edited by Henri Basnage, the *Bibliothèque Universelle*, edited for a time by Jacques Bernard, and the *Journal Littéraire* (with six editors). These journals were an important medium for the dissemination of the ideas of the early Enlightenment.

These journals were not the specialized publications with which we are familiar today but periodicals offering "news of the republic of letters," to quote the title of the most famous of them, the *Nouvelles de la République des Lettres*, published in Rotterdam by an exiled printer, Henri Desbordes, over three years, 1684–87, and edited by one of the leading intellectuals in exile, the philosopher-historian Pierre Bayle. An autodidact of wide-ranging curiosity, Bayle wrote his journal by himself.[74] The "news" reported in these journals extended from book reviews (a new invention) to the obituaries of scholars. The connections of the exiles with their homeland and with refugees in other countries formed networks that proved invaluable in providing the journals with material and spreading information more generally. Bayle, for instance, obtained news about the scholarly scene in Britain from correspondents living there, including his fellow journalist Daniel de Larroque, the surgeon Paul Buissière, and the physician Paul Silvestre.

Impartiality

The importance of the Huguenot diaspora for the production and dissemination of knowledge may be summed up in two words: mediation and detachment. The exiles mediated between their native French culture and the cultures of their three main host-lands, the Dutch Republic, England, and Prussia. This mediation is obvious enough in the role played by the exiles in translation, teaching, and above all in cultural journalism. The names of some of these journals reveal this aim very clearly: the *Bibliothèque Germanique,* for instance, founded in 1720 and edited in Berlin by Étienne Chauvin, Alphonse Des Vignolles, and Jacques Lenfant, or the *Bibliothèque Anglois,* edited by Michel de La Roche.

Returning to the theme of the detachment of exiles, two Huguenot historians, Basnage and Beausobre, were praised for their "impartiality" by Edward Gibbon, who contrasted them to earlier Catholic historians of the Jews and Manichees.[75] Beausobre had himself discussed the need for impartiality in the preface to his history, while Basnage's *Histoire des Juifs* itself claimed be impartial, its author declaring that "our design is neither to offend nor to flatter" the Jews. He wrote as a Christian, discussing how best to try to convert the Jews, but he sympathized with their sufferings and appreciated their devotion to learning, discussing their scholars, printers, and "academies" (*yeshivot*) in considerable detail.[76]

Again, the Huguenot Élie Benoist, historian of the Edict of Nantes, criticized his predecessors for offering "too much of an apologia and too little of a history" (*trop d'apologie et trop peu d'histoire*). He was not afraid of moral judgments but claimed that they were compatible with historical impartiality (*le désintéressement d'un historien*).[77]

Rapin-Thoyras, who wrote the history of England, also criticized his predecessors for their bias, particularly on the subject of King Charles I, noting the need for "a good neutral historian" (*un bon historien neutre*) who might extract the truth even from the most partial historians. Despite a certain sympathy for the Whigs, Rapin kept his distance from English party politics, which he regarded as an interesting phenomenon that needed to be explained to foreigners. His detachment was assisted by the fact that he was writing while living in The Hague and in German-speaking territory (in Wesel, in the Duchy of Cleves). As he expected—he was aware of English reactions to the history of England written by the Italian humanist Polydore Vergil, discussed later—Rapin was criticized in his turn for bias against the monarchy and the Church. All the same, his cool tone and relative freedom from prejudice help explain the success of his history not only on the Continent but (in two separate translations) in Britain as well, where it led the field for a generation until the publication of a rival version of the English past by the Scottish philosopher David Hume.[78]

Detachment encouraged a critical approach to the past, exemplified by the "critical history" that flourished in the late seventeenth and early eighteenth centuries, some of it written by the exiles. Bayle's *Dictionnaire Historique et Critique* has become the most famous instance of the genre.

As in the case of historical writing, the location of the exiles between two cultures assisted their impartiality, a quality already regarded in this period as a sign of the ideal journalist. The anonymous *Critique désintéressée des journaux littéraires et des ouvrages des savants* (published in The Hague in 1730) both claimed this quality for itself and also attributed it to some journals, in which the book reviews were written "without concern for the feelings of either the authors or the booksellers" (*sans égard, ni pour les Auteurs, ni pour les libraires*).[79]

The supreme example of detachment among the Huguenot diaspora was of course Pierre Bayle. An outsider, "provincial, poor and [. . .] Protestant," Bayle loved to undermine received ideas and to contrast two points of view without taking sides. When the witnesses contradict one another, he argued, it is necessary to suspend judgment. Bayle was at his liveliest when discussing the prejudices of earlier writers. "History is dished up very much like meat," he wrote in a famous passage from the *Nouvelles de la République des Lettres*. "Each nation and religion takes the same raw facts and dresses them in a sauce of its own taste, and each reader finds them true or false according to whether they agree or disagree with his prejudices." Bayle was "passionately attached to an ideal of impartiality." According to him, the history of Reformation should ideally be written neither by a Catholic nor a Protestant. If this is not possible, the text should at least be scrutinized by a reader who is neutral in the disputes, *quelque personne neutre*.[80]

For an example of Bayle's detachment in practice, we might take the famous article on "Mohammed" in his *Dictionnaire Historique et Critique*. This article, as a recent study points out, made a contribution to a view of Islam as "more coherent and respectable" than Christians had hitherto believed. As was customary with him, Bayle made his points not as assertions but as refutations of earlier, hostile views of Islam, in the notes, which he called "remarks," rather than in the text itself.[81]

One might say that the suspension of judgment comes relatively easily to someone who lives suspended between two cultures. Bayle, a Frenchman but also a Protestant, was pulled in opposite directions.[82] A twentieth-century Frenchman who was also capable of remarkable detachment, Pierre Bourdieu, described himself as having a "cleft habitus" (*habitus clivé*). This description would seem to have been equally true of Pierre Bayle.

It should be emphasized that Bayle's response to his situation as an exile was far from inevitable, as can be seen from a comparison between him and his colleague and former friend Pierre Jurieu, who, like Bayle, left France for Rotterdam in 1681. Jurieu's later work as well as his later life was shaped by the circumstances of exile, because much of his energy went into writing books against the Catholic Church and in particular the Papacy, forecasting the imminent ruin of that "antichristian kingdom." However, Jurieu was less adaptable than Bayle. His contributions to knowledge dwelt on past wrongs rather than making something out of the positive opportunities provided by exile, as Bayle did.

A book in the tradition of Bayle (whom the author and illustrator both admired) and one that may have made an even greater impact than his famous *Dictionnaire* is what we might call the encyclopedia of the religions of the world produced by Jean-Frédéric Bernard and Bernard Picart, discussed later in this chapter. *Cérémonies et coutumes* was remarkable not only for the scale of the project and the important role played by its illustrations, but also for its detachment. Presenting the religions of the world on apparently equal terms implied a strategy like Bayle's for encouraging readers to reject intolerance and to suspend their "partiality" for a particular form of religion.[83]

The Moment of Exile

It seems callous to speak about a good moment for anyone to be exiled, but some moments are surely better than others. The French refugees of the 1680s arrived in the Dutch Republic, at a time as well as in a place of relatively high receptivity to immigration. Amsterdam was a good choice of destination for these exiles for several reasons. It was a boomtown in the seventeenth century, and capital was available at low rates of interest, encouraging the founding of new businesses (and printers needed capital to buy metal type and paper). There was only a minimum of regulation of the book trade, which registered "amazing growth" in Amsterdam in the seventeenth century, from the 96 firms operating in the first quarter of the century to the 273 firms active in its last quarter.[84]

Besides the home market, including not only other francophone exiles but local elites who knew French, the export of books formed a significant part of the Dutch trading empire, including books in Latin, German, Hebrew, Yiddish, English, Swedish, Spanish, Portuguese, Czech, Russian, Armenian, and Georgian.[85] This polyglot publishing enterprise was made possible by the presence of exiles, including the Jewish printers mentioned earlier. The Dutch Republic and in particular Amsterdam may be described as a "culture of tolerance," the third of the American urban theorist Richard Florida's conditions for innovation, his three Ts (the others being talent and technology).[86]

The moment of the arrival of the refugees in the Dutch Republic in particular coincided with the rise of newspapers and learned journals. The *Gazeta de Amsterdam*, for instance, mentioned earlier, was founded in 1675, and its Yiddish equivalent appeared in the 1680s. The late seventeenth and early eighteenth centuries were also a golden age of nonspecialized intellectual journals. A number of them were edited by refugees, while other refugees wrote for them. They appeared in French in both the Dutch Republic and Prussia—this was no problem, because educated people in those countries knew French. It must be confessed that French-language journals of this kind were rare in England: the *Bibliothèque angloise* (founded in 1717) was a rare exception. Its editor, Michel de La Roche, also edited journals in English, *Memoirs of Literature* (1710–) and *A Literary Journal* (1730–), while the *Gentleman's Journal* was edited by the second-generation exile Peter Anthony Motteux.

The rise of these journals offered the exiles a niche, but in turn the exiles made a significant contribution to the process of proliferation. In similar fashion, Amsterdam offered opportunities to exile booksellers and publishers, as we have seen, but their arrival "may well have reversed a decline in the Amsterdam book industry."[87] The refugees were able to take advantage of the spread of French in the countries to which they migrated, but in their turn they helped "accélerer l'internationalisation de la langue française."[88]

The Second Generation

The spread of French throughout Europe in the seventeenth century, like the spread of English throughout the world today, discouraged the exiles from learning the language of their hostland, whether it was German, Dutch, or English. This reluctance to speak or write a foreign language persisted into the next generation.[89]

This second generation of Huguenot exiles was almost as important for the history of knowledge as the first, as a few examples from the Dutch Republic, Prussia, and England may suggest. In the Dutch Republic, one thinks of Jean Frédéric Bernard, Prosper Marchand, and Étienne Luzac. Bernard, who came to Amsterdam as a child, was a bookseller, editor, and translator. He is best known for an ambitious, seven-volume work, *Cérémonies et coutumes religieuses de tous les peuples du monde*, published over fifteen years, 1723–37, with an anonymous text and engravings by Bernard Picart, an artist who had turned Protestant and left Paris for Amsterdam.[90]

Like his friend Picart, Marchand was actually a new arrival who was a contemporary of the second generation. A convert to Protestantism, he moved to Amsterdam in 1709 and was active as a printer, journalist, and historian of printing, as well as linking Huguenots, booksellers, and journalists by means of his extensive network of correspondents.[91] As for Luzac, he was born in Amsterdam, the son of Huguenot refugees, joined his brother Johan in the bookselling business in Leiden, and also worked for the *Gazette de Leyde*, becoming the editor of the journal and the founder of a dynasty of journalists.[92]

In Prussia, Simon Pelloutier, who was born in Leipzig and became a pastor in Berlin, wrote a history of the Celtic peoples. Two pastors in Stettin (now Szeczin), Paul-Emile de Mauclerc and Jacques Pérard, edited the *Bibliothèque germanique*. One of the most prominent intellectuals of his time, Samuel Formey, was born in Berlin, the son of Huguenot refugees. Formey became pastor of a French Protestant church, professor of philosophy at the Collège Français, secretary to the academy of Berlin, and a prolific writer.[93]

In England, Pierre Des Maizeaux, who left France as a child in 1685, arrived in London in 1699 and wrote for French-language journals. The *Bibliothèque Raisonnée,* which he helped edit, was "the major source of news on English events and ideas" for the French, while Des Maizeaux became "the apostle of Bayle to the English," writing his biography and editing his letters.[94] John Theophilus Desaguliers, son of a Huguenot minister, studied at Oxford and became a Fellow of the Royal Society and a popular lecturer on science who published in both French and English, exemplifying the language skills of at least some members of the second generation of immigrants. Matthew Maty, born in the Dutch Republic, the son of Huguenot exiles, moved to London where he became a librarian and a journalist, founding the *Journal Britannique* (1750) to introduce the French to English literature. John Jortin, born in London, studied at Cambridge, became a clergyman, and published *Remarks on Ecclesiastical History* and a *Life of Erasmus.* He would seem to have been the most assimilated of the members of this group.

How far the exiled Huguenots of both generations resisted assimilation is a difficult question to answer. In London, where they were numerous, they could if they wished live in a kind of ghetto, or at least socialize predominantly with one another. It is known that the community's intellectuals liked to meet in a particular coffeehouse, the Rainbow in Fleet Street, the haunt of Desmaizeaux and Desaguliers, for instance; of Pierre Coste, the translator of Locke; and of the mathematician Abraham de Moivre, who wrote on probability theory and was close to Newton. Like the Russian exiles after 1917 who will be discussed in Chapter 5, the Huguenots had their own churches and schools. Assimilation was slow, although it eventually took place.

The two obvious tests of assimilation are language and marriage. Pierre Bayle, who lived in Rotterdam for a quarter of a century, never learned Dutch (he never learned English either, but for foreigners to know that language was still exceptional at this time).[95] Samuel Formey confessed that for a long time, despite living in Berlin, he knew no German: "La langue du pays m'est demeurée inconnue."[96] On the other hand, Henri Basnage was able, after some years in the Netherlands, to review books in

Dutch and English in his journal.[97] As for marriages, we may contrast Matthew Maty, who came to England at the age of twenty-two and married twice, both times to Huguenots, with Renatus Jordain, who married an Englishwoman and was the father of the assimilated John Jortin mentioned earlier.

Cultural Exchanges

To sum up: the individuals who formed part of the Huguenot Refuge exemplify mediation in various forms. Henri Justel was a cultural mediator between French and English scholars even before he moved to England in 1681, a little before the Revocation. It was Justel, for instance, who arranged for the translation of the transactions of the Royal Society into French for the benefit of Pierre Bayle.[98] Translation between languages was one major form of mediation; the dissemination of information and cultural translation were others. The historian Rapin de Thoyras explained the English political system to foreigners in his *Dissertation sur les Whigs et les Tories* (1717).

For the exiles themselves, the consequences of emigration were far-reaching. Myriam Yardeni has suggested that in the Dutch Republic, the freedom of expression, so much greater than in France, "fait libérer un potential intellectuel explosive, enseveli depuis des décennies [liberated an explosive intellectual power that had been buried for decades]."[99] As was suggested earlier, exile encouraged detachment in Pierre Bayle and some of his colleagues.

In the case of the host countries, a relatively small number of refugees were able to make a relatively large impact on Dutch, Prussian, and British culture. Thanks to the prestige of French culture at the time, the exiles were welcomed as "ambassadors of French learning" (*Sendboten der französische Erudition*).[100] For their part, the exiles increased or deepened the knowledge of French culture in the places in which they settled. They contributed in particular to an important development in the history of European knowledge, the rise of the Dutch Republic and especially of its largest city, Amsterdam, as a center of information and an intellectual entrepôt.[101]

The credit for this rise should not go to the exiles alone. Amsterdam was already a center of news and newspapers in the early seventeenth century, and also of mapmaking, while the Dutch East India Company, the VOC, maintained an important information network linking Amsterdam with Goa, Batavia, Nagasaki, and elsewhere, as we shall see in Chapter 4.[102] One might therefore say that the Huguenots benefited from the rise of Amsterdam as an information center, although they contributed to this rise as well.

Turning to the consequences of the diaspora for knowledge in France, two opposite points need to be made. On the negative side, the loss of skills and intellectual capital (not to mention financial capital) is clear enough. On the positive side, though, the French acquired more knowledge of the outside world, especially Britain, thanks to exiles who wrote in French or translated foreign works into French. Because censorship was much less strict in Britain and the Dutch Republic than it was in France, the exiles could express themselves with relative freedom. Their books were frequently smuggled into France, allowing subversive ideas to circulate.[103]

So far as hybridization is concerned, a theme that will be important in Chapter 4, the obvious question involves Descartes and Locke and the philosophical traditions out of which they emerged and which they in turn fortified. Thanks to the exiles Jean Leclerc and Pierre Coste, it was at least possible for French readers to have access to the *Essay Concerning Human Understanding* in their native language, while the British could read Descartes in Latin versions by translators such as the Huguenot pastor Henri Desmarets and his Swiss colleague Etienne de Courcelles, both refugees in the Dutch Republic.

There is at least enough evidence of French interest in Locke to undermine any simple contrast between French rationalism and British empiricism. Among Locke's French admirers were Voltaire, who appreciated what he called the *esprit sage* of the English philosopher; the publisher-author Jean-Frédéric Bernard, who was also an enthusiast for Bacon; and the historian Paul Rapin.

Although Rapin showed less interest in the essay on *Human Understanding* than in Locke's political writings, his approach to history may be described as empiricist, justifying his interpretations with frequent quotations from original documents. All the same, there are few signs of real synthesis between the ideas of Descartes and Locke or more generally between the French and British philosophical traditions.[104]

To end on a positive note: just as Italian Protestant exiles spread the culture of the late Renaissance, so the Huguenot exiles, notably Bayle, Bernard, and Picart, spread the culture of the early Enlightenment, as well as contributing to the internationalization of learning and strengthening the Republic of Letters in other ways.

4 : THREE TYPES OF EXPATRIATE

As the introduction pointed out, the topic of exiles has generated a substantial historical literature. By contrast, expatriates have received relatively little attention from historians. The term "expatriates" is used here to refer to individuals who are not forced to move away from home but choose to move, often because they are attracted by working conditions abroad. Some of them migrate on their own initiative, but many accept invitations from the host country. The relative neglect of this topic by historians (with a few distinguished exceptions, to be discussed later) contrasts with the interest in it on the part of sociologists and economists. It was in the context of expatriates that the term "brain drain" was coined in a report by the Royal Society over half a century ago. Since then, comparisons of the net gain and loss of brains in different countries, mainly scientific brains, have become common.[1]

Today, the movement of brains is obvious enough, not only in the natural sciences but in the humanities as well, including the historical profession. Think, for instance, of the British historians currently working in the United States (among them Simon Schama, Niall Ferguson, Linda Colley, Paul Kennedy, and Geoffrey Parker), or the Indian historians active outside India, from France to Australia (including Ranajit Guha, Dipesh Chakrabarty, Gyan Prakash, and Sanjay Subramanyam).

In certain periods and in certain places, demand for certain kinds of knowledge has been particularly high. The expatriation of scientists and scholars is frequently linked to the imitation of foreign models. It is part of a response to a particular conjuncture, a moment when the ruler or the government views the country as intellectually backward and so in need of foreign knowledge in order to catch up.[2] Sometimes rulers send missions abroad, like Tsar Peter the Great's "Great Embassy" to Western Europe in 1697–98, when the tsar acquired the knowledge he needed to modernize the Russian Navy; Muhammad Ali's dispatch of forty-five Egyptian students to France in 1826 to learn what the West had to teach; or the Iwakura Mission sent around the world in 1871 by the new Japanese regime to learn about industrial technology.

Alternatively, governments may invite foreign scientists, scholars, and technical experts, such as engineers, shipbuilders, or army officers, to come and work in their country. During the Renaissance, Italian humanists were invited to a number of European courts as well as teaching in universities outside Italy. In the eighteenth century, the Russian government, especially during the reigns of Peter and Catherine the Great, issued many invitations to foreign scholars, especially Germans, to teach or carry out research in Russia. German was their usual medium of communication, in lectures at the Academy of Sciences in St. Petersburg as well as in the books they published in Russia. Similarly, in late nineteenth-century Japan, expatriate academics were requested to lecture in their mother tongue in order to encourage students to learn Western languages.[3]

On other occasions, the initiative came from the other side, as in the case of Christian missionaries or the secular missions sent by the French government to Brazil. What follows will describe a few famous cases of collective expatriation, discussing not only the knowledge that the expatriates brought with them but also what they learned from their sojourns abroad. Three types of expatriate will be distinguished: the commercial, the religious, and the academic, concerned for the most part, though not exclusively, with different kinds of knowledge for different purposes.

Commercial Expatriates

A large group of expatriates lived abroad in order to trade. Commercial networks were also networks of knowledge, which was disseminated along established trade routes, within Europe and beyond it.

From the point of view of the dissemination of knowledge, printers played an important role in this group, from the late fifteenth century onward. The practice of printing was itself disseminated, or "transferred," as historians of technology put it, by German expatriates; to Subiaco and Rome by Konrad Sweynheym and Arnold Pannartz, for instance, to Venice by Johann and Wendelin von Speyer, to Seville by the Kromberger family, and so on.[4]

Other expatriates lived abroad as representatives of a family business, like the Florentines in Bruges and the Venetians in Istanbul or Aleppo, sending information home in letters. Some went further afield, like two Portuguese, Duarte Barbosa and Tomé Pires, both of whom wrote accounts of their travels. Both men developed what has been called "an ethnographical practice," concerned with the formal and informal rules for civilized behavior to be found in different places, sometimes adopting local terms to describe them.[5]

Duarte Barbosa was active in India in the early sixteenth century as a commercial agent, a clerk, and an interpreter. He wrote about Indian trade, cities, and the customs of their inhabitants and those of Southeast Asia in a text known, emphasizing its direct witnessing, as "The Book of What I Saw and Heard" (*O livro do que viu e ouviu*). Barbosa is eloquent, for instance, on the number of junks (*juncos*) in the harbor of Malacca and their various cargoes, and offers a vivid description of food, clothes, and houses in Java, as well as the character of the Javanese: "extremely proud, passionate and treacherous, and above all very cunning."[6]

Tomé Pires, an apothecary with a humanist education, lived in Malacca from 1512 to 1515, visited Java and Sumatra, led the first Portuguese embassy to China, and wrote the *Suma Oriental*, a report addressed to the king of Portugal that included much information about what is now Malaya and Indonesia. In the case of Malacca, where he lived for a time, Pires recounted the history of the region in detail and described its trade and administration. In the case of Java, he described the social system, the practice of suttee, and the interest of the Javanese in gambling. He was also the first Westerner to explain the action of "running amok" (*amoco*), when an individual suddenly attacks anyone in his path.[7]

Before the age of the commercial companies began around the year 1600, the Portuguese and Spaniards had already created institutions for collecting, storing, and analyzing geographical knowledge. In both countries, cosmographers were appointed by the rulers with titles such as *Cosmógrafo de Indias*, specialists who were expected to supply information on astronomy, geography, and navigation. Maps and charts were stored in the "Warehouse of Guinea" (Armazém de Guiné) and "India House" (Casa da Índia), both in Lisbon, and in the Casa de Contratación ("House of Trade") in Seville. Spanish officials tried to keep this information secret, making some cosmographers swear oaths not to share their knowledge with foreigners, but their efforts were, predictably, unsuccessful.[8]

The Age of the Companies

Later, in the seventeenth and eighteenth centuries, many expatriates worked as agents of a commercial company. English merchants formed the Levant Company (1592) and the East India Company (1600), for instance, while the Dutch founded the "United East India Company" (Vereenigte Ost-Indische Compagnie, or VOC for short) in 1602 and the "West India Company" (West-Indische Compagnie) in 1621. To succeed, the merchants in these companies obviously required knowledge of various kinds: about the commodities in which they traded, such as spices, sugar, coffee, or woolen cloth; and about the countries with which they wished to trade, their rulers, their languages, and the goods that their inhabitants might wish to buy from the West.

Merchants also needed to know about the best routes for ships sailing to these places. Soon after its foundation, the East India Company appointed two mathematicians to lecture to their members about navigation. In similar fashion, the VOC organized the teaching of navigation and the examination of pilots by experts such as Cornelis Lastman, author of "The Pilot's Art" (*Kunst der Stuerluyden*, 1621).

The VOC also appointed a series of official cartographers, including Petrus Plancius, a refugee from the South who was mentioned earlier, and two members of the Blaeu family, Willem and his son Joan. Maps, charts, and the logs of the VOC's vessels were stored in the offices of the company, Oostindisch Huis in Amsterdam (the northern equivalent of the Casa da Índia in Lisbon), a house that might be regarded as a "center of calculation," or at least a center for the collection of geographical knowledge. The VOC also established an office or workshop to make and store maps and charts in Batavia (now Jakarta), the local headquarters of the East Indian enterprise.[9]

Like some early modern governments and the House of Trade in Seville, the VOC took pains to keep the company's knowledge secret, but much of it seeped into the public sphere of printed atlases, thanks to pilots who sold information to outsiders. In an archive in Paris, the Service Hydrographique de la Marine, there remains a chart annotated on the reverse with the words "bought from a Dutch pilot."[10] Printed atlases included the famous ones produced by Joan Blaeu, who combined the not altogether compatible roles of official cartographer to the VOC and successful publisher. For this reason the policy of secrecy was criticized by a director of the company as "pig-headed," because "what is known by so many people can hardly be hidden."[11] The archives of the West India Company, in contrast, were more accessible. Because Johannes de Laet was one of the directors, it is only to be expected to find that he had access to the company archives, but it is more surprising that he was allowed to publish the results of his research.[12]

As the volume of trade increased, the headquarters of these companies in London or Amsterdam needed more and more information about what was happening in the local branches or "factories" in Aleppo, for instance, in Surat, in Batavia (now Jakarta), and so on. Already in 1609, the court of the East India Company of London ordered a register of letters to and from the company to be kept. All the same, so far as information is concerned, the VOC stands out for its success. The VOC has been described as a "multinational," with information requirements not unlike those of an early modern empire, and its competitiveness has been attributed in part to the "efficient communications network" of the company, without equal among its rivals in this respect.[13]

What was most remarkable in the information system of the VOC was its use of regular written reports. From the outset, captains in its service were required to keep a daily log (*daghregister*) noting the speed of their ships, the prevailing wind, sightings of other ships, and so on. What is more, the log was also required to be kept when the sailors were on land, and to be handed over when the ship returned to base. In short, writing was an "essential tool" for the VOC.[14]

The company's reports often included statistics. The heads of individual factories reported to the governor-general in Batavia, and he in turn sent annual reports to the directors of the VOC in Amsterdam. The directors, especially Johannes Hudde, who was also a leading mathematician and a burgomaster of Amsterdam, appear to have been more acutely aware than their rivals of the importance of marketing strategies in the systematic collection of information, especially statistical information. Thanks to Hudde, sales figures were already being analyzed in 1692 in order to determine the future policy of the company concerning pricing and also the ordering of pepper and other commodities from Asia.[15]

In the case of Britain, surveying and mapping became important to the East India Company after it began to administer India in 1857. Two major figures in this collective enterprise were James Rennell and Colin Mackenzie. Rennell, a naval officer in company service, was appointed surveyor-general of Bengal in 1764 and his efforts resulted in the publication of the *Bengal Atlas* in 1879. Mackenzie, who worked in the South, carried out surveys of Madras and Mysore before becoming surveyor-general of India in 1815.[16]

Practical Knowledges: Languages and Laws

Knowledge of local languages was acquired by various members of the companies in order to trade, govern, and convert. For example, a Dutch-Malay dictionary was published in The Hague in 1623, the work of Caspar Wiltens, a pastor in the service of the

VOC ("Malay" was the term used to refer to the language now known as Bahasa Indonesia). Wiltens was expected not only to minister to the Dutch community in the East Indies but also to turn the indigenous inhabitants into Christians. A dictionary of Tamil, *Malabaarsche Spraakkunst,* was published in 1672 by Philipp Baldaeus, another pastor in the service of the VOC who worked in South India and Ceylon (now Sri Lanka).

In the eighteenth century, a grammar of Bengali was published by Nathaniel Halhed, a British administrator and translator who emphasized the value of the language as a "medium of intercourse [. . .] between the natives of Europe, who are to rule, and the inhabitants of India, who are to obey."[17] A grammar of Sanskrit was published by the scholar-printer Charles Wilkins; a dictionary and grammar of what he called "Hindoostanee" (now divided into Hindi and Urdu) by John Gilchrist, a surgeon turned linguist; a grammar of Telugu by Alexander Campbell; and a dictionary of Marathi by James Molesworth, an army officer. All four men were employed by the East India Company. The grammars were intended for use in India itself, but the knowledge of all these languages was of interest to scholars at home as well.

In India, where the company began to administer the country after 1757, the new rulers needed a knowledge of Hindu laws, which were translated into English (from a Persian translation of the original Sanskrit) as the *Code of Gentoo Laws* (1776) and (directly from the Sanskrit) as *Institutes of Hindu Law* (1794). Expatriates such as Nathaniel Halhed and William Jones (as well as local scholars, as we shall see) were involved in this enterprise of mediation.[18]

Pure versus Applied Knowledges

The Flemish humanist Caspar Barlaeus gave his inaugural lecture as professor at the Athenaeum in Amsterdam in praise of the "wise merchant" (*Mercator sapiens*) and the alliance between Mercury, the god of trade, and Pallas Athena, the goddess of wisdom. What his listeners thought about his arguments is not known, but neither the Dutch commercial companies nor the

British ones showed much interest in the acquisition of knowledge for its own sake.

On the other hand, some individuals in their service did display this interest, especially in the case of the VOC, as we shall see. Johannes de Laet, one of the founding directors of the Dutch West India Company, was a scholar in his leisure hours and produced a *Description of the New World* (1625) as well as editing a number of volumes for the leading Dutch publisher Elsevier, including a collection of reports on the Mughal Empire (1631). Nicolaes Witsen was not only a burgomaster of Amsterdam and a director of the VOC but also a polymath (writing on topics ranging from shipbuilding to Siberia) and an active correspondent with a variety of scholars. However, Witsen complained to the Dutch antiquary Gijsbert Cuper that the VOC was not interested in "learned curiosity about the Indies." "It is just money, not learning that our people seek there" (*het is alleen gelt en geen wetenschap die onse luyden soeken aldaer*).[19] The councillors in Batavia confirmed the bitter verdict of Witsen some sixty years earlier when they wrote in 1781 (perhaps thinking of the alliance recommended by Barlaeus) that "it is a general rule in these parts to sacrifice to Mercury, but never to Pallas."[20]

On occasion the VOC even obstructed the dissemination of knowledge, of not only routes to the East Indies but also the studies of the botany of Amboina by their employee Georg Rumpf (studies that were only published in 1741, thirty-nine years after the author's death). Even the manuscript reports that the linguist and botanist Herbert de Jager sent from the Indies never reached Nicolas Witsen, to whom they were addressed, because the VOC had confiscated them en route, probably because they wanted to keep the information secret in case it might be useful to their rivals.[21]

The British East India Company was no better, at least until the later eighteenth century, when it became a political as well as a commercial enterprise in India. In the seventeenth century, both the natural philosopher Robert Boyle and Henry Oldenburg, secretary of the Royal Society, had tried in vain to persuade the company to collect information about the lands with which it traded.[22] It was only relatively late in the company's history that it founded posts such as historian (1769) and botanist (1778), or commissioned the publication of books by its employees, such as Patrick Russell's *Account of Indian Serpents* (1796), or the botanical papers of William Griffith (1847).

Unofficially, on the other hand, some expatriates in the service of the companies — clergymen, surgeons, physicians, soldiers, and administrators, many of whom were university graduates — devoted their leisure to acquiring and disseminating knowledge about both nature and culture in the locations to which they had been posted. In the case of the VOC, contributions range in time from 1603 to 1798 (when the company was declared bankrupt), but they clustered most densely in the 1670s and 1680s. In the case of the East India Company, the golden age of knowledge production came a century later, in the 1770s, 1780s, and 1790s.

The best-known part of this story concerns the contribution made by physicians and surgeons, who studied tropical diseases previously unknown to them and also the local remedies, including the herbs that led some of these expatriates to study botany for its own sake. In the case of the VOC, ten individuals stand out: Jacob Bontius, Georg Rumpf, Andreas Cleyer, Engelbert Kaempfer, Willem Ten Rhijne, Herman Niklas Grimm, Paulus Hermann, Hendrik van Reede, Jacob Radermacher, and Carl Peter Thunberg. Bontius, for instance, a physician in company service in Java, wrote on tropical diseases, published a book on local remedies, and studied the plants on the island, correcting the work of García de Orta and acknowledging the help of local informants.[23]

Curiously enough, only four of these ten individuals in the service of a Dutch company were Dutch themselves (Bontius, Ten Rhijne, Van Reede, and Radermacher). Four were German (Rumpf, Cleyer, Kaempfer, and Herman), while Grimm and Thunberg were Swedish. Serious contributions to botany were made by seven, who between them studied in India, Ceylon, Java, Sumatra, Amboina, and Japan. The aristocrat Van Reede, who was governor of Malabar, organized the collective research, involving about 100 contributors, both European and Asian (Vinayaka Pandit, for instance), that appeared in twelve volumes under his name as the "Garden of Malabar" (*Hortus Malabaricus*) between 1678 and 1693. The medical traditions of Ceylon, China, and Japan were studied by Grimm, Cleyer, and Ten Rhijne. Acupuncture in particular aroused the curiosity of Europeans, abroad and at home.[24]

Some of the British in India were also enthusiastic botanists, among them two Scottish surgeons, Patrick Russell and William Roxburgh, and an officer in the company's army, Robert Kyd, who proposed the foundation of a botanical garden in Calcutta in 1787 and became its superintendent. Important contributions to the study of Indian plants were also made by two foreigners: the German Johan Koenig, a former pupil of Linnaeus who joined the company as botanist in 1778, and the Dane Nathaniel Wallich, who became professor of botany at Calcutta Medical College. Thanks to Joseph Banks, with whom some of these botanists corresponded, London, or more exactly Kew Gardens, might be described as a center for the production and dissemination of the knowledge of tropical plants, while Batavia and Calcutta were important local centers.[25]

By the early nineteenth century, some of the British physicians working in India, nicknamed the "Orientalists," were taking an interest in Ayurvedic medicine. Publications such as Whitelaw Ainslie's *Materia Medica of Hindostan* (1813) and John Royle's *Antiquity of Hindoo Medicine* (1837) testify to this interest, both practical and historical.[26] Meanwhile other British physicians, the "Anglicists," increasingly confident in the superiority of Western knowledge, dismissed Indian medical practices as unscientific, as some Western physicians still do.

The attention of historians has focused on the medical and botanical contributions to Western knowledge of Asia. They were undoubtedly important, but other fields should not be forgotten. Some employees of both companies tried to stay in touch with the European Commonwealth of Learning by founding their own societies, concerned with knowledge for its own sake.

In Batavia, Radermacher, best known for his work on the flora of Java but a man of wide interests, founded a society for "arts and sciences" (Bataviaasch Genootschap van Kunsten en Wetenschappen, 1778), which published a journal of its "transactions." In Calcutta, Jones and his friends founded the Asiatic Society (1784), to read papers to one another and publish them in the society's journal. The model was followed in the Literary Society of Bombay (1805) and the Madras Literary Society (1817).[27]

In the case of astronomy, employees of both companies made a contribution. Johan Maurits Mohr, a German pastor in VOC service in Batavia, observed the transit of Venus in 1761 and 1768, the second time from an observatory he had built for the purpose. Mohr asked to be appointed official astronomer to the VOC, but nothing came of his request. A few years later, Samuel Davis, who held a number of administrative posts in Calcutta and elsewhere, made a study of Indian astronomy that gained him a Fellowship of the Royal Society. Other members of the East India Company introduced Newtonian science, which coexisted with traditional Indian astronomy.[28]

Asian languages were studied by expatriates not only to aid trade or conversion, but also to acquire knowledge for its own sake. On the British side, the most famous contribution came from William Jones, a polymath who served in India as a judge. His awareness of similarities between Sanskrit, Greek, Latin, Persian, and the Celtic languages led Jones to the idea of an "Indo-European" family of languages. He chose to ignore, or more likely was unaware of the fact that other Europeans in India had remarked on some of these similarities before him, notably the French Jesuit Gaston-Laurent Coeurdoux, who had sent a memoir on the subject to the French Academy of Inscriptions in 1767. The work of Jones is well known and has often been studied, while that of Coeurdoux was rediscovered relatively recently. More generally, "Protestant Orientalism," especially its British version, has been much more visible to the eyes of posterity than an earlier "Catholic Orientalism," whether it was the work of Italians, Spaniards, French, or Portuguese.[29]

In similar if less ambitious fashion to Jones, Francis Whyte Ellis, who was posted to Madras, studied South Indian languages along with a few colleagues and formulated the so-called Dravidian hypothesis of the common origins of Tamil, Telugu, Malayalam, and Kannada, rejecting the view that the languages of South India were derived from Sanskrit.[30]

A few expatriates extended their interest in languages to the cultures of the peoples they encountered, collecting their antiquities and studying their customs. Some missionaries, both Catholic and Protestant, attempted to go beyond the stereotype of "pagans" or "idolaters" and present a fairly detached account of what we call Hinduism, as we shall see.

As for the British in India, John Zephaniah Holwell, who was employed by the East India Company as a surgeon, published a study in 1767 of what he called "the mythology, cosmogony, fasts and festivals of the Gentoos" (in other words, the Hindus), while Alexander Dow, an officer in company service, wrote, or translated, a history of Hindustan (1768). Both men played a role in what came to be known as "the British discovery of Hinduism," to be discussed later.[31] The surveyor Colin Mackenzie studied not only the topography of Mysore but also the different peoples of that region, their history, their social organization, and their material culture. Mackenzie collected local antiquities and so did James Prinsep, who worked at the mint in Calcutta and Benares and specialized in numismatics and inscriptions. Prinsep's *Essays on Indian Antiquities* was published posthumously in 1858.

Following an embassy to China sent by the VOC, one of its members, the German Johan Nieuhof, published a description of that country which was translated from Dutch into French, German, Latin, and English and has been described as "probably the most successful book about China published in Europe since Marco Polo's travelogue."[32] All the same, some of the most remarkable additions to European knowledge of Asia came from a series of employees of the VOC who were posted to Japan.[33] One was the Huguenot François Caron, whose *Beschrijvinghe van het Machtigh Coninckryck Japan und Siam* (1636) was translated into

German and also into English in 1663 as *A True Description of the Mighty Kingdoms of Japan and Siam*. A second observer was Engelbert Kaempfer, a man of extraordinary curiosity who had already traveled widely in Russia and Persia before entering the service of the company as a physician and was posted to Deshima (or Dejima) in Japan, an island off Nagasaki to which Dutch merchants had been confined since the year 1641, apart from official visits to the capital, Edo. As the locale for encounters between Westerners and Japanese, Nagasaki may be described as a center for the accumulation, dissemination, and transformation of knowledges.[34]

Kaempfer took part in two of these visits in the early 1690s, giving him the opportunity to take notes for a detailed description of Japan, written in German but first published posthumously in English translation in 1727. His sharp eyes focused not only on the court of the shogun but also on chopsticks ("instead of knives, we were given two small sticks"), on the bare rooms in the inns with "sliding paper windows," and on "farmers hoeing their rice fields up to their knees in mud and water." Kaempfer's studies of Japanese flora have also attracted the attention of historians.[35]

A third observer, the last of the "three learned men of Deshima," was Carl Peter Thunberg, a Swedish botanist and former pupil of Linnaeus. Thunberg served as a surgeon and physician in the service of the company and lived in Deshima in 1775–76, later publishing an account of his travels as well as the *Flora japonica* (1784). A fourth learned man of Deshima was Isaac Titsingh, surgeon, diplomat, and scholar, who reached Japan in 1779, learned Japanese, formed an important collection of Japanese artifacts, and published his memoirs of Japan in French in 1820, more than two decades after the VOC's bankruptcy. Thanks to accounts by these four individuals, Western readers could learn about Japanese customs ranging from Shinto to *seppuku*.[36]

The contribution of these expatriates may be summed up by returning to the central themes of mediation, distanciation, and hybridization. Obvious examples of mediation are the dictionaries and grammars of local languages produced by members of both companies, not to mention the translations of classical Sanskrit literature made by William Jones and Charles Wilkins, translations that were influential not only in Britain but in Germany and elsewhere. Another mediator was James Robert Ballantyne, the superintendent of Sanskrit College Benares, who wrote introductions to Hindu thought for Europeans and to Christianity and Western science for Indians.[37]

Distanciation may be illustrated from an account of the religion of the Hindus by Abraham Rogier (or Rogerius), a Dutch minister in the service of the VOC who worked for some years in Madras and published *De Open-Deure tot Verborgen Heydendom* ("The Open Door to Hidden Paganism," 1651). This book has been characterized as "remarkably objective and dispassionate." A similar point might be made about Kaempfer's description of Japan. An observant traveler and a man driven by curiosity rather than by the desire to change other cultures, Kaempfer has been described as someone who tried "to approach Japanese attitudes and thought processes in an unbiased way."[38]

It is, however, hybridization that is or should be the dominant theme in this case study. For a long time the expatriates were viewed, at least in Europe, as making their discoveries and interpretations virtually by themselves. Over the last generation, on the other hand, scholars in both Europe and India have become increasingly aware of the contribution made by indigenous informants, including local scholars, who did much more than provide "raw" information. The expatriates relied on their local assistants not only to carry out research but also to inform them about local classification systems, some of which the Europeans adopted or tried to combine with the system of Linnaeus. As a historian of science recently observed, "South Asia was [. . .] an active, though unequal, participant in an emerging order of knowledge."[39]

Some local scholars, such as Kavali Venkata Borayya (or Boria), who assisted Colin Mackenzie, have recently been given, or given back, an important place in the history of "Oriental

Studies." All the same, we shall never know how much the British physicians owed to the *hakims* (Islamic doctors) and *vaidyas* (ayurvedic doctors) with whom they worked, or the British lawyers to the *pandits* (specialists in Sanskrit) and *munshis* (specialists in Persian), or indeed whether they regarded these colleagues as useful tools or as fellow scholars.[40] Again, the encounter between individuals practicing medicine within different cultural systems (Indian, Chinese, and Japanese) led, if not to syncretism, then at least to pluralism, encouraging or at least allowing some physicians to switch between systems on occasion.

Even Engelbert Kaempfer, who wrote in the main about what he had seen for himself, admits that he had learned much from talking to Japanese who visited his house in Deshima, especially the young interpreter Imamura Gen'emon Eisei.[41] Conversely, at least a few Japanese acquired some Western knowledge, especially knowledge of geography and medicine, from conversations with the Dutch at Deshima and from the books that the foreigners brought with them. The Japanese called this knowledge *Rangaku*, in other words, the learning (*gaku*) that came from Holland (*Oranda*). In short, the VOC should be regarded as an intellectual as well as an economic broker between East and West, an institution that helped to create the conditions in which certain Europeans and Japanese could engage in the tasks of both linguistic and cultural translation.[42]

Early modern Western knowledge of Japan was relatively sparse. Knowledge of China, on the other hand, was fuller in these centuries because it was disseminated by a much larger group of Westerners, most of them Jesuit missionaries.

Religious Expatriates: Missionaries

Missionaries, whether Buddhist (as we have seen), Christian, or Muslim, are an important variety of expatriate mediator, because they have long believed in the value of personal encounters as a means of conversion. The Christians have often brought secular knowledge, especially that of Western science, to the mission field. From the sixteenth century onward, some of them have been convinced of the need to study what might be called the "target culture," its language, religion, ideas, customs, and so on. As an unintended consequence, they have made important contributions to oriental studies, for instance, to linguistics, and to other fields of knowledge.

In the early modern period, the age of the so-called Counter-Reformation, the Catholic Church not only attempted to reconquer the territories in Europe that had been lost to the Protestants but also to take the initiative in Asia, Africa, and the Americas, in the hope of a spiritual conquest of the globe. Like the historians of the British in India, the scholars studying these missions have recently made what might be called a "cognitive turn," focusing more sharply than before on knowledge, especially the encounters between the knowledges that the missionaries brought with them and those of the peoples whom the missionaries were attempting to convert.[43] One result of this approach has been the discovery of the cognitive turn made by the missionaries themselves, who found that they needed not only to learn local languages but also to become familiar with local cultures in order to present the Christian message in a manner that was both intelligible and appealing.

Besides the Jesuits, other religious orders such as the Franciscans, Capuchins, Dominicans, and Augustinians were involved in evangelization and acquired and sometimes disseminated knowledge of the various peoples among whom they worked. A famous example is that of Fray Bernardino de Sahagún, a Spanish Franciscan who arrived in New Spain (now Mexico) in 1529. He remained there until his death over sixty years later, learned Nahuatl, and began to investigate the culture of the Aztecs with the help of a dozen indigenous informants and four assistants.[44]

Sahagún has often been described as a pioneer anthropologist or as a proto-anthropologist, although interest in foreign manners and customs goes back to Herodotus, if not further, while the transformation of this interest into an intellectual discipline was a gradual one, in several stages, rather than a sudden "birth." Whatever we call him, Sahagún's voluminous "History of the

Things of New Spain" (*Historia de las cosas de Nueva España*) was an important contribution to knowledge that was translated from Nahuatl into Spanish, circulated in manuscript, and finally published in the nineteenth century.

Some Protestant missionaries were also active outside Europe, especially from the eighteenth century onward. The Moravian Church was particularly active in this way in the Caribbean, the Arctic, North and South America, Africa, and elsewhere. A serious contribution to knowledge was made by the Pietist missionary Bartolomäus Ziegenbalg, who worked in South India, learned Tamil from a local teacher named Aleppa, corresponded in that language with local Hindus, and with their help produced a "Description of the Religion of the Hindus of Malabar" (*Beschreibung der Religion der malabarischen Hindous*), written in 1717, although it was only published in 1791.[45]

The Jesuits

However, the cognitive turn is particularly visible in the history of the Jesuits, whose contribution stands out not only for the numbers of missionaries who belonged to this rapidly growing religious order, but also for the sophisticated manner in which the order organized the collection and transmission of different kinds of knowledge, a manner not unlike the practice of the VOC.[46] In the first place, leading Jesuits such as the general of the order required information about the order itself. They instructed rectors of colleges and heads of missions to report regularly and frequently to the "provincial," the head of their province (including details on the performance of individuals). In their turn, provincials were required to report to the general of the order in Rome. Printed forms and questionnaires were employed to compile *informationes,* in other words, dossiers.[47]

In the second place, the Jesuits were very much concerned with academic knowledge. From early days the order invested heavily in education, founding colleges all over Catholic Europe and later in the mission field as well (in Mexico City, Arequipa, São Paulo, Goa, Macau, Amakusa, Manila, Luanda, and so on), teaching not only rhetoric, logic, and theology but also "natural philosophy," now known as science. Jesuit missionaries not only sent information to Rome (from their observation of comets to their discovery of plants unknown in Europe), but also sent information to one another, thus building up a powerful network.[48]

In theory, at least originally, the study and transmission of secular knowledge had a religious aim. It was all, in the words of the Jesuit motto, "to the greater glory of God" (*ad majorem dei gloriam*). Following the advice of their founder, St. Ignatius (who was in turn following St. Paul), the Jesuits adopted the policy of "accommodation," in other words, of being "all things to all people" (*omnia omnibus*) in order to secure conversions or simply to obtain support. "All people" included learned people. However, Ignatius himself, unlike some theologians, did not condemn curiosity ("a certain curiosity that is not evil and is wont to be found among men"), and it has been argued that some Jesuits acquired knowledge for its own sake. Indeed, their "pious pronouncements" on acquiring knowledge for religious purposes have been dismissed as "rationalizations."[49] I suspect that in some cases at least, although study was begun for religious reasons, the student was bitten by the bug of curiosity. In any case, whether or not individual Jesuits experienced conflicts of aims, the mission navigated between what was described at the time as "curiosity" and "edification," attempting to combine the two.[50]

Following their principle of accommodation, Jesuits in the mission field tried to present Christianity as compatible with local cultures. They were therefore obliged to study these cultures as well as to learn the local languages, which many did, though some resisted.[51] Important contributions to Western knowledge of non-Western languages came from some Jesuits who were active in South America, though not from them alone. The Dominican missionary Domingo de Santo Tomás, for instance, published the first grammar of Quechua in 1560, while the Franciscan Alonso de Molina published a *Vocabulario en lengua castellana y Mexicana*, in other words, a Spanish-Nahuatl dictionary, in 1571.

Between 1555 and 1645, six Jesuit missionaries in Spanish and Portuguese America published their studies of local languages. José de Anchieta, a Spaniard who worked in Brazil, wrote a grammar of Tupí in 1555, published in 1589 as *Arte de gramática da língua mais usada na costa do Brasil.* Antonio de Rincón, who was active in Mexico, was himself a native speaker of Nahuatl who published a grammar, known as the *Arte mexicana,* in 1595. His work was carried on by an Italian missionary, Horacio Carochi, whose *Arte de la lengua Mexicana* was published in 1645. Carochi also studied another Mexican language, Otomi. Meanwhile, a Spanish missionary, Luis de Valdivia, published his *Arte de la lengua de Chile* (in other words, Mapudungun) in 1606, while another Spaniard, Diego González Holguín, published a grammar of Quechua in 1607 and a dictionary in the following year. A combined grammar and dictionary of another Peruvian language, Aymara, was published by an Italian missionary, Ludovico Bertonio, in 1612.

It has been remarked that there is an "inherent contradiction" between the enterprise of conversion and that of studying a culture on its own terms, and that "missionary knowledge is produced according to its own logic," in the sense of serving the enterprise.[52] The grammars and dictionaries just mentioned were produced to help colleagues in the field and became essential tools for later missionaries. However, missionary knowledge was often appropriated by other people according to their own logic and for their own ends. These texts provided valuable information for European scholars interested in languages and would eventually assist the rise of comparative linguistics.

The missionaries made use of their knowledge of Western natural philosophy to attract local elites, as well as making use of their knowledge of various parts of the globe — India, China, Japan, Mexico, South America, and so on — to awaken the interest of Europeans. Hence the Jesuit practice of publishing what they called "edifying reports" from the field. These reports, together with descriptions of different parts of the world based on them, were major sources of information for early modern Europeans, about the Americas and East Asia in particular. The thirty-four volumes of the *Lettres édifiantes et curieuses,* published between 1702 and 1776, spread information about Jesuit missions in many places and were translated into other languages, notably German.

In the case of the Aztec and Inca Empires, a key source was produced by the Spaniard José de Acosta, the provincial of Peru, who published his *Natural and Moral History of the Indies* in Seville in 1590, drawing on his own experience and also on that of other expatriates such as the royal official Juan Polo de Ondegardo. This work has been described as "a programme for comparative ethnology" and it also made an important contribution to natural history.[53]

Some Jesuits were active in Africa, notably three Portuguese in Ethiopia in the seventeenth century: Luis de Azevedo, Pedro Paez, and Manuel de Almeida, who made a contribution to Western knowledge of that country, although this was not their principal aim.[54] More Jesuits were active in the Americas, North and South. One of the most famous of them is Jean-François Lafitau, who was sent to Quebec in 1711 and worked for six years among the Iroquois, gathering the information that he would present in his "Customs of the American Savages" (*Moeurs des Sauvages Amériquains,* 1724), a book that was translated into Dutch and German by the middle of the eighteenth century. The majority of the Jesuit missionaries in the Americas, however, worked in the Spanish viceroyalities of Mexico and Peru, studying the history and natural history of their region as well as learning local languages. Many Jesuit missionaries worked in Asia, from the time of Francisco Xavier onward: in India, Tibet, Indo-China, Siam, China, and Japan. Besides learning the local languages, including Tamil, Telugu, and Tibetan as well as Chinese and Japanese, some members of the order, like their Protestant counterparts, tried to describe and understand the ideas of the Brahmins and Buddhists, as we shall see.

The China mission is the best known of these enterprises. The Jesuits were not alone in their missionary efforts, because some

Dominicans arrived in China in the 1580s, while some Franciscans had begun to work there as early as the thirteenth century. Again, the Jesuits were not the only order to contribute to Western knowledge of China. Juan González de Mendoza, for instance, an Augustinian friar, published his *Historia de las cosas más notables, ritos y costumbres del gran reyno de la China* in 1586. In fact González had never been to China, basing his book on a journal kept by the Spanish soldier Miguel de Luarca, who had spent a little more than two months in the country as part of a diplomatic mission. The book sold well, however, and within a decade it had been published in six translations: Italian, French, English, German, Latin, and Dutch.

All the same, it is the story of the Italian Jesuit Matteo Ricci, who arrived in Macau in 1582, that has become famous. At the beginning of his mission, Ricci dressed as a Buddhist priest, but finding that this did not win him respect, he changed into the clothes of a Confucian scholar in order to accommodate the Christian message to Chinese culture. Like other Jesuit missionaries, Ricci concentrated on converting members of the local elite, appealing to their curiosity by displaying a European map of the world, by demonstrating the Renaissance art of memory, and by presenting Christianity as in harmony with the ideas of Confucius. In collaboration with two Chinese converts, Xu Guangqi and Li Zhizao, Ricci translated texts on mathematics and astronomy by Euclid and the Jesuit scholar Christoph Clavius.[55]

Ricci was a leading figure in the first phase of the Jesuit mission, which might be called the Italian phase (despite the importance of the Pole Michał Boym and of Flemings such as Nicolas Trigault) and lasted from the 1580s to the 1660s. Leading Italians included Ricci's colleague Michele Ruggieri, and later, Martino Martini. All these missionaries made significant contributions to the dissemination of knowledge.

In one direction, Ricci introduced Chinese scholars to Western natural philosophy and mathematics, while another Italian, Giacomo Rho, translated Western books on astronomy into Chinese and helped Chinese colleagues in the reform of their calendar. Chinese scholars accepted the idea that the earth was a globe, while adapting, or, shall we say, "accommodating" information from the foreigners to their own traditions.[56] In the other direction, Ricci's journal, translated into Latin and published by Nicolas Trigault, played a major role in informing Western scholars about China. Together with his colleague Ruggieri, Ricci also compiled a Chinese-Portuguese dictionary, while Ruggieri translated some Confucian texts into Latin. Michał Boym published books on Chinese flora and Chinese medicine, as well as compiling a Chinese-Latin and a Chinese-French dictionary.

As for Martini, he produced a Chinese grammar, which was published posthumously in 1696. He is better known, though, for his work on history and geography. He published an account of the displacement of the Ming dynasty by the Qing in 1644 (when he was already living in China), as well as a general history and an atlas of the country. The atlas was based on Chinese maps and so "rectified much of the erroneous information concerning China's interior geography."[57] Information provided by Martini (his former student) and also by Boym was used by the German Jesuit polymath Athanasius Kircher in his *China Illustrata* (1667). Kircher would have liked to have been a missionary in China but remained in Rome, a central place that allowed him to acquire knowledge of many subjects, from music to magnetism.[58] Information from the mission to China was also published regularly in the *Annual Letters* of the Jesuits, written in Italian and translated into Latin, German, Portuguese, and French.[59]

In India too, Jesuits not only learned the local languages but also wrote grammars and compiled dictionaries. For example, the Englishman Thomas Stephens, active in India from the 1580s, wrote a Konkani grammar that was published posthumously in 1640. The German Jesuit Heinrich Roth, active from the 1650s, learned Persian, Kannada, and Hindustani but is best known for his study of Sanskrit, which he learned from a Brahmin in Agra. On his return to Europe, he supplied Kircher with information, lectured in Germany about the Mughal Empire, and attempted to publish his Sanskrit grammar (an attempt that was vetoed by the head of his order). The Italian Costanzo Beschi, who arrived in India in 1711, wrote a grammar of Tamil, while the Frenchman Gaston-Laurent Coeurdoux, who arrived in 1732, learned not only Tamil but Telugu and Sanskrit as well.

Rome, the Jesuit headquarters, functioned as a center for the dissemination of knowledge acquired on the Jesuit missions, thanks not only to Kircher but also to Giampietro Maffei, author of a massive Latin history of the Jesuit missions in Asia (1588), and Daniele Bartoli, another Jesuit who would have liked to be a missionary himself but wrote, in Italian, about the missions of his colleagues instead, devoting a volume to Japan (1660) and another to China (1663). The central position of Rome in the enterprise of conversion was fortified by the foundation by Pope Gregory XV, in 1622, of the Congregation "On the Propagation of the Faith" (*De Propaganda Fide*). The Congregation organized missions, sometimes in competition with the Jesuits. It had its own press, producing catechisms in many languages.[60]

Another center for the dissemination of knowledge about China was Amsterdam. One might have expected Martini to publish his new atlas of China in Rome, but it was actually published, in Amsterdam in 1655, by the printer Joan Blaeu, a specialist in atlases who (as we have seen) worked for the VOC, thus linking the story of the Company of Jesus with that of the United East India Company.[61] Kircher's *China illustrata* was also published in Amsterdam by Blaeu's rival Jan Janszoon, in 1667.

In the second phase of the China mission, from the 1670s to the early eighteenth century, the Italians lost the initiative to the French, while the delicate balance between edification and curiosity shifted in favor of the latter. One reason for the shift was the intervention in the mission by Louis XIV, who sent six Jesuits to China in 1685, charged not only with the conversion of the Chinese but also with providing the French Academy of Sciences with information. In this phase, the attention of later historians has focused on astronomy. Their knowledge of this discipline made missionaries such as the Frenchman Jean de Fontaney and the German Adam Schall welcome at the court of the Chinese emperor, while their observations of the stars were sent to astronomers in Europe.

However, the Jesuits active in China in this phase made important contributions to other kinds of knowledge. Fontaney, the leader of the 1685 mission, planned a division of labor in which one colleague was responsible for history and language, another for natural history and Chinese medicine, a third for liberal and mechanical arts, and a fourth for the study of Chinese law and government, while Fontaney himself took charge of astronomy and geography. Things did not work out in exactly this way, but one of Fontaney's colleagues, Louis Le Comte, on his return to France, presented the Academy of Sciences with a map of Tartary, drawings of plants and fish and astronomical observations, as well as publishing the *Nouveau mémoire sur l'état présent de la Chine* (1696).[62]

Later, two Jesuits, Jean-Baptiste Régis and Antoine Gaubil, played a major role in the mapping of the Chinese empire, an imperial project that the order claimed to have inspired. The Jesuit botanist Pierre Nicolas d'Incarville, who arrived in China in 1740, introduced European plants to China and Chinese plants to Europe (he was the first European to describe the kiwi fruit). All the same, the best-remembered Jesuit book from the second phase is the collective work *Confucius Sinarum Philosophus* (1687), a translation of classics of Chinese philosophy by a team led by the Francophone Fleming Philippe Couplet. It is thanks to this book that the Chinese philosopher Kung Fu Tze is known in the West to this day as Confucius.

In this second phase, Rome and Amsterdam were replaced by Paris as the center for dissemination of knowledge about China, thanks in particular to the *Lettres édifiantes et curieuses*, published in thirty-four volumes in Paris from 1702 onward and edited by two stay-at-home Jesuits, Charles Le Gobien and Jean-Baptiste Du Halde. Du Halde drew on this and other material for his famous *Description de la Chine* (1735–36), naming no fewer than twenty-seven missionaries whose "memoirs" he used. His description was shaped by a list of thirty-four questions that had been drawn up in 1684 by the French Academy of Sciences at the request of the powerful minister the Marquis de Louvois, a list that (like a similar list drawn up by the German polymath Gottfried Wilhelm Leibniz in 1689) reveals the growing interest in Chinese culture in the West.[63]

Looking back at the history of the mission, the role of the Jesuits as mediators is obvious enough, informing the Chinese about Western knowledge and sending information about China, including the work of Chinese scholars, to Europe, not only to Du Halde but also to Leibniz. Many early modern Jesuits were active as translators, and the members of the China mission were no exception, translating both from and into Chinese.[64] Detachment is less obvious—after all, their apostolate was the main reason for the Jesuits to travel. As for hybridization, the Jesuits were accused in Rome and elsewhere of having been converted by the Chinese, rather than making them into Christians. A fascinating example of hybridity is provided by the text *Confucius Sinarum Philosophus*. Faced with the problem of translating the fundamental Chinese concepts of Yin and Yang into Latin, the Jesuits, well trained in scholastic philosophy, had recourse to the Aristotelian categories of Matter and Form.

In short, early modern Jesuits made a major contribution to Western knowledge of the rest of the world, especially East Asia and the Americas, as well as a significant contribution to knowledge of the West in other cultures. In some respects at least, this contribution may be viewed as one more historical example of the importance of unintended consequences. The principal aim of the Jesuits was, as their motto *Ad Majorem Dei Gloriam* proclaims, the greater glory of God, and the aim of the missionaries was saving souls—their own, and those of their converts.[65] To do this, however, they needed to learn the local languages and to understand the local cultures or "customs," as they called them. For some missionaries, as we have seen, the means became an end in itself.

This collective contribution to knowledge took several forms. The best-known part is the collection of information and its dissemination via letters, in manuscript and print, as well as other publications. Another part involved changing people's ideas about different parts of the world. For example, Acosta divided the peoples outside Christian Europe into three groups, with the most civilized, such as the Chinese, at the top; then groups with states but without writing, such as the Aztecs; and at the bottom the "savages," such as the tribes of Indians in Brazil.[66]

Lafitau, who has been variously described as "precursor of scientific anthropology" and as "the writer who made the most imaginative use of Acosta's ideas," not only described Iroquois culture in detail but also criticized those Europeans who judged it by "our manners and our customs." He studied the Iroquois on their own terms and utilized their vocabulary. Lafitau also compared their customs with those of the ancient Greeks and argued for the use of what the historian Marc Bloch, two centuries later, would call the "regressive method," using his own observation to make what he called the manners of the "first ages" more intelligible. Like Sahagún, Lafitau has been described as an anthropologist *avant la lettre*. One might say that Sahagún was more like Franz Boas, with his systematic collection of information, while Lafitau resembled Alfred Radcliffe-Brown, with his interest in comparative analysis.[67] All the same, phrases like "the first anthropologist" or "the father of anthropology" (as Claude Lévi-Strauss called Jean-Jacques Rousseau) are misleading. The process in which an interest in manners and customs was institutionalized, professionalized, and turned into an academic discipline was a protracted one.

Again, missionaries outside Europe helped their colleagues at home to see that homeland in a new light, to realize that many ordinary people in Catholic Europe knew no more about their religion and were in as much need of evangelization as the inhabitants of the Indies and other mission fields. Francesco Giuseppe Bressani, for instance, was a Jesuit who worked among the Iroquois of Canada before returning to Italy. Giovanni Francesco Romano was a Capuchin who worked in the Congo before doing the same. Phrases like "other Indies" (*otras Indias*), applied to Spain or Italy, began to be common. The Jesuit Cristoforo Landino, for instance, a missionary in the Apennines and Corsica, was inspired by what he had read about the missions outside Europe and referred to Corsica as "my India."[68]

At the level of what we would call theory, Jesuits such as Ricci and Nobili contributed to knowledge by reflecting on what were the essentials of Christianity, and what was simply European cultural baggage that might be discarded elsewhere. They were among the missionaries who helped Christians to view other religions in more positive terms than the recurrent stereotypes of "paganism" and "idolatry," as the "discovery of Hinduism" suggests.

The Discovery of Hinduism

Expatriates of very different kinds helped Europeans to view what we now call Hinduism as a religious system, one of the major world religions. In that limited sense, they "constructed" what they described.[69] In English, the first references to "Hindoo religion" and to "Hindooism" date from the late eighteenth century, in the writings of Alexander Dow, Nathaniel Halhed, and Charles Grant, all of whom worked for the East India Company. They were followed by the Baptist missionary William Ward, who studied the "religion" of the Hindus as a "system."[70]

The discovery was not a monopoly of the British. Missionaries from other parts of Europe were thinking in similar terms at about the same time. The Italian Capuchin Marco della Tomba worked in North India. In his *Diversi sistemi della religione dell'Indostano,* written in 1766, della Tomba contrasted the "system" of what he called the "heathens" (*Gentili*) with those of the Christians and Muslims. Again, in his treatise *Moeurs et coutumes des Indiens* (1777), the Jesuit Gaston-Laurent Coeurdoux (best known today for his linguistic studies, discussed earlier) described not only the customs of the Brahmins but also their divinities and what he called the "system" of transmigration (the term "system" was used more and more frequently from the late eighteenth century onward to describe both ideas and societies).

However, the idea of Hinduism as a religion comparable with Christianity or Islam rather than as a variety of local cults usually described by pejorative terms such as "idolatry" and "paganism" goes back still earlier and may well have been learned from Indian Muslims. In the seventeenth century, an account of the religion of the "Banians" or Gujarati merchants was published in 1630 by a chaplain of the East India Company, Henry Lord; a Frenchman who had lived in India, François Bernier, referred to "the doctrines of the Hindus"; and Abraham Rogier attempted, as we have seen, a detached if not a systematic account of the beliefs (*Geloove*) of the Brahmins as well as of their rituals. He drew on traditional texts such as the Vedas, on personal observation, and on conversations with a Brahmin called Padmanabha.

Rogier's book, the "Open Door," attracted considerable interest in Europe and was rapidly translated into French and German. It was followed by a book about the Brahmins by another Dutch minister in the service of the VOC, Philip Baldaeus, who worked in Ceylon (now Sri Lanka), had discussions with Brahmins, and published a "Careful Description of Malabar and Coromandel" (*Nauwkeurige beschrijving van Malabar en Choromandel*, 1672). However, much of his book was already known in the eighteenth century to have been plagiarized from a manuscript by a Portuguese Jesuit.[71]

Once again, the Jesuits were pioneers (together with a Portuguese Augustinian friar, Agostinho de Azevedo). In the early seventeenth century, before Rogier and Baldaeus, five Jesuits active in India had already offered descriptions of the "ceremonies" of the Brahmins: Giacome Fenicio, Antonio Rubino, Diego Gonçalves, Gonçalo Fernandes, and Roberto de Nobili. This remarkable cluster of reports has been explained as a response to the disappointing results of the Jesuit mission.[72]

Fenicio, for instance, wrote but did not publish a treatise on what he called the "sect" of the East Indies (*Livro da seite dos Indios orientais*). In a treatise published in 1616, Gonçalo Fernandes referred to the combination of rituals and beliefs as "this machine of Brahmanism" (*esta maquina do bramanismo*), apparently using the term "Brahmanism" for the first time.[73] The Jesuits wrote in order to refute Hindu doctrines, and Rubino went so far as to call the Brahmins "ministers of the devil." On the other hand, the Italian Jesuit Roberto de Nobili called them "wise men" (*sapientes*) and expressed respect for their various forms of knowledge (*scientiae*), as he did for the ideas of the ancient Greek philosophers to whom he sometimes compared them (comparisons of the doctrines of the Brahmins with those of Pythagoras and his followers were common in the seventeenth century).[74]

Despite differences in the context of the descriptions of Hinduism by Catholic and Protestant missionaries, who wrote to help their colleagues in the task of conversion, and the more detached studies made by lay officials of the East India Company, these descriptions were all produced in the course of interaction between the outsiders and the Brahmins themselves, and in their different ways they all contributed to the growing awareness of Hinduism as a religious system, a world religion rather than a collection of local cults. Although outsiders often misunderstand details, they sometimes see the big picture more easily than insiders. Social and intellectual systems are more visible from outside than from within. Thanks to outsiders, some Hindus became aware of their own practices as part of a larger religious system.

As in the case of the religion of the Hindus, Western missionaries contributed to the "discovery" of Buddhism, or as one scholar claims, its "imaginative creation," attributing this creation to the British in the nineteenth century.[75] Once again, however, earlier Westerners, notably Jesuits active in Japan, China, and India, including Francis Xavier, Matteo Ricci, and Robert de Nobili, had already attempted to describe Buddhist ceremonies and beliefs, often by conversing with bonzes. Again, during his stay in Japan, Engelbert Kaempfer took an interest in what he called the "doctrine of Siaka" (in other words, Buddhism) as well as in Shinto, the "old, and probably original religion of the Japanese."[76] In the encounters between Christians and Buddhists, there were misunderstandings on both sides. Just as missionaries saw Buddhism as a distorted version of Christianity (when they did not describe it as "atheism" or "paganism"), the bonzes regarded Christianity as a distorted version of Buddhism.[77]

In the book about the philosophy of Confucius mentioned earlier, Philippe Couplet gave an account of the religion of "Fo" (in other words, Buddha).[78] However, the great Jesuit specialist on the subject was Ippolito Desideri, who arrived in Tibet in 1716, learned Tibetan, and studied for five years in what we might call a Buddhist theological college in Lhasa. He wrote a report on Tibet that included a lengthy discussion of what he called "the false sect of the unique religion observed in Tibet" (*Della falsa setta di religione particolarissima che s'osserva nel Thibet*).[79] Desideri has been praised for his "openness to learning the exact details and meaning of his opponents' religious beliefs, albeit in order to refute them."[80] In the context of the European discovery of religions, his use of terms such as *setta* and *religione* is worth noting, as well as his analysis of what he calls "dogmas" (*dogmi*). All the same, he was unable to contribute to the international debate on this topic. For whatever reason, Desideri was not allowed to publish his report when he returned to Rome. It appeared in print only in the twentieth century.

Academic Expatriates

The third of our types of expatriate is the scholar. During the Renaissance, Italian humanists as well as artists were much in demand elsewhere in Europe, rather like Greeks in ancient Rome. The Italian Protestant exiles mentioned in the previous chapter were preceded by Italian expatriates. Some of them were active in foreign universities, others in foreign courts. For example, the Sicilian Luca Marineo taught at the University of Salamanca, Stefano Surigone of Milan taught at Oxford, and Gregorio Tifernate, a Tuscan of Greek descent, at Paris.

Turning from universities to courts, it is well known that King Afonso V of Portugal summoned two Italian humanists to court to teach his son, the future João II: Stefano di Napoli and Domenico Baldini. Other rulers, especially if they belonged to new dynasties, were more interested in appointing Italians as secretaries or as official historians, in order to propagate a favorable view of their regime or their nation in letters or books written in the elegant classical Latin that these humanists were the first to revive. King Matthias Corvinus of Hungary, for instance, commissioned Antonio Bonfini to write the *Rerum Hungaricarum Decades*. Ferdinand and Isabella of Spain summoned Luca Marineo to court to write the praises of Spain and the biography of Ferdinand's father, Joan II of Aragon. The emperor Charles V continued to employ Luca as well as appointing another Sicilian, the friar Bernardo Gentile, to be his chronicler. Charles VIII and Louis XII of France appointed Giovanni Filangieri and Paolo Emili as their official historians. The humanist poet and secretary Filippo Buonaccorsi (nicknamed "Callimachus" after the ancient Greek poet whose style he imitated) fled from Rome to Poland in 1468 after participating in an unsuccessful conspiracy against Pope Paul II, and reconstructed his career as secretary to King Kasimierz IV. Another humanist poet, Andrea Ammonio, who was sent to England by Pope Julius II, became Latin secretary to King Henry VIII. It seems that appointments of this kind were eagerly sought. At any rate, leading humanists such as Flavio Biondo and Angelo Poliziano wrote to the king of Portugal to offer their services.[81]

All the same, the detachment of exiles sometimes prevailed over the pressure on these humanists to produce the kind of history that their royal employers wanted. Polydore Vergil, for instance, who came from Urbino, was sent to England in 1502 to collect some revenues due to the pope and remained there for half a century. Received warmly by King Henry VII on his arrival, Polydore began work on a history of England, the *Anglica Historia*, published in 1534. In good humanist fashion, Polydore expressed skepticism about narratives for which reliable sources were lacking, including the story of Britain being founded by Brutus the Trojan and also the story of King Arthur, which he compared to "old wives' tales" (*anilibus fabellis*), despite its importance for the legitimation of the Tudor dynasty. Polydore's detached account of accepted "mythhistory" provoked angry attacks by native scholars who accused him of destroying sources and of "polluting our English chronicles."[82]

Returning to the argument presented in the introduction, that the movement of people was and is a more effective means of transmitting knowledge than the movement of books, I suggest that the presence of these Italian scholars in foreign courts and universities was a major factor in the dissemination of humanism, especially in its early stages in the fifteenth century. This view seems to have been shared by contemporaries. In the sixteenth century, the most famous humanist of all, Erasmus, was invited to stay in a number of countries, from Spain to Poland, and in fact lived for some years and died in Basel.

Professors in Russia

The welcome given to expatriates depends on the receptivity of their hosts, which in turn often depends on awareness, especially by governments, of cultural backwardness and the need to catch up with rival states. In sixteenth-century Denmark, for instance, King Christian III conducted what has been called an "extensive recruitment drive" abroad to find professors for the University of Copenhagen. During his reign, about half of the forty-one professors were foreigners.[83] In the case of seventeenth-century Sweden, although the initiative came from a private individual, Eric Schroder, who set out his plan in a book dedicated to Karl IX in 1606, it would not be far from the mark to speak of an official "translation campaign" in the age of Gustav Adolf, undertaken with the aim of helping the Swedes to catch up with cultural developments elsewhere in Europe.[84] Gustav Adolf's daughter and successor Queen Christina invited foreign scholars to court, most famously (and fatally) Descartes, who died in Sweden, probably from pneumonia, but also (among others) the Huguenot biblical scholar Samuel Bochart, Bochart's friend and pupil the Catholic Pierre-Daniel Huet, the classical scholar Claude Saumaise, and the Dutch polymath Isaac Vossius.

Farther reaching in their effects on both sides, however, were the German scholars who went to Russia in the eighteenth century, invited there as part of the program of Westernization and modernization undertaken by the Tsar Peter the Great and his successors: Catherine I, Peter II, Anna, Elizabeth, and especially Catherine the Great. The scholars were preceded by an earlier wave, or even "flood," of military specialists who had arrived in Russia between the 1630s and the 1670s. However, the new program was more ambitious. It followed the famous "Great Embassy" of 1697–98, when Tsar Peter visited the Dutch Republic and England, including on his itinerary the lecture rooms of the Royal Society as well as the shipyards of Chatham and Zaandam. Later, the tsar met Leibniz, who produced a report for him about the acquisition of knowledge, recommending a survey of Russian plants and animals, the translation of Western books into Russian, and the establishment of an academy of sciences.[85]

The translation program began under Peter, when at least sixty-nine translators were active. Boris Volkov produced Russian versions of French books on geography, navigation, artillery, and even gardening, while Vasily Kiprianov organized a kind of workshop of translators as well as himself turning Vignola's treatise on architecture into Russian. Catherine the Great's commission for translation was established in 1768, lasted for fifteen years, and published over 100 books, including William Robertson's history of Charles V, which the empress had read and admired in its French version.

All the same, the movement of people had more far-reaching consequences than the movement of texts. Some Russians were sent to study abroad: Grigory Teplov, who became the administrator at the Academy of Sciences, to Berlin; and Alexander Radischev, later exiled for his criticisms of the government, to the University of Leipzig. There was much more traffic in the opposite direction. A group of German scholars transformed the Russian intellectual landscape, in the humanities as well as in the natural sciences.[86]

Germans were not the only knowledgeable expatriates active in Russia at this time. In 1707, for instance, three printers from Amsterdam arrived in Russia: Indrich Silbach, Johann Foskul, and Anton Demey.[87] Vitus Bering, the naval officer who led the scientific expeditions to Kamchatka in the far east of Russia, was a Dane; Jakob Lindenau, who also studied Kamchatka, the mineralogist Johann Ferber, and Erik Laxmann, professor of chemistry in St. Petersburg, were all Swedes; the astronomer-geographer Joseph-Nicolas Delisle was French; while the British included the naval architect Samuel Bentham (brother of the more famous Jeremy), who spent a decade in Russia, and the Scot John Robison, who was briefly professor of mathematics at Kronstadt.[88]

Peter the Great's enthusiasm for ships and navigation is well known, and his reign has been described as a time of a "naval revolution" or "nautical turn." The Russian word for science, *nauk*, is a reminder of Peter's interest in practical knowledge, because it derives from "navigation" in Latin (*navigatio*) and Dutch (*navigatie*). Foreign sailors were welcomed in eighteenth-century Russia, and an English historian has described the "invasion" of Russia by British naval officers at this time. British experts in technology were also welcome. James Watt was invited to Russia, for instance. He did not accept, but less famous technical experts, from shipbuilders to cannon founders, did so. Expatriate scientists and scholars formed part of a larger wave of skill migration.[89]

A majority among these expatriates were Germans or at least German speakers, working in Russia in a long eighteenth century, from 1698 to at least 1826 and associated for the most part with the Academy of Sciences (Akademiya Nauk) in St. Petersburg, founded by Peter the Great at the end of his life, in 1724, following the advice of Leibniz and taking the Berlin Academy and the French Academy of Sciences as models. The Academy of Sciences of St. Petersburg was concerned not only with the discovery of new knowledge but also with its dissemination. Besides carrying out research, the academicians were instructed to summarize information from foreign publications, to teach at the university, and to give public lectures.[90]

Generous salaries were paid, while talent scouts or headhunters were sent abroad to find suitable individuals to invite, assisted by suggestions from Leibniz and from the philosopher Christian Wolff. The newcomers, many of them graduates from the universities of Leipzig and Göttingen, usually lectured and published in their native German, which was probably the best-known foreign language in Russia, at least in the domain of learning, until its displacement by French in the second half of the eighteenth century. Indeed, *nemetsky* ("German") was the Russian word for foreign, referring in particular to foreigners from Northern Europe such as the Dutch, British, or Scandinavians.

Following the prosopographical method discussed in the introduction, I shall now present eighty German-speaking expatriates who arrived between 1700 and 1826 and made serious contributions to knowledge in Russia. The group consists of seventy-one Germans, eight Swiss, and one Austrian. Some arrived when they were young and were quickly promoted. Some left after a few years or died young, whether from natural causes in the harsh climate of Siberia or, in the case of the astronomer Georg Moritz Löwitz, murder by Cossacks during the peasant revolt led by Yemelyan Pugachev (1773–74). However, a number of expatriates remained in Russia for the rest of their lives—as much as fifty-eight years in one case, that of the historian Gerhard Friedrich Müller.

The obvious question to ask about this group concerns their disciplines. Despite its name, the Academy of Sciences included not only expatriate academics but also translators, architects, librarians, cartographers, and one artist. One of them, academician J.-E. Zeiher, lectured on the manufacture of telescopes. The official encouragement of the exploration and mapping of the Russian Empire undertaken by some of the expatriate scholars was another sign of the pragmatic interests of the government. Eleven members of the group worked as naturalists (especially botanists), nine as mathematicians, eight as physicians or surgeons, seven as physicists, four as chemists, and two as astronomers.

The best known of these expatriate scholars were mathematicians and scientists, including the Swiss mathematician Leonhard Euler; the naturalist Johann Georg Gmelin, who took part in the second Kamchatka expedition; Georg Wilhelm Steller, a physician who also took part in the expedition and was a pioneer in the study of the natural history of Alaska; the chemist J. G. Lehmann; the physicist Georg Wolfgang Krafft; the physiologist Caspar Wolff; and Peter Pallas, another naturalist, who became professor of natural history at the Academy of Sciences. Pallas spent six years traveling the Russian Empire, studying plants, animals, fossils, and rocks.[91]

Some scholars practiced several disciplines or were employed on or became interested in topics remote from their original expertise. For example, Daniel Messerschmidt, originally hired as the tsar's physician, went on to make discoveries in botany and natural history, while the naturalist Pallas was ordered by his employer Tsarina Catherine to collect information about all the languages of the world and to edit a multilingual dictionary, *Linguarum totius orbis vocabularia* (1786).[92]

Here as elsewhere in this book, there will be more to say about the expatriates who worked in the humanities; seven scholars mainly concerned with languages and literatures, five with law, two with philosophy, and one with politics (*Staatswissenschaften*). No fewer than eighteen German expatriates were active in the field of history, even if one of these, Jacob Stählin, was originally invited to Russia on account of his knowledge of fireworks. The large number of historians may seem surprising, but Peter the Great was convinced that the study of the past was, like shipbuilding or cannon founding, of practical value.

Gottlieb Bayer, a polyglot orientalist, wrote about the Chinese, the city of Edessa in Mesopotamia, the ancient kingdom of Bactria (in what is now Iran and Uzbekistan), the Scythians, and the origins of Russia, making particular use of evidence from coins. His books were published in Latin in St. Petersburg in the 1730s.[93] Hartwig Bacmeister translated the history of Russia by Mikhail Lomonosov into German and published essays on Peter the Great as well as editing the first bibliographical journal in Russia, the *Russische Bibliothek*, from 1772 onward. The Austrian Philip Dilthey, professor of history and law in the new University of Moscow, published in 1762 a textbook of universal history for the use of young nobles.

A more important figure was Gerhard Friedrich Müller, who became the official historian of the Russian Empire and the author of "Collected Sources for Russian History" (*Sammlungen zur russischen Geschichte*, 1732). Müller arrived in Russia at the age of twenty, became a professor of history at the age of twenty-six, and remained in Russia until his death. In his teaching and research, he emphasized a critical approach to sources. He edited Russian chronicles, hunted for documents in archives, and emphasized the evidential value of items of material culture. In his capacity as historian of the Russian Empire, he studied its many peoples, especially in Siberia.[94]

Hardworking as he was, Müller needed assistance in his many enterprises. One of these assistants, Johann Fischer, published a history of Siberia in 1768. Another, the most famous, was August Ludwig Schlözer.[95] Schlözer came from the University of Göttingen, at that time a center of new approaches to the past, and had studied with the famous orientalist Johann David Michaelis. He was an ambitious young man in a hurry, who arrived in Russia at the age of twenty-six, originally thinking of the country as nothing but a stage on his travels further east. Soon after his arrival, he changed course and quickly learned Russian. However, he gave up his oriental ambitions with regret, missed Göttingen, and was unhappy with his role as assistant to Müller, preferring to write his own history and writing a report to the Academy of Sciences, two years after his arrival, about the way in which Russian history should be written (*Gedanken über die Art, die Russische Historie zu traktieren*).[96] Schlözer dismissed the polymath Mikhail Lomonosov, who was working on a rival history of the country, as a mere "chemist." Although he made enemies of both Lomonosov and Müller, he was able to remain at work thanks to the support of Tsarina Catherine.[97]

Schlözer spent only six years in Russia before returning to Göttingen, where he was appointed professor of Russian history and remained for more than forty years. He became one of the most famous historians of his time, combining his interest in Northern Europe (including the history of different ethnic groups within the Russian Empire) with a global approach to history, incorporating, as Müller had done, the history of material culture, including the history of the potato, tobacco, sugar, tea, and coffee. One might sum up Schlözer's career by saying that he first brought Göttingen to Russia and then brought Russia to Göttingen.

What were the effects on the Russians of this influx of expatriates? In the first place, once again, mediation, including the "transfer" of knowledge, especially technical knowledge: in other words, the dissemination of what was already known in the West, bringing the Russians up-to-date by means of public lectures at the Academy of Sciences, by teaching in the gymnasium attached to it (which had 342 students in its first five years) or at the new University of Moscow, founded in 1755. Expatriates who came to practice as architects or engineers were expected to train Russians in their fields of expertise. From the Russian point of view, hiring expatriates was a necessary but also a temporary expedient. In any case, Russian scholars, the famous polymath Mikhail Lomonosov for instance, were considerably less receptive to foreigners than their tsars were. Thanks in part to the efforts of Lomonosov, the Academy of Sciences, originally a virtual monopoly of foreigners, gradually became more Russian.[98]

In the second place, as was mentioned earlier, the senior expatriates were expected to carry out research and to publish their conclusions, often in the proceedings of the Academy of Sciences and in Latin, so that the learned world would know about the contributions to the work of the Commonwealth of Learning that were being made in Russia.

For Russian scholars, encounters with the expatriates were an education, bringing them up-to-date on new methods for studying both nature and culture. For example, Müller and Schlözer produced scholarly editions of medieval Russian chronicles, notably Nestor's chronicle, otherwise known as the Russian Primary Chronicle. Schlözer introduced the practice of methodical source criticism, describing it in his "Thoughts on the Manner of

Dealing with Russian History" (*Gedanken über die Art, die russische Historie zu traktieren*, 1764).[99] Müller asked his assistants to search in archives for information (even if his work marked a decisive shift in the balance between chronicle and record sources, Leopold von Ranke was not the first historian to carry out research in an archive). Gottlieb Bayer, who had been trained as a classicist, studied the ancient Scythians through the remains of their material culture. Müller too was concerned with what he called *Antiquitäten*, and he collected weapons, coins, holy images, and other objects in order to use them as sources for Russian history.

I have left until last what may well be the most important of the research achievements of these German expatriates. Messerschmidt, Müller, Pallas, and others took part in expeditions to remote areas of the Russian Empire (including Kamchatka, Orenburg, and the Caucasus), studying not only the local rocks, fauna, and flora but also the religion, manners, and customs of the inhabitants. The first and second expeditions to Kamchatka between 1728 and 1743 are the most famous, but the physician Daniel Messerschmidt had explored Siberia, on the orders of Peter the Great, from 1720 to 1727, while an expedition to the south of Russia, led by Pallas, set out in 1768, at the same time that Captain Cook was leaving for the South Pacific. These expeditions, in which surveying and mapping played a key part, were the result of a pragmatic concern with the resources of the empire, natural and human, but the leaders also collected information without any obvious practical use, including information about local antiquities.[100]

Among the major contributions to knowledge that resulted from these expeditions were the ones made to what became known as "Finno-Ugrian" studies, after the structural similarities between Hungarian, Finnish, and some Siberian languages such as Vogul and Ostiak had been demonstrated. On his expedition to Siberia, Daniel Messerschmidt, together with the Swedish prisoner of war Philip von Strahlenberg, collected information about the local languages.[101] Müller was also interested in these languages, while his assistant Johann Fischer compiled a "Siberian vocabulary" with the help of the Swede Jakob Lindenau. Fischer was aware of some similarities between these languages and Hungarian, and so was Bacmeister, a linguist as well as a historian who published an essay on links between languages before Sámuel Gyarmathy published his demonstration of the affinities between Hungarian and Finnish in 1799.[102]

Knowledge also traveled in the opposite direction. We know less than we would like about what the German scholars who took part in these expeditions owed to their Russian assistants as well as their Siberian informants. Many recent studies of scientific expeditions have emphasized that although the credit went to the foreign leaders, the role of their local informants was extremely important. A famous example is that of George Hunt, who helped Franz Boas with his famous studies of the Kwakiutl people of Northwest Canada.[103]

In the case of history, Müller and Schlözer learned from their Russian predecessor Vasilii Tatishchev and also from their local assistants, known as "adjuncts." In Schlözer's case, he was indebted, in the study of Russian chronicles, to his assistants Semyon Bashilov and Alexei Polenov.[104] And take the case of Stepan Krascheninnikov. Krascheninnikov was a student on the second Kamchatka expedition, but he carried out independent investigations and published a "Description of the Land of Kamchatka" (*Opisanie zemli Kamchatki*) that was used without proper acknowledgment by Steller. Krascheninnikov also helped Gmelin in the study of flora. Yet again, Pallas worked with a number of Russian assistants, such as Nikolai Rytschkov, who accompanied him on the expedition to South Russia, as well as some students who later became academicians in their own right.[105]

To sum up: mediation is obvious enough in the case of these German expatriate scholars. For the expatriates themselves, the years they spent in Russia were an education, widening their horizons and allowing them to discover new plants, new animals, new languages, new peoples, and so on, as well as to discover Russian history, little known in the West at this time. For Russian scholars too, the years these foreigners spent in their country were an education in the sense of bringing them up-to-date on new methods for studying both nature and culture. The tribute to Schlözer by Nikolai Gogol, who was not only the author of *Dead Souls* but also a professor of history at the University of St. Petersburg, is well known: "Schlözer was the first to feel history as one great whole [. . .] His writing was like the lightning that illuminates objects almost at once."[106] Schlözer's work was also an inspiration to a later generation of Russian historians of Russia, notably Nikolai Karamzin.

The consequences of this migration for German culture were also important, especially, once again, in the case of Schlözer. On his return to Göttingen he published *Allgemeine nordische Geschichte* ("General History of the North," 1772), translated the famous medieval Russian chronicle by Nestor, and taught and wrote on world history, culminating in his *Weltgeschichte nach ihren Haupttheilen im Auszug und Zusammenhange* ("The Main Parts of World History, Excerpts and Connections," 1792–1801). He was among other things an effective popularizer of Russian history abroad, especially in the German-speaking world.

Some expatriates also exhibited the usual distanciation. Distance encouraged comparison, so it should not surprise us that expatriates took the lead in the study of language families, in this case Finno-Ugrian. In contrast to Russian scholars such as Lomonosov, Müller and Schlözer—together with fellow expatriates such as Gottlieb Siegfried Bayer and Johann Philipp Krug (uninhibited by patriotism, like Polydore Virgil in England)—suggested that Rurik, the heroic founder of the Russian nation, and his followers had been "Normans," in other words, Scandinavians. Schlözer also cast doubt on the identification of the Slavs with the ancient Scythian and Sarmatian peoples.[107]

Although the relation between German and Russian scholars was not always harmonious, as we have seen, a kind of hybrid knowledge emerged from their encounter. The joint achievement of these expatriates was the creation of new knowledge that would later form part of a new discipline, ethnography. The books and articles that resulted from the scientific expeditions in which the expatriates took part made major contributions to knowledge in a number of established disciplines as well as in a few that were just beginning to emerge.

For example, Müller's unpublished treatise describing the manners and customs of various Siberian peoples was a pioneering study of what he called "the description of peoples" (*Völker-Beschreibung*), which would soon be known as ethnography. Indeed, Müller was recently described (like Sahagún and Lafitau) as "the first ethnographer." It was Müller's former assistant Schlözer who launched the terms *Völkerkunde* ("the study of peoples") and *Ethnographie* in academic discourse when he returned to the University of Göttingen (the word "ethnology," *ethnologia,* was introduced at much the same time). New words such as these encouraged the transformation of the old interest in manners and customs into a new discipline.[108]

There was of course a long tradition of travelers, merchants, and missionaries describing, as we have seen, the customs of the people they encountered, as Lafitau, whose work Müller took with him to Siberia, had done in the case of the Iroquois and Kaempfer in that of Japan. Voltaire's *Essai sur les moeurs* (which Müller had also read) described changes in European manners over the long term. What was new was the "systematic description" (*eine systematische geographische Beschreibung von Sibirien,* as he called it) that Müller gave and encouraged his assistants to give by drawing up an extremely detailed questionnaire. As in the cases of Sahagún and Lafitau, the work of Müller suggests that the emergence of what we still call ethnography was not so much a sudden break with tradition in the early twentieth century, the age of Malinowski, as a more gradual development.

Late Modern Expatriates

The Russian case offers an early example of a government that sees the country as backward and invites foreigners to provide the knowledge that will help it catch up. Another well-known example is that of Japan after 1868, when a land that had been almost closed to foreigners for centuries suddenly opened and invited foreigners to help with the modernization of the country.

In Turkey, which achieved independence after World War I, the president of the new Republic (proclaimed in 1923), Kemal Atatürk, launched a campaign of modernization by following Western models, which increased the receptivity of the country, officially at least, to foreigners. As part of this campaign, in 1931 a Swiss professor of education, Albert Malche, was asked to reform Turkish universities, and among his recommendations was the hiring of European scientists and scholars. Germany was the obvious country to approach, given the reputation of German science and scholarship at this time and the tradition of close relations between the Ottoman Empire and Germany.

In other words, at just the moment that Jewish professors were being dismissed in 1933, there was a demand for them in Turkey. By the beginning of the academic year 1933–34, forty-two refugee professors had been appointed to posts at the new University of Istanbul. Erich Auerbach and Leo Spitzer were the most famous of the German professors who moved there, Spitzer for three years and Auerbach for eleven, but they were part of a larger group who might equally well be described as exiles or as expatriates, invited to Turkey at the very time that they were forced to leave Germany or Austria.[109]

Besides students and colleagues of Auerbach and Spitzer, among them Rosemarie Burkart, Herbert and Liselotte Dieckmann, and Hans Marchand, the group included scientists, such as the astronomer Wolfgang Gleissberg (who remained in Istanbul for a quarter of a century), and specialists in Ottoman studies such as Andreas Tietze and Peter Sugar.

At least some of these expatriate-exiles had considerable influence on Turkish academic culture. Hans Reichenbach, philosopher of science, introduced the students of the University of Istanbul to the ideas of the Vienna Circle. The classicist Georg Rohde, together with his student Azra Erhat, initiated a program of translations into Turkish. A lawyer, Ernst Reuter, introduced a new approach to the study of politics at the University of Ankara, while another lawyer, Andreas Bertholan Schwarz, trained a generation of Turkish legal scholars. Similarly, former students of Auerbach and Spitzer, among them Süheila Bayrav and Şara Sayin, carried on their philological and comparative approach, extending it to Turkish literature in what Renaissance humanists would have called a *translatio studii.*[110]

The exiled scholars did not always enjoy their time in Turkey: Auerbach complained of his isolation, while Liselotte Dieckmann wrote about the atmosphere of distrust. Both of them remarked on the lack of books, at least in their particular fields. The situation was remedied in part thanks to another refugee, the librarian Walter Gottschalk, who arrived in Turkey in 1941 and was given the job of supervising all the libraries at the University of Istanbul.[111] Despite these problems, their exile brought benefits not only to Turkey but also to some of the scholars themselves, most obviously to the orientalists. The lawyer Oscar Weigert, who later taught comparative law in Washington, is likely to have learned something of value from his three years in Ankara. In the case of Auerbach, as we have seen, he—and the world—owes his most famous book, *Mimesis*, a general study of the representation of reality in Western literature, to his years in Istanbul away from the libraries that would have allowed him to continue his philological research.

The French in Brazil

Unlike Spanish America, Brazil had no universities in the colonial period, so that it was necessary to travel to Coimbra to study for a degree. In the nineteenth century, faculties of law and medicine were founded in several cities, often on a French model, because French culture enjoyed great prestige in the country at this time—and, to some extent, still does. The Instituto Histórico e Geográfico Brasileiro in Rio (1838) imitated the French Institut Historique. The Escola Normal and the Escola Politécnica followed the model of the French *Grandes Écoles*.

The French model was important once again when the University of São Paulo (USP) was founded in 1934, with the help of the owners of a leading newspaper, the *Estadão*. A year later, in 1935, the University of the Federal District (UDF) was founded in Rio de Janeiro, which was still the capital of the country. In both these universities, French expatriates played a major role. They were members of a so-called French mission, the same term that had been used in 1818 for a *mission artistique* and in 1921 for a military mission.[112]

Returning to prosopography, what follows concentrates on forty-six expatriate Frenchmen who made significant contributions to knowledge, almost entirely in the humanities and social sciences (by contrast, the posts in the natural sciences were generally filled by Germans and Italians). The group consisted entirely of men: Claude Lévi-Strauss's first wife Dina, who was also an anthropologist, was not invited in her own right, although she accompanied her husband on expeditions and also taught in São Paulo. As in the case of the Huguenot exiles in the Dutch Republic or Prussia, language was not a problem for these expatriates, because the Brazilian elite, from whom most of the students came, were familiar with French.

The group of forty-six included eight historians, seven geographers, and six sociologists or anthropologists. As in the case of the Germans in Russia, they were mainly young and ready for new experiences (not all scholars would have been prepared to leave France for a country so distant, three weeks away by sea at this time). As in the German case, they were often recruited by talent scouts, sometimes at extremely short notice—Lévi-Strauss, a former student of a French academic involved in the foundation of USP, told the story that he accepted the invitation to teach there following a telephone call requiring him to make a decision by the following day.[113] Most of the recruits went to the two Brazilian universities already mentioned, USP and UDF.

Sixteen professors from the Sorbonne went to UDF, including the economic historian Henri Hauser, who had just retired from his chair at the age of seventy, and Émile Bréhier, the well-known historian of philosophy, who was sixty. The new university lasted for only two years. It was closed following opposition by the Church (smelling Communism) and suspicion by the state—the minister of education, Gustavo Capanema, was opposed to the university, while 1937, the year of closure, was the year that Getúlio Vargas converted his presidency into a dictatorship known as the *Estado Novo*.

It is, however, the group that went to USP, twenty-one in all, that is best known and was most influential in the long term. The group included Braudel, Lévi-Strauss, the geographer Pierre Monbeig, and the sociologists Paul Arbousse-Bastide and Roger Bastide. To have two people named Bastide in this small group might have created confusion, but the Brazilians solved the problem by giving them nicknames. Roger, who was small and thin, was known as "Bastidinho," while Henri, who was a big man, was called "Bastidão." Most of the group did not stay long. Braudel (aged thirty-two in 1934) and Lévi-Strauss (aged twenty-six) were young scholars with a great future before them, but not in Brazil. Braudel returned to France in 1937, joined the army in 1939, and spent most of the war in German prison camps, while Lévi-Strauss returned in 1939, was dismissed from his position as teacher in a *lycée* because he was Jewish, and escaped to the United States. Monbeig, on the other hand, lived in Brazil from 1935 to 1946, while an older man, Roger Bastide, who was forty when he arrived in 1938, remained in the country until 1951.

Brazil made a strong impression on some at least of these expatriates, while a few of them exercised considerable influence on Brazilian students and scholars.[114] Although Hauser spent relatively little time in Brazil, he produced a number of articles on Brazilian history, ranging from slavery to the Brazilian disciples of the social theorist the Count of Saint-Simon. Braudel had already widened his horizons by teaching for ten years in a *lycée* in Algeria, learning to view the Mediterranean from the other side. His three years in Brazil, which he later described as the best years of his life, made his vision still more global. As was noted earlier, Braudel came to emphasize the value for historians of detachment, what he described as *dépaysement*.[115]

For his part, Paul Arbousse-Bastide once gave a lecture entitled

"What I Learned from Brazil," saying his time there had changed his life by giving him a different sense of space and time, while he viewed São Paulo as "a marvellous meeting-place of cultures."[116] As for Lévi-Strauss, it was in his years at USP, which gave him the opportunity to visit Mato Grosso and the Amazon, that he discovered the indigenous peoples of Brazil, such as the Bororo and the Nambikwara, whom he spent much of his later life studying.

The most dramatic example of the impact of the new environment on the expatriates is surely that of Roger Bastide, who changed his research topic soon after arriving in Brazil and became a specialist on Afro-Brazilian religion. In this respect he resembled his compatriot Pierre Verger, who was not a member of the group of academics but a photographer who became an authority on *candomblé* as well as a leading figure in this Afro-Brazilian cult. Bastide, by contrast, was more detached, focusing on *candomblé* as an example of syncretism or what he called the "interpenetration" of cultures, taking his cue from the Brazilian historian-sociologist Gilberto Freyre. Braudel too admired Freyre's work and wrote an enthusiastic review of it, published in *Annales* when he was a prisoner of war in Germany. In 1953, introducing Freyre's *Casa Grande e Senzala* to an Italian public, he was still more enthusiastic, speaking of the author's "acute intelligence" and of the work as "a masterpiece," part of a series of "stupendous books." "The crucial miracle is to have known how to combine a precise and careful historical narration with an immaculately subtle sociology."[117]

In their turn, some of the expatriates made considerable impact on the intellectual life of Brazil. In the case of history, Sergio Buarque, one of the leading Brazilian historians in the 1960s and 1970s, declared, "From Hauser I learned much."[118] The new French approach, incarnated and transmitted by Braudel when he was in São Paulo, has been and still remains influential in Brazil, especially for historians of the colonial period such as Fernando Novais, author of a study of the crisis of the colonial system; Luiz Felipe de Alencastro, who has written on the slave trade and replaced Brazil in its Atlantic context; and Laura de Melo e Souza, who has written on the history of mentalities and in particular on witchcraft.

In the case of geography, a new discipline in Brazil in the 1930s, the French approach remains influential, thanks to Pierre Monbeig in particular.[119] Lévi-Strauss remains an intellectual model for leading Brazilian anthropologists today, among them Roberto DaMatta and Eduardo Viveiros de Castro. Roger Bastide remains a central figure to cite, whether to agree or disagree, in Brazilian studies of *candomblé* or more generally, of religious syncretism. One of the country's leading sociologists, Maria Isaura Pereira de Queiroz, is a former student of Bastide's, while another, Fernando Henrique Cardoso, was once his assistant, although he is better known as a former president of Brazil.

As for the effect of the expatriates on their homeland, Braudel's enthusiasm for the study of colonial Brazil and Latin America was communicated to his students, among them Pierre Chaunu, much of whose voluminous output deals with the history of the New World, and Frédéric Mauro, author of a study of Portugal and the Atlantic world in the seventeenth century. The tradition has been carried on by younger French historians such as Nathan Wachtel and Serge Gruzinski, both of whom have studied Portuguese as well as Spanish America.

Unlike the exiles, many of the expatriates discussed in this chapter did not normally think of themselves primarily as mediators. Mediation often happened while they were thinking of something else, such as teaching physics or converting the heathen. The following chapter will return to exile and self-conscious mediation.

5 : THE GREAT EXODUS

Where the early modern story of diasporas was dominated by exiles for the sake of religion, the story after 1789 is largely one of political exiles or of victims of ethnic cleansing.

Revolution and Exile

Following the French Revolution and especially the "Terror" of 1793–94, a wave of opponents of the new regime went into exile, some 180,000 of them altogether, moving over the frontiers to Colmar, for instance, to Brussels and to London. It was at this time that the term *émigré* came into regular use not only in French but in other languages as well.

This large group included a few intellectuals, notably Viscount Bonald, who moved to Heidelberg, and Viscount Chateaubriand, who chose London (and lived for a time in a garret in Holborn); Madame de Staël, who moved to Switzerland and then to England; and Joseph de Maistre, who took refuge in Lausanne, Cagliari, and St. Petersburg. As so often happens, the movement of these émigrés was accompanied by the movement of ideas, while for at least some members of the group, exile was a form of education, because they learned something of the diversity of Europe, from Ireland to Russia, and eventually produced a shelf of travel books. If their impact on their hosts is a less obvious one, this may have been because French culture was already well known abroad at this time.[1]

The case of Poland is rather different. After 1789 or 1793, the next major date in the history of European diasporas is 1830–31, following the defeat of the Polish rising against Russian rule. In what Poles call the Great Emigration (*Wielka Emigracja*), over 70,000 people left the country, mainly for Paris. They included Frédéric Chopin, Adam Mickiewicz, and Joachim Lelewel. Mickiewicz, already known as a poet, became a journalist and a lecturer at the Collège de France, where the French government created a post for him as professor of Slavic languages and literatures. The historian Lelewel was not so fortunate. In 1833, ordered to leave Paris on account of his political activities, Lelewel walked to Belgium, where he lived for nearly thirty years. Both Mickiewicz and Lelewel acted as ambassadors of Polish culture, Mickiewicz in his lectures, published later in five volumes, and Lelewel in a history of Poland that was published in French in 1844. Fernand Braudel once explained his own warm international reception, contrasting with that of his gifted Polish colleague Witold Kula, by his access to the "French loud-speaker," a more effective means of communication than its Polish equivalent. Similarly, it has been argued that Paris provided the Polish rebels of the Great Emigration with the language, the publishing houses, and the other facilities that they needed to spread their ideas across Europe.[2]

The next important date in the history of European exiles is 1848, the year of the "springtime of nations," of revolutions in France, the German states, the Habsburg Empire, and elsewhere. Following the failure of the revolutions of that year, a diaspora of Central Europeans spread across the world. Some went to the United States, others to South America (to Brazil, for instance, or Chile), but the majority remained in the more peaceful parts of Europe, settling in Zurich, in Brussels, and above all in London (part of which became known at this time as "Little Germany"). London has been described as "probably the refugee capital of Europe" at that time.[3]

Karl Marx has become the best known of the new Londoners, following his years in Paris, but other revolutionary intellectuals who made the same choice included Louis Blanc, whose books on French history were based on his research in the British Museum; the orientalist Theodor Goldstücker, who was appointed professor of Sanskrit at University College in 1852; Friedrich Althaus, who translated Carlyle and eventually became professor of German, again at University College; the art historian Gottfried Kinkel, who came to England after escaping from prison in

Spandau and taught at University College and at Bedford College for Women before moving on to Zurich; and the Hungarian Gustav Zerffi (a former secretary to the nationalist leader Lajos Kossuth), who lectured at the National Art Training School in South Kensington.[4]

The role of these exiles and other expatriates as mediators is obvious enough, whether they were translating British writers such as Carlyle or introducing new German methods of art history to the English. In the case of natural science, a well-known example is that of August Wilhelm von Hofmann, a chemist who, thanks to Prince Albert, was invited to be director of the new Royal College of Chemistry in London in 1845. Hofmann remained for twenty years and spread the knowledge of German scientific methods, publishing a description in English of the chemical laboratories at the Universities of Bonn and Berlin. The Italian Antonio Panizzi, a former revolutionary who became principal librarian at the British Museum, ensured that the museum's holdings of Italian books were adequate as well as reforming the catalogue, helping design the new reading room, and pressing the government to spend more money on its national library.[5]

Conversely, at least some of the exiles learned from their hosts. It has been argued, for instance, that "it was French history that encouraged Marx to think about the nature of revolution, the limits of political reform and the importance of economic forces in the process of historical change."[6] In similar fashion, his thirty-four years in England gave Marx a ringside seat to watch the development of capitalism, industrialization, and imperialism in the age of the Great Exhibition in London (1851), the Indian "Mutiny" and rising against the British (1857), the Lancashire "Cotton Famine" (1861–65), and so on.

Three examples of Latin Americans abroad confirm the idea of exile as education. Andrés Bello was sent to London by Simón Bolívar in 1810, to raise money for the movement for independence, and lived there for nineteen years. At this time, as the titles of his publications suggest (*Biblioteca Americana*, *Repertorio Americano*), he came to think in terms of South America as a whole rather than of his own region (which became Venezuela). As in the case of the Poles in Paris after 1830, Bello's years in London gave him access to a major printing center from which to spread his ideas. A London publisher, Rudolf Ackermann, himself a German expatriate, decided to open bookshops at this time in Mexico, Guatemala, Colombia, Argentina, and Peru, selling textbooks that had been translated into Spanish by exiles living in London.[7]

It has been said of the Chilean historian Benjamín Vicuña MacKenna, who spent the 1850s in exile in Europe, that his years abroad would "shape the great questions that throughout the decades of 1860 and 1870 will stimulate his intellectual work."[8] And it was in his years of exile in Paris and London in the 1850s that the Colombian journalist José María Torres Caicedo coined the term "América Latina." The timing suggests that Caicedo needed to leave that large region in order to see it as a whole.

Much more could obviously be said about the intellectual consequences of the diasporas of 1789, 1830–31, and 1848, but this chapter will concentrate on two case studies from the twentieth century. The first is concerned with intellectuals who left Russia following the Bolshevik Revolution. The second and longer case study focuses on what some scholars describe as the Great Exodus of the 1930s, though from a Jewish point of view it was their third major exodus, while Laura Fermi called it "The Great Wave."[9]

The Russian Diaspora

An even more memorable date in the history of exiles than 1685, when French Protestants faced the alternatives of expulsion or conversion, is 1917. All the same, a focus on that year is misleading. It was only as the Russian Civil War came to an end in 1919 that the opponents of the Bolshevik regime began to flee in large numbers. Estimates of the total number of Russian refugees from these years vary greatly, between 700,000 and 3 million.[10] They went to a variety of places, "from Paraguay to Manchuria," but among the most important were Berlin, Paris, and Prague.[11]

In these cities in particular many of the refugees were able to resist assimilation, establishing themselves in certain quarters, such as Grenelle and Clignancourt in Paris, frequenting certain cafés such as the Leon, on Nollendorfplatz in Berlin, publishing their own newspapers, and establishing their own schools and churches. Finding employment was difficult, and although the stories of Russian princes turned Paris taxi drivers are largely mythical, real examples can be found.[12] In the early years especially, many exiles expected the Bolshevik regime to collapse quickly, allowing them to return.

In the case of intellectuals, although some — among them the literary critic Gleb Struve and the historians Elias Bickerman and Anatole Mazour — fought for the Whites in the civil war and had to leave after their defeat, the crucial year for departure was 1922. More than 150 scholars were deported at that time, many of them on the now famous "philosophers' ship" to Germany. The philosophers expelled included Nikolai Berdyaev, Semyon Frank, and Nikolai Lossky, accompanied by other academics such as the sociologist Fyodor Stepun, the biologist Mikhail Novikov, the theologian George Florovsky, the economist Sergei Prokopovich, and the historian Aleksandr Kizevetter.[13]

Some of these scholars found employment as professors in Sofia and Belgrade, but the main center of intellectual emigration was Prague, which became known as "the Russian Oxford." The Czechoslovak government invited about seventy professors to remain there, working in newly founded institutions such as the Russian Law Faculty, the Russian People's University, the Russian Business School, and the Ukrainian Free University.[14] Following the German invasion of Czechoslovakia in 1939, the group was scattered. A number of refugee intellectuals lived a kind of nomadic existence, moving from city to city for either political or economic reasons. The economist Paul A. Baran, for instance, who was born in the Ukraine, left what would soon become the Soviet Union in 1921 for Poland, Germany, France, England, and finally the United States, where he is said to have been the only Marxist professor of economics with tenure (at Stanford University). Elias Bickerman left Russia for Berlin, Paris, Marseilles, and New York before coming to rest in Israel. George Florovsky, expelled from Russia in 1920, lived in Sofia, Prague, Paris, New York, and at Harvard and Princeton. Similar examples of "re-emigration" are to be found among the diaspora of the 1930s.

Unlike the scholars among the Huguenot diaspora, the Russians faced a serious problem of language. If they wrote in Russian, they would be read only by their fellow refugees, because their books had little chance of publication in the USSR. The many small publishing houses founded by the Russian exiles in Berlin and elsewhere catered primarily to other exiles.

On the other hand, if the exiles chose to write in a foreign language, they needed to master it. German was not too difficult, at least for the scholars who had studied in Germany in their youth, like the sociologist Fyodor Stepun or the literary historian Dmitry Chizhevsky. English, on the other hand, posed problems. The ancient historian Mikhail Rostovtzeff, who arrived at the University of Wisconsin–Madison in 1918, was one of the leaders in his field, but when he lectured, the students complained that they could not understand his English. A few years later, when he was trying to bring his former student George Vernadsky to Yale University, Rostovtzeff warned him of the need not only to speak but also to publish in English.[15] Other exiles were more adaptable than Rostovtzeff, at least so far as language was concerned. The art historian André Grabar published in French while he was living in France, and later, in the United States, in English. The historian Robert Vipper learned to lecture and write in Latvian during his stay in Riga between 1924 and 1941, when Latvia was an independent state.

Despite the problems, the refugee scholars had a considerable impact on at least some of the host countries. Russia's loss was the gain of many other countries, most obviously Bulgaria, Yugoslavia, and Czechoslovakia. For example, the study of zoology was stimulated by the arrival of Novikov and some of his Russian colleagues at the Zoological Institute at the Charles University of Prague.[16] Again, the study of linguistics and literature owed a good deal to the presence in Prague of gifted refugees such as Nikolai Trubetzkoy and Roman Jakobson, while psychoanalysis was launched in Czechoslovakia by the Russians Nikolai Osipov and Fyodor Dosuzhkov.

Mediation was important to the exiles because they saw themselves as defending Russian traditions that were under threat from the Bolsheviks. This work of mediation was particularly important in France, Britain, and the United States, where Russian culture had been relatively little known. At Yale, Vernadsky introduced American students to Russian history, while the former diplomat Mikhail Karpovich did the same at Harvard and Anatole Mazour at Stanford. In Paris and at Harvard, André Grabar introduced his listeners to the art of the Orthodox Church. At the University of London, Dmitri Mirsky introduced English students to Russian literature. At Oxford, Isaiah Berlin, who arrived in Britain as a child in 1921, explained the history of nineteenth-century Russian thought and inspired enthusiasm for the ideas of an earlier Russian exile in England, Alexander Herzen, as well as lecturing on political philosophy. Berlin became more fluent in English than most of the English themselves, but he never lost his Russian accent.[17]

The experience of exile also made an impact on the refugees, most obviously on young ones such as Mikhail Postan, who became a specialist on the history of his hostland, England, but on older scholars as well. The theologian George Florovsky, who taught at Harvard and Princeton, reinvented himself as a cultural historian of Russia. George Fyodotov, a former specialist on the French Middle Ages, became known in exile for his study of *The Russian Religious Mind*, while Konstantin Mochulsky turned from Romance languages and literatures to Russian studies and produced an important biography of Dostoyevsky.

The catastrophe (as they saw it) that the exiles had experienced stimulated their search for explanations. In Sofia, the linguist Nikolai Trubetzkoy and the geographer Pyotr Savitsky, together with Florovsky and Vernadsky, responded to the Bolshevik Revolution with the theory of "Eurasianism." According to this theory, Bolshevism was a form of Westernization that was doomed, because it had appeared at the time of the decline of the West and the rise of Eurasia, a trend in which Russia, located culturally as well as geographically between East and West, was destined to play a leading part. Other exiles, among them the historian Pavel Miliukov and the politician-economist Pyotr Struve, also brooded on and wrote about the reasons for the rise of Bolshevism, while Rostovtzeff looked at the crisis of the third century from the perspective of the crisis of the twentieth.

These responses were very far from being detached. Despite this, it can be argued, and indeed it has been argued, that the detached viewpoint of the outsider underlies what has been called "the enormous importance of exile and emigration for the birth of modern literary theory in East and Central Europe." The star witness to this effect is the literary critic Viktor Shklovsky, who emphasized the artistic value of what he called "defamiliarization" (*ostranenie*), a literary or artistic technique encouraging readers or spectators to see their familiar surroundings in a new light. Shklovsky spent a few years in Berlin before returning to Russia, and his theory may well have been inspired by his experiences there, because many exiles have commented on the culture shock they experienced abroad, discovering that what they had taken for granted was unfamiliar to their hosts, while what their hosts took for granted surprised the new arrivals.[18]

Signs of hybridization also became visible in the decades that followed the diaspora of 1919–22. Novikov has been described as offering a "productive combination of German and Russian biological traditions," though he may have already been combining them before he left Russia. A stronger example comes from linguistics. The Prague Circle of the 1920s, famous for its contribution to the rise of semiotics, was composed of both émigré Russians (Jakobson, Trubetzkoy, the folklorist Pyotr Bogatryev) and Czech scholars such as Vilém Mathesius, who co-founded the circle in 1926, and Jan Mukařovský. The history of the Prague Circle illustrates the way in which new ideas may emerge from encounters between people coming from different cultures and speaking from different standpoints.

Meanwhile, events in Hungary were taking the opposite course from events in Russia. In 1919, the short-lived Red or Soviet republic, led by Béla Kun, was followed by the White regime of Admiral Miklós Horthy, unleashing a movement of "White Terror" that was directed against both Communists and Jews. In response, many Hungarians took refuge abroad, in Germany in particular. They included the physicist Leó Szílárd, the chemist George de Hevesy, the sociologists Oskar Jaszi and Pál Szende, the economist Karl Polanyi (followed some years later by his younger brother Michael), and some leading members of an intellectual circle that had formed around the philosopher-critic Georg Lukács and used to meet at his house on Sundays. Among the members of this "Sunday circle," Karl Mannheim, his future wife the psychologist Júlia Láng, the art historian Arnold Hauser, and the philosopher Béla Fogarasi all took refuge in Germany, while another art historian, Frederick Antal, fled to Italy. Following the rise of Nazism and Fascism, Fogarasi moved to the USSR, while Mannheim, Láng, Hauser, and Antal all took refuge in Britain. Lukács himself, who became a minister in the Hungarian Soviet Republic, fled to Vienna in 1919 and moved to Moscow in 1930, only returning to Hungary after World War II.[19]

The Great Exodus

The really "great" exodus of the twentieth century (though the phrase has sometimes been applied to the Russians after 1917 and the Poles after 1830) was that of refugees from Hitler's *Reich*, for the most part Central European Jews, who left Germany after 1933, Austria after 1938, and Czechoslovakia after 1939. Gentile scientists and scholars who opposed Hitler for political reasons also emigrated at this time. Other scholars left Mussolini's Italy, and yet others fled from Spain either at the beginning or in the aftermath of the civil war.

As in the case of the Huguenot diaspora of the 1680s, it is illuminating to view the Great Exodus of the 1930s as part of a longer trend. In the case of Jewish refugees, one might begin the story as far back as the flights from the pogroms that were taking place in the Russian Empire from the early 1880s onward. Intellectuals were not particularly prominent in this massive movement—some 2.5 million people left Eastern Europe between 1880 and 1914—but some of the children who left with their parents became distinguished scholars in England, where over 120,000 Jews settled in this period, and also in the United States.

Among the refugees who came to England, the sociologist Morris Ginsberg, for instance, who was born in Lithuania when it was part of the Russian Empire, arrived as a teenager in 1904 and became a professor at the London School of Economics a quarter of a century later, in 1929. The economist Abba Lerner, born in Bessarabia, again when it was part of the Russian Empire, came to London with his family at the age of three, in 1906, migrating to the United States in 1937 and becoming a professor at the University of California–Berkeley, Columbia University, and elsewhere. The political scientist Herman Finer was also born in Bessarabia and came to England with his parents. He later left for the United States and a chair at the University of Chicago, while his younger brother Samuel, born in London, became a well-known professor of government at the University of Manchester. Lewis Namier, born in Russian Galicia in 1888, came to England to study in 1907. He too became a professor at the University of Manchester, in his case in the department of history. Namier became one of the most famous historians in Britain and acquired a number of disciples, the "Namierites."

The children of exiles from Central and Eastern Europe were still more important in the intellectual life of the United States. For example, the anthropologist Paul Radin, who ended his career as chair of his department at Brandeis University, had arrived as a baby in 1884. Meyer Schapiro, who was to become a professor at Columbia and a distinguished art historian, arrived in 1907 at the age of three, while Louis Wirth, later a central figure in the Chicago School of sociology, arrived from Germany in 1911 at the age of fourteen. Even more significant in the history of knowledge was a group of children born in the United States to parents who had arrived relatively recently. As adults, these children became leaders in their academic fields. In the case of politics, one thinks of Gabriel Almond, for instance; in psychology, of Jerome Bruner; in anthropology, of Melville Herskovits; in philosophy, of Sidney Hook; in economics, of Milton Friedman and Paul Samuelson; in history, of Daniel Boorstin and Oscar Handlin (author of two studies of emigration); and in sociology, of Daniel Bell, Morris Janowitz, Robert Merton, and Edward Shils — quite a galaxy.

Despite these earlier examples, the emigrants of the 1930s have a special place in the history of knowledge, given their large numbers and also the way in which their careers made the consequences of displacement for knowledge particularly visible. A brief account of Italian and Spanish exiles will be followed by a longer section that focuses on refugees from Germany and Austria.

The Italian Exiles

The literature on the Italian diaspora is relatively sparse, despite the importance of the movement, at least in intellectual history, as a few famous names will suggest. The most politically involved of the exiles was probably the historian Gaetano Salvemini, who left Italy as early as 1925 (three years after Mussolini came to power) and lived in France and England before going to Harvard in 1934, where he studied and taught until 1948. Salvemini viewed Harvard as an "enchanted island" and the Widener Library in particular as "paradise." He was described by a former assistant as a "voluntary recluse." All the same, Salvemini's fluent English, together with his affinity with Anglo-American empiricism, allowed him to influence scholars and students alike.[20]

In any case, this "recluse" was active in politics. A former student of medieval Italian communes and of the French Revolution, Salvemini turned in exile to the study of Fascism. He orchestrated an anti-Fascist campaign in the United States that spread knowledge of the situation in Italy to Americans. He also produced a trilogy about the history of Italy in his time, *The Fascist Dictatorship in Italy* (1927), *Mussolini Diplomatico* (1932), and *Under the Axe of Fascism* (1936).

Salvemini was only one member of a group of distinguished Italian intellectuals in exile. The economist Piero Sraffa, another opponent of Fascism, moved to Cambridge, England, in 1927 and remained there until his death. The political philosopher Max Ascoli, who was Jewish, left Italy for the United States in 1931. He taught at the New School for Social Research and published books on justice, liberty, and Fascism. The political scientist Mario Einaudi, son of Luigi, later president of Italy, was dismissed from his post at the University of Messina for refusing an oath of loyalty to Fascism. He arrived in the United States in 1933 and taught at Harvard and Cornell as well as writing about Communism, Christian Democracy, and what he called the "Roosevelt Revolution."

The art historian Lionello Venturi also refused to take the oath of loyalty and moved to Paris, where he made a living by advising art dealers, as well as writing about Impressionism. After the German invasion of France, he left for the United States, where he taught at a number of universities. Another opponent of the regime was Renato Poggioli, whose field was Russian literature. Soon after his arrival in the United States, Poggioli became president of the anti-Fascist Mazzini Society, whose members included Ascoli and Salvemini.

The dismissal of Italian academics of Jewish origin in 1938, following the model of Germany in 1933, was followed by the emigration of more scholars and scientists (in 1938, 9 percent of Italian university teachers were Jewish).[21] The physicist Enrico Fermi, for instance, arrived in the United States in 1939 and was offered a post at Columbia University before playing a leading part in the Manhattan Project. Fermi helped a younger scientist, the microbiologist Salvador Luria (who was twenty-eight when he arrived in the United States in 1940), to obtain a Rockefeller Fellowship while he established himself. Other distinguished exiles included the physiologist Carlo Foà, who moved to Brazil; the mathematician Beppo Levi, who moved to Argentina; and the physicists Bruno Rossi and Emilio Segrè, who both moved to the United States. Rossi, like Fermi, took part in the Manhattan

Project, while Segrè was awarded a Nobel Prize when he was working at the University of California–Berkeley.

In the humanities, Giorgio Levi Della Vida, a linguist and historian specializing on the Near East, moved to the University of Pennsylvania, while the ancient historian Arnaldo Momigliano chose England and, after some years in Oxford and Bristol, was appointed to a chair at University College London.

Some scholars had trouble finding a niche in their hostland. Leonardo Olschki, who contributed to both Romance and oriental studies, had a particularly difficult time in exile. Born in Verona, Olschki obtained a chair of Romance philology at the University of Heidelberg. Dismissed from his chair in 1933 because he was Jewish, he returned to Italy, only to leave again in 1939 for the United States. There, he held a succession of temporary posts and complained about the difficulty of carrying out research for its own sake "in this pragmatic world." Finally he joined the faculty at Berkeley, only to be asked to swear the loyalty oath. Olschki refused, and returned to Italy once more for some years until he was able to resume his position in the United States. No wonder, then, that he was attracted to the study of another Italian wanderer, Marco Polo.[22]

Promising younger Italian émigrés included Roberto Lopez, a historian of the Middle Ages who later became a professor at Yale; Giorgio de Santillana, a historian and philosopher of science who taught at MIT; Uberto Limentani, a specialist on Italian baroque literature who was appointed to a chair at the University of Cambridge; Bruno Zevi, who was only twenty when he left Italy in 1938, still to make a reputation as a historian and critic of architecture; and Franco Modigliani, the same age as Zevi, who was to become a professor of economics at MIT and a Nobel Prize winner. Some young scholars moved out of the academic world. The historian Paolo Treves worked as a journalist in London, while his cousin, Antonello Gerbi, a historian, philosopher, and economist, worked for a bank in Lima.

In some cases at least, the effect of exile on the work of these scholars is clear enough. It was in Peru that Gerbi, for instance, became interested in the history of the New World, leading to his classic study *The Debate over the New World* (*La disputa del nuovo mondo*, 1955) and other studies. Again, it was in exile that Salvemini, as we have seen, turned to the study of Fascism. In the United States, Renato Poggioli extended his teaching and writing from Russian to comparative literature, and became known for his *Theory of the Avant-Garde*, which appeared in Italian in 1962 and in English translation six years later.

The intellectual impact on their hostlands of at least some of these scholars is also manifest. At Harvard, Mario Einaudi helped establish the study of comparative politics, while Renato Poggioli did the same for comparative literature. As for Arnaldo Momigliano, he became legendary in both London and Chicago (where he also lectured) for his extraordinary learning, his mastery of many languages, his innumerable articles, and his sharp wit. The British students who were taught or at least inspired by him, often by attending his seminars at the Warburg Institute and elsewhere, included leading ancient historians such as Michael Crawford, Keith Hopkins, Sally Humphreys, Fergus Millar, and Oswyn Murray. Momigliano helped to deprovincialize British scholarship and to persuade historians to make use of the ideas of social theorists such as Max Weber and Emile Durkheim (together with Sally Humphreys, he introduced a course on ancient history and anthropology at University College). Following an Italian tradition, Momigliano also encouraged ancient historians to study their predecessors, the scholars, including the antiquarians, who had written about ancient Greece and Rome from the Renaissance onward.[23]

Spanish Exiles

Unlike the Italian case, the story of the Spanish exiles during and after the civil war has been told many times. There were many more of the Spaniards. Calculations vary between 160,000 and 500,000, including some 5,000 individuals with academic degrees or similar qualifications (500 were members of the medical profession).[24] Of the academic population, 42 percent left Spain at this time.[25] Some left early, to avoid the war, like the philosopher José Ortega y Gasset, the historian Claudio Sánchez-Albornoz, and the scholar-physician Gregorio Marañón (who had received death threats). A greater number left in 1939, when it was clear that the Republicans had lost.

France was a popular destination (chosen by both Ortega and Marañón in 1936), but 1939 turned out to be a bad moment for taking refuge there, because the Germans invaded the country in 1940. Those exiles who were able to do so moved on, usually to a Spanish-speaking country, which others had chosen in the first place: to Cuba, for instance, like the philologist-historian Ramón Menéndez Pidal or the philosophers José Ferrater Mora and Maria Zambrano; to Venezuela, like the physiologist Augusto Pi i Sunyer; to Santo Domingo, like the literary historian Vicente Lloréns; to Ecuador, like the philosopher Juan David García Bacca; or to Argentina, which accepted some 2,500 refugees and was chosen by scholars such as Ortega y Gasset, Sánchez-Albornoz, the philologist Amado Alonso, and the sociologist and essayist Francisco Ayala.

Mexico was the most welcoming hostland to these exiles. President Lázaro Cárdenas had supported the Republicans during the civil war and accepted an unlimited number of refugees, in practice about 20,000, about half of whom came in ships chartered by the Republican government. The first of these ships "offered courses in Mexican geography and recent history" to prepare the refugees for their new environment.[26]

At a time when higher education was expanding, intellectuals were particularly welcome in Mexico, as they were in Turkey at this time, while Spain was still widely viewed as the cultural metropolis of the hispanophone world. Some leading Spanish scholars were invited to Mexico, and the Casa de España (soon to become the Colegio de Mexico) was founded in order to give the exiles a place to work. Among the best known of the new arrivals were the historians Pere Bosch-Gimpera, Lluís Nicolau d'Olwer, and Josep Maria Miquel i Verges (all three Catalans); the philosophers José Gaos and Joaquin Xirau; and the lawyer-sociologists José Medina Echevarría and Luis Recásens Siches.[27]

A few Spanish scholars took refuge in England, like the diplomat-historian Salvador de Madariaga, and also, for a time, Juan Negrín, a former professor of physiology who became prime minister of Spain during the civil war. Negrín "could never decide whether, and how, to resume his career as a physiologist," but he did make a rather unusual contribution to knowledge when he was in exile, volunteering as a guinea pig in the physiological experiments carried out by the British scientist J. B. S. Haldane "on the effects of cold, darkness and varying water and air pressures on the human body."[28]

Many more Republicans went to the United States. For some, this was their first choice, as in the case of Américo Castro, discussed earlier, the former minister Fernando de los Ríos, who became professor of politics at the New School in New York, the literary historian Angel del Río, who taught at Columbia, and the poet-critics Pedro Salinas and Jorge Guillén (both of whom taught at Wellesley College). For others, such as Amado Alonso and José Ferrater Mora, the United States was a later choice.

For the homeland, the brain drain, which has been called "the destruction of science," was a serious one.[29] Spaniards were even cut off from the work that their compatriots published in exile. Américo Castro's reflections on Spanish history, for instance, were published in Buenos Aires and Princeton, but not in Spain itself.

What did the exiles learn from this variety of experiences? Unlike the German-speaking refugees in Britain and the United States, the Spanish exiles in Latin America did not have to struggle with a foreign language, even if some of them found the culture more foreign than they had expected. Individual reactions to the hostlands varied from misery to enthusiasm. Sánchez Albornoz wrote to Ortega from Argentina that "my life in this extremity of the world is a sequence of unhappy days."[30] On the other hand, José Gaos adapted well to life in Mexico, declaring, as was remarked in the introduction, that he was not so much uprooted (*desterrado*) as transplanted (*transterrado*), while Angel del Río wrote of himself as "fully and equally identified" with the cultures of Spain and the United States.[31]

Some exiles shifted from studies of Spain to studies of their hostland. Gaos wrote a book about the history of ideas in Mexico; d'Olwer, who had studied the history and literature of Catalonia before becoming a minister, turned to the sixteenth-century missionary Bernardo de Sahagún and to the economic history of his adopted country at the turn of the nineteenth and twentieth centuries; the philosopher Adolfo Sánchez Vázquez wrote a book about Rousseau in Mexico, that is, his influence on the ideology of the movement for independence.[32] The historian Manuel Isidro Méndez, who had lived in Cuba as a child before returning there as an exile in 1936, wrote a biography of the Cuban national hero José Martí. Another historian, Miquel i Verges, aged thirty-six when he arrived in Mexico, followed his earlier studies of Catalan literature with a book on the role of the press in the age of Mexican independence. For these exiles, the encounter with Spanish America led to a widening of their intellectual horizons.

What did the émigré scholars contribute in return? Above all, different kinds of mediation. In 1965, Angel del Río noted his "thirty years of interpreting Spanish culture in the United States." Américo Castro, who taught at the Universities of Wisconsin, Texas, and at Princeton, placed Spanish American history on the mental map of his students, while Juan Marichal, a sixteen-year-old exile in 1938, did the same for Spanish literature in his courses at Harvard in the 1950s. The exiles in Mexico, Argentina, and elsewhere mediated between the cultures of Europe (not only Spain but also Germany, where a number of them had studied) and those of Spanish America.

Some of the scholars in exile acquired disciples in their hostlands. For example, Gaos influenced two students who became leading Mexican intellectuals: the historian Edmundo O'Gorman and the philosopher Leopoldo Zea; Gaos conducted dialogues with both of them in print as well as in conversation.[33] In similar fashion, Sánchez Albornoz encouraged the study of medieval history in Argentina and also inspired historians of other periods, notably José Luis Romero, who ranged from the ancient world to the twentieth century, and Túlio Halperín Donghi, who wrote on Latin America from colonial times onward.

Mediation naturally took place through books as well. Like earlier exiles, some of the new arrivals in the New World turned to translation. The philosopher Eugenio Ímaz, who arrived in Mexico in 1939, devoted much of his time to translating the complete works of Wilhelm Dilthey. José Gaos translated a number of books by German philosophers: Eduard Husserl, Max Scheler, Martin Heidegger, and Karl Jaspers. José Medina Echevarría translated Max Weber. These translations, published in Mexico, circulated throughout the Spanish-speaking world—with the exception of Franco's Spain.

A number of exiles were involved in publishing. In Mexico, some small publishing houses were founded by the newcomers, just as small publishing houses had been founded by Russian émigrés in Berlin and elsewhere, although in contrast to the Russian case, the readership of the books published in Mexico was not confined to the diasporic community. The Fondo de Cultura Económica, established by Spanish exiles, published translations of historical classics such as Marcel Bataillon on Erasmus and his Spanish followers, Marc Bloch's *Historian's Craft*, and Fernand Braudel's *Mediterranean*.[34]

In Argentina, exiles were involved in publishing on a grander scale, with large firms such as the rivals Espasa-Calpe and Losada. Calpe, which published more traditional titles, was a branch of a Spanish publisher that became independent in 1937. Losada, founded in 1938 by Gonzalo Losada, a former employee of Calpe, was more adventurous. The first book published by the firm was a Spanish translation of Kafka's *Metamorphosis*.[35] At a time of civil war and its aftermath, publishers in Spain were unable to compete successfully with these Argentine firms. In publishing—and not only in publishing—the civil war led to the provincialization of Spain, the former cultural metropolis of the hispanophone world.

Germany and Austria

The exodus of intellectuals from Germany and Austria was a movement on a much greater scale than the others discussed here. Nearly 1,700 German scholars and scientists were dismissed in the early years of the Hitler regime, and over 75 percent of these academics were Jewish.[36] Besides scholars of Jewish origin (at a time when to have one Jewish grandmother was sufficient to warrant dismissal), the refugees included individuals with Jewish wives and others who were members of the Communist and Socialist parties. Altogether, over a fifth of German university teachers were dismissed.

Some of the refugees (Erich Auerbach among them, as we have seen) went to Turkey; others to Palestine (among them the historian Yitzhak Baer and the philosopher Hans Jonas); yet others to Sweden (the philosopher Ernst Cassirer); Japan (the philosopher Karl Löwith and the urban planner Bruno Taut); Panama (the sociologists Franz Borkenau and Paul Honigsheim); or Egypt (the sociologist Siegfried Landshut). Most of them, however, went to France (moving on after 1940), Britain, or the United States.

The group whose migration had the greatest consequences for the hostlands was surely that of the natural scientists, including famous figures such as Erwin Schrödinger, who went to Ireland; Enrico Fermi and Leó Szílárd (in his second emigration), both of whom worked on the Manhattan Project in the United States; and Albert Einstein, who was offered a post at the Institute for Advanced Study in Princeton, together with his friend the mathematician Kurt Gödel and the polymath John von Neumann. In the case of physics, it has been argued that the organization of the discipline "was uniquely suited to provide niches for newcomers" (that is, a high degree of receptivity), while the émigrés themselves have been described as "bridge-builders," who made a "synthesis" between the German theoretical tradition and the more empirical Anglo-American tradition of experiment.[37] In other words, the physicists exemplified the hybridization that has been noted so often in this book. In what follows, however, I shall concentrate on examples from fields in the humanities and social sciences.

As in the case of the Protestant refugees discussed earlier, many of the exiled scholars experienced difficulties in their search for employment. Once again the supply, in this case of professors rather than pastors, exceeded the demand. Academic jobs were scarce in both Britain and the United States, and there was resistance to the appointment of foreigners when natives were unemployed. Some scholars had to wait a long time before their future was secure. The sociologist Norbert Elias received short-term grants for research after his arrival in Britain, but he was fifty-seven when he was finally appointed to a permanent post, as a lecturer at the University College of Leicester. The medievalist Hans Liebeschütz, who arrived in Britain in 1939, was interned during the war and had to wait until 1946 for his appointment as assistant lecturer at the University of Liverpool—like Elias, at the age of fifty-seven. The gifted economic historian Fritz Redlich arrived in the United States in 1936, but did not find a permanent post until 1952, when he was sixty.

Other scholars suffered a loss of academic status. Karl Mannheim rather resented his reduction to the ranks of lecturer at the London School of Economics after his stint as a full professor at Frankfurt. And on his arrival in England, the ancient historian Victor Ehrenberg, who had been a full professor at the German University in Prague from 1929 to 1939, worked as a classics master in two schools before becoming a lecturer and later reader at Bedford College London. Eugen Täubler, who had been a professor of ancient history at the University of Heidelberg, moved to a less prestigious post at Hebrew Union College–Cincinnati. Still less fortunate was Richard Laqueur. Dismissed from his chair of ancient history in Halle, Laqueur fled to the United States but could find work only "as a packager in a large bookstore."[38]

Teachers of *Germanistik* were especially difficult to place in their new homes, as the example of Richard Alewyn suggests. Alewyn, a professor at the University of Heidelberg and a leading specialist on seventeenth-century German literature, was dismissed from his chair because one of his grandmothers was Jewish. After spending time in France, England, Austria, and Switzerland, he moved to the United States in 1939 and finally secured an appointment at Queens College, in Flushing. Specialists on Italian were somewhat easier to place. Uberto Limentani, for instance, who arrived in England in 1938, a victim of Mussolini's race laws, became a teacher and eventually professor of Italian at Cambridge.

A number of refugees took a second doctorate in the hostland, in case their foreign qualifications were not taken seriously by potential employers. This group included the lawyer and sociologist Franz Neumann, the political scientist Karl Deutsch, the art historian George Hanfmann, the philosopher Olaf Helmer, the sociologist Ernest Manheim (Karl's cousin), and the historian Robert Kann.

For the first time in the case studies examined here — and perhaps for the first time in history — the exiled scholars comprised a substantial number of women (including those listed in the appendix to this book).[39] The development of opportunities for women to study and teach in universities was slow, but its effects are visible on the individuals mentioned in this list. That said, it must be added that female exiles had even more difficulty than their male counterparts in finding permanent employment. The appendix to this book, with its brief biographies of 100 female academic exiles from the 1930s, should make these difficulties clear. Helene Wieruszowski, for instance, a historian of the Middle Ages who lived in Spain and Italy after her dismissal from the post of librarian at the University of Bonn, arrived in the United States in 1940 at the age of forty-seven and held a succession of temporary posts before she was appointed professor at the City University of New York, not long before her retirement.[40]

A number of women who eventually became university teachers, especially in the United States where opportunities were greater, had found employment earlier in a greater variety of jobs than the men. Some became babysitters, waitresses, or maids, whether because they had less choice of occupation than their male colleagues or because they were more adaptable. For example, Louise Holborn, sister of the exile Hajo Holborn, had studied political science at Heidelberg before fleeing to the United States in 1934 and taking her doctorate at Radcliffe in 1938 at the age of forty. She supported herself by babysitting, working in a library, giving German lessons, and acting as a research assistant before securing a teaching post, first at Wellesley College and then at Connecticut College for Women. Another example is the historian Gerda Lerner (née Kronstein) from Vienna, who left for the United States in 1939 at the age of nineteen. In New York she worked as a waitress, a clerk, and an X-ray technician. After becoming a student again in the late 1950s, at the New School for Social Research and then at Columbia University, she finally found a post at Sarah Lawrence College in 1968, where she established a degree program in women's history.

On the positive side, it has been pointed out that Brooklyn College in particular was unusually hospitable to female refugee historians, offering posts not only to Wieruszowski but also to Emmy Heller and Charlotte Sempell. Indeed, "some fourteen women who had emigrated from German-speaking Europe as a result of Nazi policies" became professors at American colleges and universities, "almost as many as all women historians in Germany," where there were few opportunities for females in the academic world.[41]

In other places and in other disciplines, female exiles were not so fortunate. In England the Czech sociologist Viola Klein, who arrived in 1938, worked as a nanny or a servant before taking a second doctorate at the London School of Economics.[42] Despite her two doctorates and a book on *The Feminine Character* (1946), Klein had to work as a translator and a teacher before she was finally appointed as a lecturer in sociology at the University of Reading, aged fifty-six, in 1964. In 1965 she published *Britain's Married Women Workers*, perhaps her most important study, in the series formerly edited by Karl Mannheim.

After arriving in the United States, the art historian Sabine Gova earned her living as a cleaner and by giving language lessons before she found academic employment at St. Peter's College, Jersey City, and at Fordham University. Another German art historian, Ilse Falk, never found a post in a university but worked as a translator and also as a secretary to another exiled art historian, Richard Offner. Anita Orienter was yet another exiled art historian who was unable to find an academic post. She made a living as an artist and a restorer of paintings as well as by giving language lessons.[43]

A substantial group of refugees migrated more than once, sometimes because their country of first choice, such as France or Austria, had become too dangerous, and sometimes because they had not succeeded in finding stable employment. For a number of scholars, including leading political scientists as well as historians of the caliber of Hans Baron, Felix Gilbert, and Hans Rosenberg, England turned out to be no more than a staging post on the way to the United States. The Marxist art historian Frederick Antal would have followed the same path had he not been denied entry because he was viewed as a Communist.[44]

Turning now to the intellectual consequences of the diaspora, it appears that the humanities and even the social sciences were more firmly rooted in national cultures than were the natural sciences, and as a result they did not travel as easily, with the possible exception of economics. Cultural differences often led to misunderstandings in the short term, as we shall see. In the long term, on the other hand, it might be argued that the newcomers were in a position to contribute more to their disciplines in their hostlands precisely because they were different. They knew different things, asked different questions, employed different methods, and in short, offered alternative approaches to the ones that were dominant in their new homes.

As we have seen in other cases, the tension between the desire for assimilation to the culture of the hostland on one side and the desire to resist assimilation on the other is very clear in the biographies of individuals who formed part of this diaspora. One group, generally relatively young when they went into exile, learned a new language without too much trouble and also adapted themselves to the local culture more or less easily. Some even became specialists on the culture of their hostland, on its history, literature, philosophy, and art.

Alfred Neumeyer, for instance, a German art historian who moved to California, began to write about art in both North and South America as well as continuing to work on European artists. The historian Erich Eyck wrote about Gladstone and also about Bismarck. Ernst Cassirer, who left Germany for Sweden when he was sixty, learned Swedish, debated with Swedish philosophers, and wrote books on Swedish topics before emigrating again, this time to the United States. Nikolaus Pevsner shifted his interests from Central European art to English architecture, and is now best remembered for his *Buildings of England*.[45] Compared to the Russian exiles after the Bolshevik Revolution, the exiles of the Great Diaspora seem to have found it easier to adapt themselves to their new environments, perhaps because the Jews had had plenty of practice in assimilating.

There were exceptions, however. Some German émigrés after 1933, like many of the Russians after 1919, wanted nothing more than to continue their past life in a new environment. They continued to speak their native language whenever and wherever this was possible, to frequent other exiles, and to concentrate on studying the culture of their homeland. Their reaction may be described as the opposite of internal emigration. Where the internal emigrants live in their homeland as if it were a foreign country, these resisters lived in a foreign country as if they were still in their homeland.

This contrast in responses to displacement may be illustrated by two relatively extreme examples. For an instance of what Franz Neumann called the "assimilation" of exiled scholars, we may take the historian Geoffrey Elton, who was born in Germany, grew up in Prague, and was originally known as Gerhard Ehrenberg. Elton began one of his books with the confession that when he arrived in England in 1939, at the age of seventeen, "within a few months it dawned on me that I had arrived in the country in which I ought to have been born." He never lost his German accent, but he devoted his life to English history, especially the reign of Henry VIII.[46] Elton identified himself with English culture, and used his inaugural lecture as Regius professor to argue that the history of England should form the "backbone" of historical studies in Cambridge, encouraging the "rekindling of a certain respect for a country whose past justifies that respect."[47]

What is more, Elton's approach to history was marked by an enthusiasm for "the true facts" and a hostility to theory (including "obtrusive theoreticians") that some people would regard as typically English.[48] He liked to advise students to enter the archives without having questions in mind or hypotheses to test, just an "initial choice of main area of study or line of approach" (questions were supposed to come later and needed to be "suggested by the evidence").[49] In short, like many younger émigrés, Elton was trying hard to assimilate, indeed to become more English than the English themselves. He was not the only historian from Germany to be attracted by British empiricism. Francis Carsten, for instance, who became familiar with Marxism while he was still in Germany, "much preferred the British tradition of factual narrative." Again, John Grenville (formerly Hans Guhrauer) paid tribute to his English "training in the British school of history," describing it as "pragmatic, not obsessed by theories."[50]

His attempt to assimilate does not mean that Elton derived no benefit from his condition as a foreigner in Britain. It may have been easier for him to formulate original ideas about Henry VIII and Thomas Cromwell because he had not learned the conventional wisdom at school. As for his central idea of "the Tudor Revolution in Government," it looks very much like a case study in what another Central European, Max Weber, called the process of bureaucratization.[51]

Other scholars refused to adapt. For an extreme example of what Neumann called "resistance" to the host culture, we may take the philosopher Theodor Adorno. Adorno began his exile in Oxford, working on a study of the thought of Edmund Husserl and supervised by a very different kind of philosopher, Gilbert Ryle. Adorno was unhappy in his new home, complaining about the difficulties of making his kind of philosophy intelligible to the English (*Schwierigkeiten [. . .] meine eigentlich philosophischen Dinge den Engländern begrifflich zu machen*), so that he had to speak at "child's level" (*ein Kinderniveau*).[52] Although he lived in England for four years and in the United States (as a member of the Institut für Sozialforschung) for twelve more, Adorno continued to write in German and also to speak it whenever possible. He described himself as "European through and through" and considered it "natural," as he put it, "for me to preserve the intellectual continuity of my personal life" while living in the United States. His friend Paul Lazarsfeld said of him that "he behaves so foreign that I feel like a member of the Mayflower Society."[53]

Resistance to assimilation became particularly visible when groups of scholars migrated together, along with the organization in which they had been working, as in the case of two interdisciplinary research institutes, the Kulturwissenschaftliche Bibliothek Warburg and the Institut für Sozialforschung, best known for their respective contributions to art history and sociology but in no way confined to those disciplines.

Two Immigrant Institutions

The Russians in exile in Prague in the 1920s set up their own academic institutions, as we have seen, but in two famous cases, the German exiles of the 1930s brought their institutions with them. These examples of collective displacement illustrate with particular clarity both the initial resistance to assimilation on the part of the refugees and their later impact on their hostlands.

The staff of the Kulturwissenschaftliche Bibliothek Warburg in Hamburg, formerly the private library of the Jewish polymath Aby Warburg, were transported to London in 1933 along with its books (about 60,000 of them). The library, incorporated into the University of London in 1944 under the name of the Warburg Institute, employed leading art historians such as the Austrian Fritz Saxl and the German Edgar Wind.[54] The Institut für Sozialforschung in Frankfurt moved to the United States after 1933, first to New York and then to Los Angeles, changing its name to the

Institute for Social Research. Both institutions functioned, especially at first, as enclaves, foreign bodies lodged in the University of London and Columbia University, helping to insulate their learned inhabitants from the local cultures.

In early 1934, for instance, the Warburg Institute was hosting lectures in German, "mostly attended by Germans."[55] As late as the 1960s, as I remember, German was still spoken by the staff in the reading room. It was only in 1976, forty-three years after the arrival of the institute in Britain, that a director was appointed whose native language was English, the New Zealander Joseph Trapp. All the same, the institute from Hamburg was more open than its sister from Frankfurt, and it was soon offering lectures in English, as well as organizing exhibitions such as "English Art and the Mediterranean." The foundation of the *Journal of the Warburg and Courtauld Institutes* in 1937 increased the visibility of the newcomers among their hosts. The transplanted institute was beginning to take root.

The Institut für Sozialforschung offers a more dramatic example of refusal to adapt. Adorno's resistance to Anglo-American culture was an extreme individual reaction (his colleague Max Horkheimer, for instance, began writing in English after his emigration) but it was supported by his micro-environment. The "self-imposed isolation" of the institute at this time, its "deliberate aloofness from its new surroundings" (despite contacts between the group and individuals at Columbia such as the sociologist Robert Lynd) has been noted more than once. This aloofness was intensified as well as symbolized by the decision to continue to publish the institute's journal, the *Zeitschrift für Sozialforschung*, in German, with exceptions for articles by Americans such as Charles Beard and Margaret Mead. Only in 1940, seven years after its transplantation, was the title of the journal changed to *Studies in Philosophy and the Social Sciences*.[56] The Institute for Advanced Study in Princeton, the academic home of Einstein, Gödel, von Neumann, and Panofsky, is also said to have "functioned almost entirely in German during the war years."[57]

As in the case of the New School, their numbers encouraged

the "insulation of the refugee academics from their surrounding milieu," and so, in the early years, did their endowment.[58] The Frankfurt group, attempting to carry on their own work in an alien environment as if nothing had happened, were not so much mediators between Germany and the United States (at least at first) as themselves in need of mediators who would explain what they were doing to Columbia University and to New York intellectuals.

On the other hand, as time went by, both the Warburg Institute and the Institute for Social Research (which moved from New York to California) became increasingly visible in their new academic worlds. They became symbols of intellectual schools and styles that had been relatively unfamiliar in their new environments but were now attracting interest, especially an art history that formed part of a wider study of culture (*Kulturwissenschaft*) in the case of the Warburg Institute, and a sociology or "critical theory" that combined ideas from Marx and Freud in that of the Institute for Social Research.

Two Disciplines: Sociology and Art History

To understand the impact (however delayed) of these two institutes on their hostlands, together with the influence of other refugee scholars, it is necessary to say something about the place of both art history and sociology in the British and American academic worlds in the 1930s. Both subjects were much more firmly established in Central Europe than they were in the English-speaking world at this time. This situation allowed the exiles to achieve a critical mass sufficient to make a contribution, quite disproportionate to their numbers, to the development of these disciplines, especially in Britain.[59]

Museums, galleries, and art schools rather than universities (apart from Edinburgh, where a chair in the subject had been founded in 1879) were the places where art history was studied in Britain, usually in the form of connoisseurship, an approach that was empirical and pragmatic. Kenneth Clark, for instance, who later became one of the best-known British art historians, read history at Oxford but learned connoisseurship at the Ashmolean Museum there as well as from Bernard Berenson, who had been born in the Russian Empire and taken to the United States as a child. Clark was employed at the Ashmolean and then at the National Gallery in London.[60]

By 1933, changes in this situation were just beginning. As late as 1944, the young art critic John Russell could assert that "English art history does not exist."[61] However, Clark, who believed that the English tradition of connoisseurship was "practically exhausted," confessed that hearing a lecture by Warburg (in Hamburg) changed his life, shifting his interests toward iconography (he later described the chapter on "Pathos" in his book *The Nude* as "entirely Warburgian").[62] Turning to institutions, a chair in art history had been established at the Slade School of Art in 1922, while the Courtauld Institute was founded in 1932, funded by the businessman Samuel Courtauld. Himself a descendant of Huguenot exiles, Courtauld played a major role in the transplantation of the Warburg Library from Hamburg to England, and he did much to help Central European scholars who sought refuge in England. There was no shortage of them — 250 art historians left Germany alone after 1933, followed by more from Austria after 1938.[63]

Among the exiles appointed to posts at the Courtauld Institute between 1933 and 1948 were Frederick Antal, Ernst Gombrich, Otto Kurz, Otto Pächt, and Johannes Wilde. Anthony Blunt (later director of the institute) and the critic John Berger both testified to the importance of the Hungarian scholar Frederick Antal for their intellectual development, while Wilde taught leading British art historians such as John Shearman. The exile Rudolf Wittkower became professor of art history at the Slade School in 1949 and was succeeded by another exile, Leopold Ettlinger, who had been a social worker for refugee children and a schoolmaster in Birmingham before following an academic career.

A new chair in art history at Oxford was founded in 1955 especially for Edgar Wind, with the support of prominent Oxford figures such as Isaiah Berlin, an exile himself. Wind soon made an impact on a wide audience. It was not possible to study, or as they say in Oxford, to "read" art history at that time, but Wind lectured to packed rooms filled with students of other subjects. I listened to these lectures in the late 1950s, and I think that I can speak for a whole generation of students when I say that we were excited to learn from Wind, as Clark had learned from Warburg, that art history included iconography, and we were fascinated by his decoding of Renaissance images by artists such as Leonardo and Giorgione.

The situation was somewhat different in the United States, because art history was more firmly established in universities than it was in Britain or Canada (where Peter Brieger, who was born in Breslau, virtually founded that academic discipline after his arrival in 1936). However, in America, art history was taught in the form of the succession of styles, while scholars in the German-speaking tradition paid more attention to the theory of art and to the iconography, and also to the cultural context of painting, sculpture, and architecture. Whether or not American art history was still "provincial," as some scholars argue, contrasts between the two traditions allowed the refugees to make a distinctive contribution to both teaching and research in the discipline. The most famous name is surely that of Erwin Panofsky, who wrote on Renaissance iconography and iconology, but his colleagues in exile in the United States included scholars of the caliber of Paul Frankl, the historian of Gothic; Walter Friedlaender, the historian of Mannerism; Julius Held, a specialist on Rembrandt and Rubens; and Richard Krautheimer, whose studies of architecture ranged from early Christianity to the baroque.[64]

Any assessment of the intellectual influence of the exiles cannot confine itself to universities but must consider publishing as well, including such presses as Praeger and Shocken Books in the United States, and Weidenfeld and Nicolson in Britain (Frederick Praeger and George Weidenfeld both came from Vienna, and Salman Schocken from Posen, now Poznań). In the case of art history, an important role was played by the Phaidon Press, founded in Vienna in 1923 by Béla Horowitz and Ludwig Goldscheider, and brought to London with the help of the English publisher Stanley Unwin. The press was made famous—and prosperous—after publishing Ernst Gombrich's *The Story of Art* (1950), which has sold over 7 million copies in its sixteen editions and thirty-odd translations. Phaidon's rival in the business of publishing books on art history, Thames and Hudson, was founded by another émigré from Vienna, Walter Neurath, in 1949.[65]

Like art history, sociology occupied a very small place in the British academic world in 1933, in contrast to German universities, where more than fifty sociologists were teaching before the dismissals began. In parallel to connoisseurship, a tradition of social surveys existed in Britain, empirical research on social conditions for practical reasons, as in the case of the studies of dockworkers and tailors in East London around the year 1900 carried out by by Beatrice Potter (who was later famous as Beatrice Webb). A Sociological Society was founded in Britain in 1903 and a journal in 1908. The first professors of sociology in the country were the Finnish expatriate Edvard Westermarck and the former journalist Leonard Hobhouse; both were appointed to chairs at the London School of Economics (LSE) in 1907. Hobhouse was succeeded in 1929 by his former assistant, the refugee Morris Ginsberg, while Thomas Marshall was appointed reader in sociology, again at the LSE, in 1930.

Serious change in the situation of sociology in Britain began after 1933. There was an attempt to transport the Institut für Sozialforschung to the London School of Economics, but the Frankfurt group went to the United States instead. However, the LSE did find a place for the sociologist Karl Mannheim (with his assistant, Norbert Elias), the criminologist Hermann Mannheim (no relation of Karl's), and refugee students such as Viola Klein and Ilya Neustadt.

Of the provincial universities, three are particularly worth mentioning. Birmingham University (where the German sociologist Wilhelm Baldamus found a post) was particularly welcoming to exiles. Manchester appointed another sociologist, Werner

Stark, until he left for the United States. Most important of all was the University College of Leicester. Ilya Neustadt was appointed lecturer in sociology there in 1949, teaching the subject on his own and then appointing the German Norbert Elias as his colleague. By the mid-1960s, there were about 180 students of sociology at Leicester, which had been promoted from a university college to a university. A number of sociologists who made a name for themselves later were students or junior colleagues of Elias and Neustadt there, including Tony Giddens, John Goldthorpe, Keith Hopkins, Bryan Wilson, and Stephen Mennell.

Turning to publishing, Karl Mannheim developed a special relationship with the firm of Routledge, editing a series of books under the title The International Library of Sociology and Social Reconstruction — notably including the sociology of art and literature — and introduced a number of Hungarian and other Central European scholars to the English-speaking world (it may be a coincidence that a leading figure in Routledge at this time, Cecil Franklin, came from a family, originally Frankl, that had migrated from Hungary to England in the eighteenth century).[66]

In the United States, sociology was already well established before 1933. Albion Small, who had studied in Germany with the leading sociologist Georg Simmel, founded the department at the University of Chicago in 1892 and the *American Journal of Sociology* in 1895. Franklin Giddings became professor of sociology at Columbia University in 1894. Robert Park, a former journalist like Hobhouse and a former student of Simmel's like Small, taught at Chicago and founded the famous Chicago School of sociology that included the émigré Louis Wirth, who arrived in the United States as a teenager from Germany. Harvard established a department of sociology in 1930, with the Russian émigré Pitirim Sorokin as the first professor, while the young Talcott Parsons, who had studied sociology in Germany, soon joined the new department as a lecturer. All the same, in 1933 the discipline was still new enough and small enough for the refugee sociologists to help shape it, rather than simply being absorbed.[67]

A Mixed Reception

Despite these positive examples, here as elsewhere it is important not to paint too rosy a picture. Misunderstanding and rejection of the exiles was not uncommon in their hostlands, especially at first. In both Britain and the United States, the language and the habitus of the German-speaking exiles was often perceived as abstract, difficult, even pretentious. The problem was exacerbated by the demonization of the Germans after 1939. In 1945, in the *New English Weekly*, a pro-French journalist, Montgomery Belgion, wrote against what he called the "Germanization of Britain," quoting as a notorious example the case of Karl Mannheim (who happened to be Hungarian, not German). The historian G. M. Young described one of Mannheim's projects as "too grandiose" and contrasted his German style with English "academic realism." Students of the exiles sometimes complained about their manner. The sociologist Jean McDonald, later Jean Floud, who took courses with Mannheim, remembered, "His dealings with us were so un-English."[68]

For his part, Mannheim complained about the problem of explaining the sociology of knowledge to the British and described American sociology as "characterized by its peculiar delight in a form of empiricism which I would be inclined to call an 'isolating empiricism,' a 'mass of secondary details' unrelated to the whole."[69] He wrote to a Hungarian friend in 1937 that he was "trying to change the English." Norbert Elias also complained of the "endless struggle" of sociology for recognition, adding that this recognition was "particularly difficult in Great Britain."[70]

In other disciplines too, art history among them, the relatively methodical and theoretical approach of the exiles met with resistance from some natives. As Saxl remarked after arriving in his new home, "Theories are abhorred by the English in general and by the learned in particular."[71] A notorious clash of cultures took place between two writers on architecture: John Betjeman, a poet and self-consciously amateur art critic, and the highly professional Nikolaus Pevsner, whom Betjeman called "that dull pedant from Prussia" and nicknamed "the Professor-Doktor."[72] In the case of literature, René Wellek, a Czech exile in England, criticized the native Frank Leavis, writing to him, "I could wish that you had stated your assumptions more explicitly and defended them more systematically."[73]

Indifference was another reaction to the influx of foreigners. The historian Eric Hobsbawm — who grew up in Vienna and Berlin and came to England in 1932 — commented on what he called the "extraordinary provincialism of the British in the 1930s," who "paid next to no attention" to the ideas of Frederick Antal, for example, or those of the economist Karl Polanyi (the brother of Michael).[74] In Britain, the work of Norbert Elias, who taught at Leicester from 1954 to 1977, was long neglected in his adopted country (longer than in the case of the Netherlands, for instance, Germany, and France). The ancient historian Arnaldo Momigliano famously complained that if you mentioned ideas to British historians, they would simply give you the address of the Warburg Institute.

In the course of time, however, a few exiles received signs of recognition, while some transplanted ideas took root in foreign soil. The Hungarian economists Thomas Balogh and Nicholas Kaldor both became English barons, like the Austrian publisher George Weidenfeld. Pevsner became Sir Niklaus and Gombrich became Sir Ernst. Gombrich was also appointed a member of the prestigious Order of Merit, while Pevsner became "a British institution" thanks to his series of architectural guides to the counties of England.[75] As we still say when puzzled by an architectural detail in a country house or parish church, "Let's look it up in Pevsner." At the Warburg Institute, the impact of Gombrich on a younger scholar, Michael Baxandall, is visible in the vocabulary that the latter employed in *Painting and Experience in Renaissance Italy* (1972). The "language" of art, the "reading" of paintings, the idea of art as an "institution" and that of the "expectations" of the viewer, all echo the language of Gombrich in *Art and Illusion*

(1960) and elsewhere. The phrase "art theory," virtually an oxymoron in the anglophone world in the 1930s, gradually became respectable or even fashionable.[76]

In the United States, the Frankfurt School gradually made an impact on intellectuals, notably in the study of what was known at the time as "mass culture," as critics such as Dwight Macdonald "drew from the Horkheimer Circle's work on commodity fetishism, conformity, authoritarianism and negation." The Marxist psychoanalyst Erich Fromm was important as a mediator. The American Marxist sociologist C. Wright Mills also learned from the Frankfurt School, as well as from his German colleague Hans Gerth, whom Mannheim had described as "one of my very best students."[77]

Mannheim himself was invited to join a club called "the Moot," allowing him to frequent members of the British Establishment, from Lord Lindsay, Master of Balliol, to T. S. Eliot, a fellow immigrant. Basil Bernstein, who became a leading sociologist of education, was inspired by Mannheim's lectures, while the Cambridge historian Peter Laslett chose him as a thesis supervisor. Mannheim's concern with situated knowledge is visible in Laslett's studies of the political thought of John Locke, which take care to place Locke's ideas in the context of the crises of the 1680s in British politics.[78] Elias, too, gradually made an impact on sociology in Britain, introducing a younger generation to a historical approach to the discipline as well as to concepts such as "figurations" or the "civilizing process."[79]

Other Disciplines

In other disciplines in the humanities and social sciences, the arrival of the refugees seems to have made less of a difference than it did in the cases of art history and sociology. History, for example, was already a big subject in both Britain and the United States before 1933, so that the newcomers who were fortunate enough to find employment, about 100 of them in my database, could be absorbed without major changes in the system. All the same, they were able to make a distinctive contribution to historical studies in their hostlands, not only because they had local knowledge of Central Europe, but also because they were driven, like some of the Russian exiles after 1919 or indeed the Jewish exiles from Iberia after 1492, by the need to explain a disaster. Francis Carsten, for instance, was stimulated by the need "to find out what had gone 'wrong'" with Prussian history.[80] Eva Reichmann wrote her second doctorate, in London on the social causes of antisemitism, thus placing her own exile in a wider perspective.

Departments of language and literature were smaller, and there can be little doubt that Leo Spitzer and Erich Auerbach made a difference, not only in Istanbul, discussed earlier, but also at Johns Hopkins and Yale Universities. However, most of the refugee philologists and critics worked on the German language and literature, a subject for which there was little foreign demand —that was Alewyn's problem, as we have seen, just as it was for Charlotte Jolles, a specialist on the novels of Theodor Fontane who taught in English schools before she was appointed a lecturer at Birkbeck College at the age of forty-six.

Two Germanists who made successful careers for themselves despite these difficulties both came, by coincidence, from German-speaking Jewish families in what is now the Czech Republic. Joseph Peter Stern was a professor of German at University College London, while Erich Heller became a professor of German first at the University College of Swansea and later at Northwestern University in the United States. Both scholars were mediators between the modern German classics and the anglophone world. Heller brought German "modes of thinking" to England as well as adapting literary criticism in the English manner to the study of German literature.[81]

Differences between legal systems made it difficult for lawyers to transfer their expertise when they moved from Germany or Austria to Britain or the United States. Even the philosophy of law did not travel very well. The ideas of the Austrian Hans Kelsen, for instance, a leading jurist in the German-speaking world, did not receive a warm reception in the United States, where the philosophical tradition was very different.[82] To survive in their new academic environment, the refugee lawyers needed to adapt. Some of them did so with success, reinventing themselves as political scientists (assisted in this transformation by the German tradition of the sociology of law) or as specialists in the relatively new field of international relations.

Successful examples of this adaptation include John H. Herz (formerly Hans Herz); Hans Morgenthau (a former student of Kelsen's); and Franz Neumann, who will be discussed later. From a younger generation, Karl Deutsch offers an outstanding example of a scholar who made a successful transition from law to political science. American political science has been described as "increasingly parochial in outlook" in the 1930s, a weakness that the refugees were well placed to correct, not only by exemplifying an alternative approach to politics but also by the emphasis placed by Herz and others on explicitly comparative analysis.[83]

Differences in cultural traditions also posed problems for émigré philosophers. It is not easy to imagine Heidegger teaching undergraduates in a British or American university, supposing he had decided to emigrate. Adorno's problem at Oxford has already been discussed, studying Husserl under the unsympathetic supervision of Gilbert Ryle. Hannah Arendt arrived in the United States in 1941, but she did not hold an academic post (other than visiting professor) until 1959, at Princeton, a year after the publication in English of what is arguably her most famous book, *The Human Condition*. For a smooth landing, it was better to move to a place where the philosophical culture was close to German, as in the case of Groningen (which hosted Helmuth Plessner) and Gothenburg (which did the same for Ernst Cassirer). Other refugees practiced a philosophy that was close to or at least compatible with the philosophies of the English-speaking world. They included Karl Popper in New Zealand and Britain; the logical empiricists of the Vienna Circle, such as Rudolf Carnap and Carl Hempel, in the United States; and the political theorist Leo Strauss, who was taken up by American neoconservatives.[84]

By contrast, economics seems to have been easier to translate from one culture to another, thanks to the international languages of mathematics and statistics. The leading refugee economists found posts and exercised influence in their new homes. The Austrian Friedrich von Hayek, for instance, occupied a chair at the LSE for nearly twenty years, before moving to Chicago, and became a kind of guru for Margaret Thatcher when she was prime minister. Another Austrian, Fritz Machlup, who became a specialist on the knowledge economy, went to Princeton. A third Austrian, Ludwig von Mises, taught at New York University. The German Adolf Löwe (later Adolph Lowe) taught at Manchester and the LSE before moving to the United States. The Ukrainian econometrician Jacob Marschak, a Menshevik exile in 1919, moved first to Germany, then to England, and finally to the United States, holding a succession of posts at leading universities — the New School, the University of Chicago, Yale, and the University of California–Los Angeles.

The story of émigré psychologists is rather more complicated because psychologists were and are divided into a number of conflicting varieties — experimental, social, developmental, psychoanalytical, and so on. By 1941 there were 141 refugee psychologists in the United States. Their success was limited. There was a cool reception for Gestalt psychology, particularly so in the case of Karl Bühler, who never found a post in America commensurate with his former chair in Vienna. On the other hand, the social psychology of Kurt Lewin was received more warmly, while Rudolf Arnheim had a successful career as the author of *Art and Visual Perception* (1954) and as a professor of the psychology of art at Harvard.

As for psychoanalysis, it has been described as "phenomenally successful" in the United States but less so in Britain, despite the fact that Freud himself and his daughter Anna took refuge in London.[85] The immigrant analysts arrived in the United States at the right moment, when, according to one of them, Franz Alexander, American psychology was ready for Freud. The American climate of opinion also seems to have been more favorable than the European one to analysts who differed in some respects from Freud; witness the careers of Erich Fromm, for instance, Karen Horney,

Erik Erikson, Sándor Radó, and Wilhelm Reich—though Reich died in a Pennsylvania penitentiary after his methods of sexual therapy were declared to be fraudulent.

In classics, German scholarship had a formidable reputation that worked to the advantage of some outstanding figures, such as Werner Jaeger, who moved from his chair in Berlin to one at the University of Chicago and then at Harvard, and Eduard Fraenkel, who moved from Freiburg to Oxford. Jaeger's three-volume study of Greek culture, *Paideia*, written in German but completed in the United States, is most widely known in its English translation, while Fraenkel's book on the poet Horace was first published in English. Another gifted classicist, Karl Lehmann, professor of archaeology at the University of Munster before his dismissal by the Nazi regime, adapted well enough to his new environment in the United States to write a study of Thomas Jefferson, viewing him as an American humanist. Among classicists from other countries, the Italian historian of the ancient world Arnaldo Momigliano spent some years at Oxford before moving to a chair at University College London, which he held for a quarter of a century.

Mediation

It is often the case that almost anything penetrating that historians can say about a particular period turns out to have been been anticipated by individuals who lived in that period. As was noted in an earlier chapter, the negative consequences of the migration of Huguenot artisans were already under discussion as early as the 1680s. Similarly, acute analyses of the situation of intellectuals in exile in the 1930s were offered by a few of them, notably Karl Mannheim and Franz Neumann.

Writing on what he called the "function" of refugees, Mannheim emphasized their opportunities for mediation between the culture of their homeland and that of the country to which they had fled.[86] Again, Neumann made the point about the fruitful interaction between the theoretical approach current in his homeland and the empirical approach dominant in his hostland, and he saw himself as a mediator between the two. Another exiled social scientist, the Austrian Paul Lazarsfeld, argued that academic innovations "can often be traced to people who belong to two worlds but who were not safe in either of them" and described himself as "a connecting cog" between European and American scholars.[87]

Many exiles chose this middle way between self-segregation and assimilation. Some of them were translators, both linguistic and cultural, introducing students from the host culture to the language and culture of their own homeland. Bernard Groethuysen made both Kafka and German sociology known in France. In the United States, Kurt Wolff translated Simmel and Mannheim, Hans Gerth translated Max Weber, and Werner Stark introduced the writings of Max Scheler, while Walter Kaufmann both translated and commented on many works by Nietzsche.[88] The German philosopher Fritz Heinemann explained existentialism to the British in book form (*Existentialism and the Modern Predicament*, 1958), while other exiles, among them George Lichtheim, performed their mediation via journalism.[89]

Yet other exiles introduced students in their hostland to the history of their homeland. German history "was not well established at American universities in the thirties."[90] A generation later, in the 1960s, the situation had changed dramatically, thanks to scholars such as Hajo Holborn, Hans Rosenberg, Fritz Redlich, George Mosse, Fritz Stern, and Peter Gay. Holborn, for instance, who became a professor at Yale, published a three-volume *History of Modern Germany* in the 1960s. In similar fashion, the Austrian Robert Kann wrote on the Habsburg Empire and Peter Sugar, a Hungarian, on East-Central Europe. In Britain the situation was comparable. Francis Carsten recalled that when he was appointed a lecturer at Westfield College in 1947, he had "at first almost a monopoly" of teaching German history at the University of London.[91] Like their Russian predecessors such as George Vernadsky, the exiles placed their homelands on the historical map in the United States, Britain, and elsewhere, and taught the following generation of native doctoral students to carry on their work.

Distanciation

Distance had positive as well as negative effects on refugee scholars, allowing the big picture to become more visible at the same time that it made more specialized research difficult, as in the cases of Erich Auerbach in Istanbul and Américo Castro in Princeton.

In a famous passage of his masterpiece *Mimesis* (1947), Auerbach warned his readers that the book had been written in Istanbul, "where the libraries are not well equipped for European studies." All the same, he admitted that "it is quite possible that the book owes its existence to just this lack of a rich and specialized library. If it had been possible for me to acquaint myself with all the work that has been done on so many subjects, I might never have reached the point of writing."[92]

Similarly, the Spanish scholar Américo Castro, a refugee from the Spanish Civil War, concentrated on medieval philology when he lived in Spain; but in exile, especially in the United States from 1936 onward, he produced his most important study, a reinterpretation of Spanish history as the fruit of a prolonged encounter between three cultures, Christian, Jewish, and Muslim, a study published in 1948 under the title *España en su historia*. Written in exile, the book could only be published in exile, because its innovative thesis was anathema in Franco's "national-Catholic" Spain. Castro's book was violently attacked by another Spaniard in exile, Claudio Sánchez-Albornoz, who has become notorious for his remark that "there is no antisemitism in Spain" (*no hay antisemitismo en España*). Sánchez-Albornoz was indeed an exception to his own claim.[93]

One form of distanciation, then, is an emphasis on the big picture. Another form, discussed earlier, is detachment. Detachment encourages comparative analysis, while comparative analysis is difficult if not impossible without some degree of detachment, so it is scarcely surprising to find, as we have seen, that émigré scholars have made a contribution to comparative politics that—as in the cases of comparative literature and comparative religion—is quite disproportionate to their numbers.

When Erwin Panofsky wrote in defense of the scholar's ivory tower as an observation post, he was probably thinking not only of his position at the Institute for Advanced Study in Princeton, but also of his place between two cultures (after his dismissal from his chair at the University of Hamburg in 1933, he returned to his native Germany only in 1967, and even then he insisted on lecturing in English).[94] Even more remarkable examples of detachment include the political scientist Franz Neumann, the historian Lucie Varga, the sociologist Norbert Elias, and the historian Eric Hobsbawm.

An American scholar who knew Franz Neumann during his exile in the United States described him as "curiously detached from his surroundings," a quality that surely assisted him in the task of a critical analysis of institutions.[95] Lucie Varga, an expatriate who came to Paris from Vienna and worked with Lucien Febvre, published an article in 1937 that made a cool "social analysis" of the genesis of Nazism all the more remarkable because Varga (née Rosa Stern) was Jewish. As for Norbert Elias, he not only practiced detachment but also wrote about it. A striking feature of his famous essay on "involvement and detachment" is that rather than pointing out the comparative advantages and disadvantages of the two approaches, Elias reserved his praise for detachment, suggesting that it is necessary for survival. The example offered is a fictional one, from a story by Edgar Allen Poe about a man who escapes drowning by keeping a cool head, but Elias was surely thinking about his own experiences in Germany in 1933.[96]

Like Américo Castro and Fernand Braudel, Eric Hobsbawm saw the big picture with more clarity than most of his professional colleagues, as his trilogy on the ages of revolution, capital, and empire vividly illustrates. He also offers a striking example of detachment. In so saying, I do not mean to suggest that Hobsbawm was incapable of commitment. Quite the opposite: his loyalty to the Left began at an early age and was maintained until the end of his life. However, this loyalty on Hobsbawm's part coexisted with a remarkable capacity for detaching himself from his objects of study and even from his surroundings. In personal encounters, Hobsbawm seemed to be at least as much observer as participant, not cold but certainly "cool." His autobiography, *Interesting Times,* includes a quotation from the diary that he kept at the age of eighteen, describing himself with almost inhuman (or is it superhuman?) distanciation as "quick on the uptake, with a considerable if superficial stock of general knowledge and a lot of original ideas [. . .] an incorrigible striker of attitudes."[97] In the same volume, Hobsbawm went on to dissect the mistakes that the Communists, himself included, had made over the decades.

This detachment is also perceptible in Hobsbawm's historical studies, most obviously in *Nations and Nationalism,* which begins by imagining the Olympian view of "an intergalactic historian" and argues for the need of viewing the subject with "a cold and demystifying eye." One is left with the impression that this cosmopolitan scholar found nationalism an odd or even a pathological phenomenon.[98]

A third form of distanciation might be described as "displacement," in the Freudian sense of a defense mechanism that replaces a threatening topic with a less dangerous one. Displacement may be detected in the work of some refugees of the 1930s as well as in that of the Huguenot refugees of the 1680s, discussed in Chapter 3. Examples include two distinguished historians of Renaissance Italy, Hans Baron and his doctoral student Nicolai Rubinstein (who became the assistant of another historian in exile, the Russian Nicolai Ottokar, in Florence). Baron stressed the civic, republican aspect of Florentine humanism, while Rubinstein confined his passion for the history of Florence to the republican period.

It does not seem too fanciful to suggest that both Baron and Rubinstein were thinking about the Weimar Republic when they wrote about the Florentine one. Baron in particular argued that "the defense of civic freedom" against the threat of invasion by the army of the Duke of Milan led to the "intellectual revolution" now known as the early Renaissance. More generally, he suggested that awareness of "the mutual dependence of politics and culture" offered a "new vantage-point" from which to view the Renaissance. Baron himself admitted that his approach was "quickened by the political experiences of our own generation," even if Florence resisted a tyrant while Weimar Germany succumbed to one.[99]

The sociologist Nina Rubinstein (no relation of Nicolai's), the daughter of Russian refugees from the Bolshevik Revolution, studied with Karl Mannheim in Heidelberg, choosing as the subject for her doctoral dissertation the French émigrés after 1789, in the place of the Russian émigrés she had originally intended to study. Unfortunately, Mannheim was dismissed from his chair by the Nazis before Rubinstein could take her doctorate, while she was forced into exile herself, first in Paris, and later in the United States, where she worked as an interpreter. This sad story had a happy ending—eventually. Rubinstein's doctorate was awarded by the University of Frankfurt in 1989, fifty-six years late. The dissertation was published in the year 2000, some seventy years after she began her research.[100]

Synthesis?

Perry Anderson once asserted that the effect of the encounters between the English and the refugees of the 1930s was not to weaken but actually to reinforce empiricism. They "systematized the refusal of system. They codified the slovenly empiricism of the past, and thereby hardened and narrowed it."[101] Whether or not this was sometimes the case, it will be argued here that at least in the longer term, empiricism was weakened, while synthesis or at least hybridization between theory and empirical research became increasingly visible.

The most important intellectual consequence of the Great Exodus was surely the encounter between the theory-laden refugees and the empirical or empiricist culture of their hosts, producing new knowledge in a way that the Huguenot refugees of the seventeenth century did not. As noted earlier, the émigré physicists of the 1930s have been described as "bridge-builders" between German theoretical and British experimental traditions. These physicists were cultural translators.

The process of hybridization or cultural translation is still more visible in the humanities and social sciences. Academic sociology may be regarded as a translation of the pragmatic knowledge of society, while academic art history translated connoisseurship. The key figures in these "translations" were the exiles, individuals who had themselves been "translated" in the sense of "transferred," the original meaning of the term. Looking back on his career, Erwin Panofsky called it a "blessing" that he had been able to "come into contact—and occasionally into conflict—with an Anglo-Saxon positivism which is, in principle, distrustful of abstract speculation."[102]

Looking back on his life, the émigré publisher George Weidenfeld declared that he had "yearned [. . .] to turn my condition of being with the English but not of the English into an advantage."[103] Pevsner really did manage this, especially in his lectures on "the Englishness of English art." These lectures drew on both a detailed empirical knowledge of the art of Pevsner's adopted country and the speculations of some German art historians, concerned with what exactly was German in German art. German scholars inspired Pevsner to ask a general question about "Englishness" that the English themselves had not thought of asking. In short, he engaged in hybridization. So did English scholars at the Warburg Institute, such as Michael Baxandall and the intellectual historians Frances Yates and Perkin Walker. This small group might be described as semi-Germanized in the sense of having learned much from the refugee scholars they encountered every day at work, but they also contributed to the gradual anglicization of the Warburg tradition.[104]

In philosophy, English-language and German-language traditions were particularly far apart in the 1930s, with the exception of a certain affinity between anglophone philosophers and their Austrian colleagues associated with the so-called Vienna Circle. Affinity turned into dialogue when the American pragmatist John Dewey met the Austrian philosopher of law Felix Kaufmann, in exile at the New School in New York. The result of their conversations, if not full hybridization, was at least a kind of interaction between the two traditions.[105] More recently, the philosopher of science Nicholas Rescher, who was taken to the United States as a child in 1938, has claimed to produce a synthesis between German idealism and American pragmatism.

In political science, Karl Deutsch, a member of the more adaptable younger generation of exiles, was at home in both the empirical and the theoretical traditions. Deutsch, who came from Prague, arrived in the United States aged twenty-six, studied at Harvard, and went on to teach at Yale, is probably best known as the author of a study of political communication, *The Nerves of Government* (1963). It has been suggested that "the trademark of Deutsch's approach is always the merging of creative theoretical ideas with the search for quantitative data to buttress his argumentation."[106]

It was in the United States, described by the sociologist Edward Shils, the child of immigrants, as "the country of legendary theorylessness," that the opposition between German theory and local empiricism was most obvious, if not most important.[107] This opposition, like so many dichotomies, should not be made too stark. Both Germans and Americans saw themselves as combining theory with facts. Even Adorno recognized that he had learned something from his American experience, declaring that he had become inclined to "critical self-scrutiny" after people kept asking him for the "evidence" for his generalizations. He even expressed a certain degree of enthusiasm for empirical research, at least for a time.[108] All the same, the two combinations differed, with a larger dose of theory in the German case, as both British and American scholars were quick to note.

Contrasting American and German approaches to the subject, the Scottish sociologist Robert McIver, one of the Frankfurt Institute's hosts at Columbia University, noted perceptively that even when they used the same term, the two groups sometimes misunderstood each other. "Method means an entirely different thing to American and to German investigators. To the American, method means primarily research technique [. . .] to the German, method is a principle [. . .] In a word, the American is eager for new facts and new verifications, whereas the German seeks new formulations and new thought-constructions." Adorno himself made a similar point, saying that during his stay in the United States, he was "disturbed" by "a basic methodological problem—understanding the word 'method' more in its European sense of epistemology than in its American sense, in which methodology virtually signifies practical techniques for research."[109]

These contrasts should not be exaggerated. The leading American sociologist of his generation, Talcott Parsons, was a theorist, while one of the leading émigré sociologists, Paul Lazarsfeld, was an enthusiast for facts who attempted "to induce Adorno to try to link his ideas with empirical research."[110] It is worth adding that Lazarsfeld was not German but Austrian, and that a tradition of empiricism and "methodological individualism" has long existed in Austria, vividly exemplified in the work of another exile, Karl Popper, but also including the economist Carl Menger and the art historian Ernst Gombrich, who famously began *The Story of Art* with the words, "There really is no such thing as art. There are only artists." In similar fashion, Margaret Thatcher, a disciple of the Austrian economist Friedrich von Hayek, once declared that "there is no such thing as society." It is tempting to speak of "Austro-Empiricism" on the analogy of Austro-Marxism, and even to suggest that this was a way for Austrian intellectuals to distinguish themselves from German ones. In any case, the affinity between this approach and Anglo-American empiricism doubtless helped the work of Popper and Gombrich as well as Hayek and Lazarsfeld to be accepted in the English-speaking world.

All the same, McIver had a point. The legal and political theorist Hans Kelsen had a cool reception in United States because he was seen as too theoretical and also because he arrived at the wrong moment, when an extremely pragmatic approach, "legal realism," was in the ascendant.[111] Horkheimer hoped to solve what he described as "the problems of empirical research and theoretical synthesis," but lamented in a letter to his colleague Leo Lowenthal (1942) that "the more empirical approach" has defeated "the more theoretical." An internal tension "destroyed the *Institut*'s hope for the unity of theory and empirical work."[112] Over the long term, on the other hand, American sociologists became more open to theory, thanks in particular to the refugees and to the children of earlier emigrants from Eastern Europe.[113]

The Authoritarian Personality

Both the achievement and the limitation of synthesis between German and anglophone traditions in sociology may be illustrated from the making of what became a celebrated study, published in the United States by members of the Frankfurt School. This study was the result of a compromise, made originally for economic reasons. Adorno's research project on antisemitism was viewed as too theoretical and too speculative by American foundations. The situation was saved by Franz Neumann, who was employed by the Frankfurt Institute as an administrator and legal adviser but was not a real insider. As a former labor lawyer in Weimar Germany, Neumann understood the art of compromise, and on this occasion he advocated what he called "a combination of the highly developed American empirical and quantitative methods with the more theoretical European methods." He negotiated for funding for Adorno's project by revising it to make it more empirical, bringing in collaborators for this purpose.[114]

The result was a hybrid book, *The Authoritarian Personality* (1950), a collective work by four main authors (Adorno, the refugee psychologist Else Frenkel-Brunswik, and the Americans Daniel Levenson and Nevitt Sanford) together with three other collaborators. The underlying theory, which emphasized the relation of the authoritarian attitudes of adults to the way they had been brought up as children, developed out of earlier studies of antisemitism but had a more general scope. The evidence for the theory came from questionnaires and interviews that were translated into statistical form by Frenkel-Brunswik and Levinson. Adorno contributed Part 4, entitled "Qualitative Studies of Ideology," while Horkheimer's preface insisted that the purpose of the study was not "simply to add a few more empirical findings to an already extensive body of information," but to introduce "a relatively new concept."[115]

As might have been expected from a study conducted by seven individuals, the marriage of two research styles was not altogether successful. In addition, in the theoretical section, the synthesis of Freud (whose contribution was acknowledged) and Marx (who was used but not cited) was not a smooth one. Despite these flaws, *The Authoritarian Personality* was and remains a milestone in the history of social psychology, as the continued use of its central concept reminds us.[116]

Loss and Gain

Turning now to the effects of the Great Exodus on the homelands of the exiles, above all Germany and Austria, what is most obvious is the loss. The exiles encouraged the deprovincialization of their hostlands, but on the other side, their homelands became more provincial without them. After the war it became clear that Germany and Austria had lost their leading position in a number of disciplines, from physics to psychology and from sociology to art history, a position that they had held before the emigration. The Germanization of the social sciences was replaced by their Americanization. In the academic study of psychology, for instance, where Germans were the pioneers, "American dominance in the field has never been challenged" since 1933.[117] The refugee historian Nicolai Rubinstein observed that the impact of the Great Exodus was "particularly destructive in the field of Renaissance history, in which German and Austrian scholars had been playing a leading role."[118] In some respects Germany and, still more, Austria have never recovered from the brain drain of the 1930s.

In partial compensation, the "remigration" of some exiles brought new ideas to Central Europe. After the war, the Institut für Sozialforschung returned to its original home in Frankfurt, but it was not the same as the institute that had left, because American traditions had left their mark. Ernst Fraenkel returned to Germany in 1951 and helped establish American-style political science there, teaching at the Berlin Hochschule and the Free University. Similarly, Eric Voegelin returned in 1958 and founded the Institut für Politische Wissenschaft in Munich. Although Franz Neumann remained in the United States after the war, he too helped establish political science in West German universities. René König, an émigré (in his case, to Switzerland) who returned to become a professor at the University of Cologne in 1949, introduced the students to American approaches to sociology.

Over the long term, empirical research in the American style has become established in Germany, although links between sociology and philosophy are still strong, as the example of Jürgen Habermas reminds us. In Italy, the physiologist Carlo Foà returned to Milan and his former chair in 1945, while Bruno Rossi, following his retirement from his position in the United States, taught at the University of Palermo from 1974 to 1980. They both helped to make Italian students more familiar with science in the American style. In short, intellectual hybridization took place not only in the United States and Britain, but in Germany, Austria, and Italy as well.

Unlike the Institut für Sozialforschung, the Warburg Institute remained in England, but the approach associated with Aby Warburg and his younger friends Erwin Panofsky and Edgar Wind was revived in Germany by a younger generation of art historians. Among them were Martin Warnke and Horst Bredekamp, students of iconography and the political history of art, who encouraged the City of Hamburg to buy Warburg's former house and turn it into a new institute, the Warburg Haus, in parallel with the institute in London. In the case of literature, Richard Alewyn, a distinguished specialist on German baroque who had taught in the United States during the war, returned to Germany and introduced comparative methods there.[119]

It might be argued that, given enough time, the empirical and theoretical traditions would have merged or at least interacted without the work of exiled scholars. However, the balanced conclusions of a study that concentrates on natural science carry conviction: "it seems unlikely that the degree of convergence and synthesis could have come about as quickly as it did without the special pressures of forced migration."[120]

The collective impact of German-speaking scholars in particular on the humanities and social sciences in the United States and Britain cannot be reduced to the encounter between empiricism and theory. Another important contribution made by these scholars, and by their Italian colleagues such as Arnaldo Momigliano, who were also trained in a historicist tradition, was to encourage what Paul Tillich (who found it lacking in the United States) called "history-mindedness," in other words, awareness of the history of one's own discipline, and in the case of the social sciences, awareness of economic, social, and political history over the long term.[121] Franz Neumann, for example, argued that the "predominance of empirical research" in the United States made it difficult for social scientists "to see problems in their historical significance." His strategy was the "integration" of philosophy and history with social science.[122] In Britain, Norbert Elias was a sharp critic of what he called "the retreat of sociologists into the present," and in response he both preached and practiced a historical sociology.[123]

Again, German scholars who had been trained in the tradition of hermeneutics (including the visual hermeneutics famously described by Panofsky as "iconography and iconology") were confronted in exile with what they considered to be an alien tradition, that of positivism. American scholars in particular followed the model of the natural sciences in the study of the social sciences and even the humanities, in fields ranging from "political science," with its heavy reliance on quantitative methods, to linguistics. Hans Morgenthau, for instance, who taught politics at the University of Chicago and the City University of New York, was a sharp critic of analogies between the natural and social sciences. In the case of psychology, there was a confrontation between representatives of the American tradition of behaviorism, such as B. F. Skinner, and the new arrivals, whose approaches varied from psychoanalysis to Gestalt psychology but generally rejected the behaviorist model.

In the case of linguistics, the divergence between the two approaches to the subject dominant in the United States and in Germany was dramatized by a famous exchange between a leading representative of each school, not so much an encounter between cultures as a collision. In a well-known article in a professional journal, Leonard Bloomfield argued that linguistics was a science, employing "only such terms as are translatable into the language of physical and biological science." He praised the work of Pavlov and the logical positivists and claimed that linguists should discard what he called "the terminology of mentalism and animism." In reply, writing in the same journal, Leo Spitzer, celebrated for his hermeneutical approach to the language and style of literary texts, criticized Bloomfield's approach as reductionist and "mechanist." Spitzer pointed out that according to his own criteria, Bloomfield ought not to be willing to use basic terms in linguistics such as "Indo-European" or "proto-Romance," let alone "stylistics."[124] Whether or not Spitzer made converts to his hermeneutic approach among American linguists, he did at least foster awareness of an alternative to Bloomfield.

To sum up: personal encounters in the age of the Great Exodus promoted a change in habitus on both sides, encouraging a closer relation between theory and empirical research. Among the various case studies presented in this book, that of the exiles of the 1930s offers the clearest as well as the most important example of hybridization.

Epilogue: After 1945

Since 1945 many intellectuals, like other people, have become either exiles or expatriates, and it would not be difficult to add to the collective examples offered in this brief conclusion. Among the exiles or refugees, some fled from Communist regimes while others escaped from anti-Communist ones, often military dictatorships.

One group of intellectuals went into exile, or refused to return home, after the establishment of Communist regimes in Central and Eastern Europe after World War II. The Polish political scientist Zbigniew Brzezinski, for instance, was living in Canada, where his father was a diplomat, in 1945. The family decided not to return to Communist Poland. Brzezinski studied at Harvard and remained there as a professor, as well as advising American presidents, from Kennedy onward, on foreign policy. Another Pole, the journalist Jerzy Giedroyć, moved to Paris after 1945 and edited the periodical *Kultura* from 1947 to his death in the year 2000. The Hungarian psychoanalyst Maria Török fled to France in 1947, the year that the Communist Party won the election in her country.

The Romanian Mircea Eliade, a major figure in studies of comparative religion, was living abroad when a Communist regime was established in his country after the war. Eliade remained in the West, living first in Paris and then moving to Chicago. Another Romanian, the sociologist Zevedei Barbu, originally supported the new regime and was working in London as a diplomat at the time when he heard that one of his best friends had been executed. He asked for political asylum, returned to academia, and taught at the University of Glasgow, the University of Sussex, and finally at the University of Brasilia.

In some cases, exile or expatriation was encouraged by the foundation of the state of Israel in 1948. Among the scholars or future scholars who moved to Israel at that time were the sociologist Yehudah Elkanah, from Yugoslavia; the historian Saul Friedlander, from Prague; the philosopher Hans Jonas, originally from Germany; and the political scientist Zeev Sternhell, from Poland. The problems of mediation were experienced particularly acutely by the art historian Moshe Barasch, who came from Czernowitz (which was in Romania at the time that he left) and became a professor in Jerusalem. Barasch, who specialized in the early Italian Renaissance, sometimes encountered difficulties when explaining Western art to students who had been brought up in an iconophobic culture in which the biblical commandment forbidding images was often taken literally.[125]

The next wave of exiles, about 200,000 of them, following the suppression of the Hungarian Uprising of 1956, included a number of intellectuals, some already well known, and others with distinguished careers abroad. The philosophers included Imre Lakatos, who studied at Cambridge and taught philosophy of science at the London School of Economics, and István Mészáros, a former student of Georg Lukács who taught at the University of Sussex. Historians included János Bak, who studied in Oxford and Marburg and taught in Canada before returning to Hungary in the 1990s; Nicholas Pronay, who became a professor at the University of Leeds and a leading exponent of historical studies of films; and Laszlo Péter, who became a professor of Hungarian history at London University. As in the case of the Russian and German exiles before them, the historians made their students aware of the place of Hungary in European history, while the philosophers both revealed and exemplified modes of thought that contrasted with anglophone empiricism.

A third wave of exiles came from Czechoslovakia in 1968, about a quarter of a million of them, following the Soviet invasion in 1968, when many intellectuals were dismissed from their academic positions. Many of those who remained worked in the construction industry, as clerks, taxi drivers, and so on. Those who chose exile were scattered, some going to Western Europe, others to the Americas (to Canada and Chile, for instance, as well as the United States). The intellectuals, besides writers such as Milan Kundera, included the literary scholar Eduard Goldstuecker, who had played a prominent part in the Prague Spring and became a professor at the University of Sussex; the Slovak historian of science Mikulás Teich (who had been exiled before, like his friend Goldstuecker, in 1938); Dalibor Vesely (a former student of the dissident philosopher Jan Patocka), who introduced students of architecture at Cambridge to the insights of Continental philosophers; and the historian Vilém Prečan, dismissed from his post at the Czechoslovak Academy of Sciences after publishing documents about the Soviet invasion of 1968 (the "Czech Black Book"). Prečan left for West Germany, returning more than two decades later to become the director of a new Institute for National History.

At about the same time in Poland, as the government became more oppressive and antisemitic, a number of intellectuals left or were expelled, among them the philosopher Leszek Kołakowski, who emigrated to Canada and then moved between Britain and the United States; the historians Bronisław Baczko and Krzysztof Pomian, who moved to Geneva and to Paris respectively; and the sociologist Zygmunt Bauman, who became a professor at the University of Leeds. These Central and Eastern European exiles (together with some expatriates, discussed later) acted as mediators, encouraging interest in their part of Europe by students in the West, and also encouraging an interest in theory, ranging from an open Marxism to semiotics, especially in its Russian form, represented by Juri Lotman and his school. Some exiles from Castro's Cuba, or their children, have become professors in the United States and made important contributions to the study of both Spanish and Spanish American culture: Teofilo Ruiz at UCLA and Carlo Eire at Yale in Spanish history, for instance, and Roberto González Echevarría, also at Yale, in Spanish and Spanish American literature. Maria Rosa Menocal, who left Cuba for the United States as a child, taught medieval Spanish history, once again at Yale. One of her books was concerned with the place of exile in the origins of the lyric.

Refugees from right-wing regimes include the South American intellectuals who fled following the military coups of 1964 in Brazil, 1973 in Chile, and 1976 in Argentina.[126] In the case of Brazil, one thinks of the economist Celso Furtado, who was minister of planning in 1964, took refuge in the Mexican embassy after the military coup, and returned to academic life in exile in the United States, France, and then England; the educator Paulo Freire (sometimes confused with Gilberto Freyre), who fled to Bolivia, moved to Chile, and then to Switzerland; and of the sociologist (and much later, president) Fernando Henrique Cardoso, who left for Chile and moved to France before his return to Brazil. The historians who went into exile in this period included José Honorio Rodríguez, who was dismissed from his position of director of the National Archives in 1964, and Emília Viotti da Costa, who was dismissed from her chair at the University of São Paulo in 1969. Both moved to the United States, where Rodríguez was professor at Columbia University and Viotti at Yale. Viotti helped to put Brazilian history on the North American map of learning, while Freire's ideas about literacy as a means of "consciousness raising" became better known abroad as a result of his exile.

The exiles from Argentina included the historian Tulio Halperín Donghi, who left following an earlier military coup, in 1966, and spent much of his life teaching in California, at Berkeley; the cultural theorist Walter Mignolo, who became a professor at Duke University; the political scientists Guillermo O'Donnell, who moved to Brazil and later to the United States, and Ernest Laclau, who taught at the University of Essex, and whose ideas remain influential today (on the *Podemos* movement and on Jeremy Corbyn, for instance); and the anthropologists Nestor Canclini, who migrated to Mexico and published important studies of its culture, and Eduardo Archetti, who chose Norway, becoming director of the department of social anthropology at the University of Oslo, while continuing to study Latin America. Archetti's study of the anthropology of the tango, polo, and football in Argentina, especially his contrast between the Latin style of football and the Northern one, illustrates the distanciation from the homeland that often follows exile. A collective example of the impact of these refugees on the host countries comes from psychoanalysis. Psychoanalysts from Argentina introduced this practice, especially the school of Jacques Lacan, to Spain from the 1970s onward.[127]

As the majority of these examples suggests, in contrast to the Spanish Republicans of the 1930s (most of whom moved to Spanish-speaking countries), the majority of the Spanish American exiles of the 1970s settled in places where they needed to learn a foreign language. More recently, the exiles have been followed by expatriates. The Colombian Carlos Jáuregui, for instance, teaches literature at the University of Notre Dame and has written about "cultural cannibalism" in Latin America, that is, the process of digesting and transforming European influences. Jorge

Cañizares-Esguerra was born in Ecuador, grew up in Mexico and Colombia, and now teaches Latin American history in Austin, Texas, emphasizing the importance of Iberian contributions to Western culture. The Brazilian Luiz Felipe de Alencastro was appointed professor of Brazilian history at the Sorbonne in the year 2000, reversing the movement of the 1930s that (as we have seen) brought distinguished French scholars to teach in Brazil. Collectively, the whole group of Latin American scholars have acted and are still acting as mediators, encouraging the study of their continent by foreigners. They have also reinforced the message of the Central and Eastern European exiles of the 1930s, 1950s, and 1960s about the importance of theory.

Midway between exile and expatriation are the intellectuals who left South Africa in the age of apartheid, usually to study and then teach elsewhere. The anthropologists Jean and John Comaroff, for instance, taught at the University of Chicago, while their colleague Adam Kuper taught at the University of London. African studies in Britain owe a great deal to scholars from South Africa: to the anthropologists Meyer Fortes, Max Gluckman, and Isaac Shapera, for instance, and to the historian Shula Marks. The sociologists John Rex and Stanley Cohen also moved to Britain from South Africa.[128] Another group of expatriates left North Africa for France: Hélène Cixous and Jacques Derrida arrived from Algeria, for instance, and the historian Lucette Valensi from Tunisia. In similar fashion, two Bulgarian semioticians, Julia Kristeva and Tzvetan Todorov, both arrived in Paris to study in the 1960s and have remained in France ever since.

Expatriates in a less ambiguous sense include a number of intellectuals from South Asia who have made successful careers for themselves in the English-speaking world. In the case of anthropology, they include the Indians Arjun Appadurai and Partha Chatterjee and two Sri Lankans, Gananath Obeyesekere and Stanley Tambiah, all four of whom became professors in the United States. In the domain of literature and cultural theory, Gayatri Chakravorty Spivak, from Calcutta, and Homi Bhabha, from Bombay, have established themselves in the United States, like the economist Amartya Sen and the philosopher Akeel Bilgrami. Particularly numerous are the expatriate Indian historians. Ranajit Guha, for instance, founder of the innovative group associated with the idea of "subaltern studies," taught at the University of Sussex before moving to Australia. Indian historians teaching in the United States include Dipesh Chakrabarty in Chicago, Gyan Prakash in Princeton, and Sanjay Subrahmanyam (after spells in Paris and Oxford) in Los Angeles. Collectively, they have put Indian history on the intellectual map of American students, as well as encouraging trends such as "history from below," "connected history," and postcolonial theory.

Thanks to scholars like these, Western students and intellectuals are better equipped to understand the movement of cultural globalization in which we all live today. To offer a thick description and deep analysis of the various effects on the world of the different diasporas that have been discussed in this book, ranging from the 1450s to the 1970s, would be an impossible task. Instead, turning to the present, I invite readers to conduct a thought experiment in virtual history. Try to imagine the state of intellectual affairs, especially in the humanities and social sciences, whether in Britain or another Western country, if the exiles, in particular the exiles of the 1930s, had not arrived when they did. My own vision of what might have been is that the various parts of Europe and the Americas would have remained much more provincial without the contribution of the exiles, just as the exiles would have remained more provincial had they remained in their homelands. What I should most like readers to remember, after they close this book, is the importance, both in recent times and in more remote periods, of this double deprovincialization.

A COMMENT ON BREXIT

When I wrote the last paragraphs of this book, early in 2016, referring to countries that would have remained more provincial without the contribution of immigrant scholars, I did not imagine that in the June referendum the British electorate would vote —by a narrow majority—to leave the European Union, in the hope of limiting the numbers of immigrants. As of this writing, it is not completely certain that Britain will leave the EU, and even if it does leave, it is not clear what the consequences of that decision will be, either for citizens of the EU who are already established in the UK or for others who would like to move there. I can only say that in my view, if Brexit takes place, it will be a disaster not only for the British economy but also, as the evidence assembled in this book suggests, for British culture.

Exiles and Expatriates argues that immigrants, from artisans to scholars, have often had a good deal to teach people in their "hostland" as well as a good deal to learn from them, in a process of "double deprovincialization." Conversely, restricting immigration is likely to lead, in the long run, to intellectual provincialism. Suppose that we compile a list of the leading intellectuals in twentieth-century Britain, dividing them into two teams—"natives," born in Britain, and "immigrants," whether exiles or expatriates. In philosophy, the native Bertrand Russell was matched by the immigrant Ludwig Wittgenstein, just as Michael Oakeshott was matched by Isaiah Berlin. In the case of history, Edward Thompson was matched by Eric Hobsbawm, and Richard Southern by Lewis Namier. In anthropology, Jack Goody was matched by Ernest Gellner, and in economics, John Maynard Keynes by Nicholas Kaldor. In art history, there was no native to match Ernst Gombrich, and in sociology, no one to match Norbert Elias.

If the flow of immigrants dries up, or at least is seriously reduced, the consequences of the loss of cognitive diversity may take some time to become visible, but they are likely to be serious. If Britain insulates itself from other points of view, it will make the British more and more insular, more provincial, less creative. The examples discussed in this book suggest that even if no one actually wants this kind of future, it would inevitably follow in the decades to come if Britain left the EU.

APPENDIX

ONE HUNDRED FEMALE REFUGEE SCHOLARS IN THE HUMANITIES, 1933–1941

The importance of art historians (half the total) is worth noting (though this figure may be the result of more intensive research on this discipline than on others). The number of female art historians who did not follow an academic career in exile but worked as artists, dealers, or curators, is also worth noting, whether they chose to do this or failed to find a position in a university. Next in order of popularity come general history, language, and literature and psychology (including psychoanalysis) with a dozen exiles each; and sociology, with half a dozen. There were also a few female scientists in exile, not listed here, of whom the most famous was Lise Meitner.

Principal sources: Werner Röder and Herbert A. Strauss (eds.), *International Biographical Dictionary of Central European Emigrés* (Munich: Saur, 1983); Ulrike Wendland (ed.), *Biographisches Handbuch deutschsprachiger Kunsthistoriker in Exil* (Munich: Saur, 1999); Susanne Blumesberger, Michael Doppelhofer, and Gabriele Mauthe (eds.), *Handbuch österreichische Autorinnen und Autoren jüdische Herkunft* (Vienna: Saur, 2002); *Dictionary of Art Historians*, https://dictionaryofarthistorians.org/.

1. HANNAH ARENDT, 1906–75, from Koenigsberg, philosopher, studied with Heidegger, Husserl, Jaspers at Freiburg, Heidelberg. Fled to Paris in 1933, to the United States in 1941.
2. ERNA AUERBACH, 1897–1975, from Frankfurt, studied art history there, fled to England in 1933, studied at the Courtauld Institute, active as a painter, writer on portraiture, and lecturer at Royal Holloway and Westfield Colleges.
3. INGEBORG AUERBACH (née Fraenkel), born 1903, art historian, studied with Panofsky in Hamburg, wrote her

dissertation on Andrea del Sarto, fled to England in 1935, gave up the practice of art history.

4. SUSAN GROAG BELL, born 1926, from Czechoslovakia, fled to England in 1939, came to know Barbara Hammond who awakened her interest in history, later moved to California where she discovered women's history and taught at Stanford.
5. THERESE BENEDEK (née Friedmann), 1890–1977, from Eger, studied in Budapest, shifted from medicine to psychoanalysis, left Hungary in 1920 for Leipzig, moved to Chicago in 1936.
6. ALICE BERGEL (née Berger), 1911–98, from Berlin, scholar in *Romanistik*, fled to England in 1939, moved to the United States in 1941, taught at University of California–Irvine.
7. MARGARETE BIEBER, 1879–1978, born in Schönau, Prussia (now Poland), classicist and art historian, professor at Giessen, moved to the United States in 1934, invited by Barnard College, remained associate professor until her retirement.
8. SENTA BIER (née Dietzel), 1900–1978, from Fürth, studied art history with Wölfflin in Munich, fled to the United States in 1938, worked as an art teacher, teacher of German, and finally as professor of art history in Louisville, Kentucky.
9. GERTRUD BING, 1892–1964, from Hamburg, art historian, worked with Aby Warburg, fled to London in 1933 with the Warburg Institute, of which she was assistant director 1933–55 and director 1955–59.
10. GERDA BLUMENTHAL, born 1923, from Berlin, specialist in *Romantistik*, fled to the United States c. 1941, studied in New York, taught French literature at Catholic University of America in Washington, DC.
11. HEDDA BOLGAR, 1909–2013, born in Zurich, psychoanalyst, studied in Vienna, moved to the United States, practiced analysis in Chicago until she was 102.
12. CHARLOTTE BÜHLER (née Malachowski), 1893–1974,

from Berlin, psychologist, professor in Vienna, fled to Norway in 1938, then London, then the United States.

13. ANNELIESE BULLING, 1900–2004, from Saxony, historian of Chinese art, studied in Berlin, fled to Britain 1935, earned PhD at Cambridge, moved to the United States in 1956, published on the architecture of the Han period, and was a translator.
14. GERTRUDE COOR (née Achenbach), 1915–62, from Frankfurt, art historian, moved to Italy after 1933, then Wales, then the United States. Worked on the Princeton Index of Christian Art, taught at the university, was research assistant to the art historian Millard Meiss, published a monograph on Neroccio.
15. HANNA DEINHARD (née Levy), 1912–84, art historian, student of Wölfflin, fled to France in 1933, then to Brazil and wrote on colonial art there, moved to the United States in 1947, taught at the New School and Queens College in New York, published on the sociology of painting.
16. HELENE DEUTSCH (née Rosenbach), 1884–1982, from Poland, psychologist, moved to Vienna in 1907, studied medicine, worked with Freud, emigrated to the United States in 1934, worked as a training analyst.
17. LISELOTTE DIECKMANN (née Neisser), 1902–94, specialist in *Germanistik*, fled to Rome in 1933, then to Istanbul, then to the United States, taught in St. Louis.
18. ILONA DUCZYNSKA, 1897–1978, from Vienna, revolutionary in Hungary, sent to Zurich, then Moscow, then Vienna, married Karl Polanyi, moved to England in 1933, then to the United States, worked as a translator.
19. ILSE FALK, born 1906, from Hamburg, art historian, studied in Berlin, wrote a dissertation on Andrea Pisano, fled to Switzerland in 1937, then to the United States, worked as a secretary to the art historian Richard Offner and as a translator.
20. ELSE FRENKEL-BRUNSWIK, 1908–58, from Lviv, psychologist, fled to Vienna in 1919, assistant to Charlotte

Bühler, fled to the United States in 1938, worked with Adorno.

21. ANNA FREUD, 1895–1982, Austrian psychoanalyst, fled to England in 1938 with her father.
22. MARGARETE FREUDENTHAL-SALLIS, born 1893, from Speyer, sociologist, studied with Karl Mannheim, wrote doctoral dissertation on the history of the family, emigrated to Palestine in 1934.
23. GISÈLE FREUND, 1908–2000, from Berlin, photographer, studied at Frankfurt with Adorno, Horkheimer, and Mannheim, fled to Paris in 1933 and later to Argentina and Mexico.
24. FRANZISKA FRIED-BOXER, born 1904, from Vienna, art historian, studied with Strzygowski, wrote on Andrea Pisano, worked at the Warburg Library in Hamburg 1930–32, returned to Austria, fled to England 1939, then to the United States.
25. TERESA GRACE FRISCH, from Vienna, art historian, a specialist on Gothic, professor at Wellesley College 1947–66, dean of the college.
26. LILI FRÖHLICH-BUME (née Caroline Bum), 1886–c. 1975, from Vienna, art historian, fled to England in 1938, became an art journalist reviewing exhibitions.
27. ERIKA FROMM (née Oppenheimer), 1910–2003, psychologist, trained in experimental psychology in Frankfurt, fled to the Netherlands in 1934, to the United States in 1936.
28. MELITTA GERHARD, 1891–1981, specialist in *Germanistik*, *Privatdozent* in Kiel, dismissed in 1933, fled to the United States in 1934, taught at Wellesley College, wrote on Schiller, Goethe.
29. FRANCIS GRAY GODWIN (Franziska Grabkowitz), 1908–79, from Vienna, art historian, student of Strzygowski, moved to the United States in 1930, studied with Richard Offner, taught at Queens College 1945–70 and was known as an outstanding teacher.

30. SABINE GOVA (née Spiero), 1901–2000, from Hamburg, art historian, fled to France in 1933, studied in Paris, was deported but escaped, emigrated to the United States in 1941, worked as a cleaner, gave lessons in French and German, professor at St. Peter's College in Jersey City, and at Fordham University.
31. HANNA GRAY (née Holborn), born 1930, from Heidelberg, daughter of Hajo Holborn, fled to the United States with her family in 1934, historian of the Renaissance and president of Yale.
32. CARMEN GRONAU (née von Wogau), 1910–99, historian of Italian Renaissance art, left Germany in 1935 for London, worked at Sotheby's.
33. YVONNE HACKENBROCH, 1912–2012, from Frankfurt, studied with Pinder, fled to England in 1937, curator at the British Museum, specialist in jewelry, moved to Canada in 1945, the United States in 1949, then returned to England.
34. ELISABETH MARIA HAJÓS, 1900–1982, born in Hungary, art historian, worked at Albertina in Vienna, taught in Budapest, fled to the United States in 1938, published on twentieth-century architecture and on the Renaissance.
35. BETTY HEIMANN, 1888–1961, from Wandsbek, Indologist, studied in Kiel and Halle, professor in Hamburg, fled to England in 1933, moved to (East) Germany in 1957.
36. EMMY HELLER, 1886–1956, historian of the Middle Ages, studied in Heidelberg, fled to the United States, taught at Brooklyn College 1937–56.
37. HERTA HERZOG, 1910–2010, from Vienna, social psychologist, moved to the United States in 1935, returned to Europe in 1976.
38. ROSEMARIE HEYD (née Burkart), 1905–2002, from Berlin, worked in *Romanistik,* student then assistant to Leo Spitzer, whom she followed to Istanbul in 1933, returned to Germany with her husband in 1942, taught languages at Darmstadt, and acted as an interpreter.
39. HEDWIG HINTZE (née Guggenheimer), 1884–1942, from

Munich, historian, studied with Meinecke, worked on the French Revolution, was offered a position at the New School but was refused entry to the United States, fled to the Netherlands in 1939, died (possibly suicide?) before being deported.

40. URSULA HOFF, 1909–2005, born in England, art historian, brought up in Hamburg, a student of Panofsky, fled to England in 1933, museum curator, moved to Australia in 1939, worked at the National Gallery Victoria and University of Melbourne.
41. LOUISE WILHELMINE HOLBORN, 1898–1975, specialist on politics, sister of Hajo Holborn, fled to London in 1933, to the United States in 1934, earned PhD in 1938, supported herself by babysitting, working in a library, giving German lessons, and as a research assistant, taught at Wellesley College and Connecticut College for women.
42. MARIE JAHODA, 1907–2001, Austrian social psychologist, emigrated to England in 1937, then the United States, studied at Barnard College and Columbia University, her PhD supervised by Lazarsfeld, became professor at Barnard in 1938, to the University of Sussex in 1965.
43. CHARLOTTE JOLLES, 1909–2003, from Berlin, worked in *Germanistik*, fled to England in 1939, worked with refugee children, taught in schools, and from 1955 at Birkbeck College, a specialist on Fontane.
44. SONJA KARSEN, born 1919, from Berlin, worked in *Romanistik*, fled to Switzerland in 1933, then to the United States, earned PhD at Columbia, professor of Spanish in several American universities.
45. VIOLA KLEIN, 1908–73, from Prague, fled to England in 1938, worked as a nanny, took a second doctorate at the LSE, worked as a translator, teacher, and finally (aged fifty-six) as a lecturer in sociology at Reading University.
46. OLGAR KOSELLEFF-GORDON, born 1904 in Sebastopol, art historian, moved to Dresden in 1906, wrote on medieval

sculpture and illumination, fled to the United States after 1933.

47. TRUDE KRAUTHEIMER-HESS, 1902–87, from Erfurt, art historian, studied in Frankfurt, fled to Italy in 1933, then to the United States, art collector, collaborated with her husband Richard on a study of Ghiberti.
48. BETTY (Bettina Dorothea) KURTH (née Kris), 1878–1948, from Vienna, art historian, studied with Dvořák, a specialist on medieval tapestry, fled to Britain in 1939, found part-time employment at Glasgow Art Gallery.
49. HILDE KURZ (née Schüller), 1910–70, from Vienna, art historian, student of Schlosser, moved to England in 1937, collaborated with her husband Otto.
50. CLAIRE LACHMANN (née Ullman), 1904–91, born in The Hague, art historian, studied in Hamburg with Panofsky, Saxl, assistant at the Warburg, fled to Palestine in 1934, became an art critic and journalist.
51. URSULA LAMB (née Schaefer), 1914–96, from Essen, historian, anti-Nazi, left Germany in 1935, studied at Berkeley, taught at Columbia, Yale, and the University of Arizona, wrote on the Spanish Empire.
52. JÚLIA LÁNG, Hungarian psychologist, fled from Germany to England in 1933 with her husband Karl Mannheim.
53. OLGA LANG (née Joffe), 1897–1992, Russian sinologist, associated with Frankfurt School, married Karl Wittfogel, moved to the United States in 1934, taught Russian at Swarthmore, wrote on the Chinese family.
54. EDITH LENEL, born 1909, historian, studied with Rothfels in Koenigsberg, fled to the United States, assistant to Hans Kohn at Smith College, librarian at Montclair State College, later taught German and became chair of the German department there.
55. GERDA LERNER (née Kronstein), 1920–2013, from Vienna, historian, anti-Nazi, imprisoned before leaving for the United States in 1939, worked as a waitress, studied at the

New School, professor at Sarah Lawrence College, set up a program for women's history.

56. AENNE LIEBREICH, 1889–c. 1940, from Westphalia, art historian, wrote on the sculpture of Sluter, fled to France c. 1933, became assistant to Focillon, killed herself.
57. ILSE LIPSCHUTZ (née Hempel), born 1923 in Württemberg, specialist in *Romanistik*, fled to Paris in 1936, then to Spain and the United States, professor of French at Vassar, chair of the department.
58. MARGARET MAHLER (née Schönberger), 1897–1985, from Sopron, psychoanalyst, studied medicine in Munich and Vienna, moved to the UK, then the United States in 1938, worked at New York Psychoanalytical Institute.
59. ERNA MANDOWSKY, 1906–70, from Hamburg, art historian, student of Panofsky, fled to England 1933 and then to the United States, published studies of Ripa and Ligorio.
60. ANNE MARIE MEYER, 1919–2004, from Berlin, fled to England with her family in 1933, worked at the Warburg Institute 1937–84 as secretary and registrar, studied the history of opera and ballet.
61. SIBYL MOHOLY-NAGY (née Pietzsch), 1903–71, from Germany, daughter of architect, married Laszlo Moholy-Nagy, moved to Amsterdam in 1934, to the United States in 1937, turned historian of architecture after her husband's death, taught at the Pratt Institute, New York.
62. ELISABETH MOSES, 1894–1957, from Cologne, studied art history in Bonn, museum curator, dismissed in 1933, fled to Italy, then to the United States in 1933, became a curator in San Francisco.
63. ALICE MÜHSAM (née Freymarck), 1889–1968, from Berlin, historian of ancient art and art restorer, fled to the United States in 1940, worked as a cleaner in New York, on art restoration at Brooklyn Museum, as a tutor at Columbia.
64. ANITA ORIENTER, 1896–c. 1990, born in Brazil, her father from Romania, moved to Berlin in 1900, studied with Wölfflin, returned to Brazil in 1939, a painter and restorer,

moved to New York in 1948, could not find job as art historian, gave language lessons.

65. DOROTHEA (Dora) PANOFSKY (née Mosse), 1885–1965, wife of Erwin, moved to the United States with him and collaborated with him.

66. LOTTE BRAND PHILIP (née Forster), 1910–86, from Altona, Hamburg, art historian, student of Panofsky, moved to the United States in 1941, jewelry designer, studied and published on the art of the Netherlands, taught at NYU and Queens College.

67. ANNEMARIE POPE (née Henle), 1910–2001, art historian, earned PhD at Heidelberg in 1931, moved to the United States, worked as art administrator in Washington, DC.

68. EDITH PORADA, 1912–94, from Vienna, archaeologist and art historian of ancient Near East, fled to the United States in 1938, worked at the Metropolitan Museum, Queens College, and Columbia.

69. LIESELOTTE PULVERMACHER EGERS, born 1904, from Berlin, art historian, studied with Walter Friedlaender, published on German sculpture, moved to the United States c. 1937, taught German and art history in various colleges.

70. BEATA RANK (née Minzer), 1886–1967, from Poland, psychoanalyst, lived in Vienna after her marriage, translated Freud into Polish, emigrated to the United States in 1936.

71. ANNIE REICH (née Pink), 1902–71, from Vienna, psychoanalyst, studied medicine, was analyzed by Wilhelm Reich and married him, lived in Berlin, moved to Prague in 1933 and to the United States in 1938, worked at New York Psychoanalytical Institute.

72. EVA GABRIELE REICHMANN (née Jungmann), 1897–1998, from Silesia, Jewish historian and sociologist, fled to London in 1939, worked as translator, earned a second doctorate at LSE on the social causes of antisemitism, director of the research department of the Wiener Library, pioneer of holocaust studies.

73. GRETE RING, 1887–1952, from Berlin, art historian, studied

with Wölfflin at Munich, became an art dealer, opened Paul Cassirer gallery in London in 1938, specializing in nineteenth-century drawings, wrote on fifteenth-century French painting.

74. HELEN ROSENAU, 1900–1984, art historian, studied in Munich with Wölfflin, fled to England in 1933, studied at the Courtauld Institute, worked at the LSE, taught at the Universities of London and Manchester.

75. GERTRUD ROSENTHAL, 1903–89, from Mayen, art historian, studied at University of Cologne, fled to England in 1938, worked at the Courtauld Institute, moved to the United States in 1940, art librarian, curator of Baltimore Museum of Art.

76. NINA RUBINSTEIN, 1908–96, from Berlin, daughter of exiled Russian (Baltic German) liberals, wrote a dissertation on French émigrés, supervised by Karl Mannheim, fled to Paris in 1933, then to New York, worked as an interpreter.

77. LEONIE SACHS (née Feiler), born 1908, from Berlin, studied *Romanistik*, fled to Spain in 1933, then to France and the United States, professor of Spanish at Hunter College.

78. ROSA SCHAPIRE, 1874–1954, from Galicia, art historian, studied at Heidelberg with Thode, collector of contemporary art, fled to London in 1939, earned her living as translator.

79. FELICIE SCHARF (née Radziejewski), born 1901, from Berlin, art historian, wrote dissertation on Romanesque sculpture, fled to England in 1933, taught German and later became an art dealer.

80. HERTA SCHUBART (née Müller, known as Susanne Carwin thanks to her historical novel *Faith and Inquisition*), 1898–1975, art historian, studied at Hamburg with Panofsky, wrote dissertation on illustrations to the Bible, fled to Spain in 1933, then to France and England in 1937, returned to Germany in 1945, worked as art dealer and journalist.

81. BERTA SEGALL, 1902–76, art historian, Jewish, studied with Schlosser, museum curator in Berlin, fled to England in 1933,

then to Athens in 1934, worked at Benaki Museum, moved to the United States in 1938, worked at the Museum of Fine Arts, Johns Hopkins, returned to Germany in 1956, keeper at art museum in Hamburg.

82. CHARLOTTE SEMPELL, born 1909, historian, published studies of the Schleswig-Holstein question and of Robespierre, anti-Nazi, moved to Paris, Uruguay, the United States, taught part-time at Brooklyn College 1947–74.

83. JUDITH SHKLAR, 1928–92, from Riga, Jewish, fled to Canada c. 1940 and then the United States, professor of politics at Harvard.

84. ERIKA SPIVAKOVSKY (née Zarden), 1909–98, from Hamburg, historian, studied in Buenos Aires and Berlin, taught Spanish at the University of Melbourne 1936–39, at Radcliffe Institute 1962–64, published a biography of Diego Hurtado de Mendoza.

85. KATE STEINITZ (née Traumann, sometimes wrote as Annette C. Nobody), 1889–1975, from Silesia, art historian, fled to the United States in 1936, art librarian and artist.

86. SELMA STERN-TÄUBLER, 1890–1981, historian, studied Jewish history, moved to the United States in 1941, archivist of American Jewish Archive, Cincinnati.

87. ALICE TEICHOVA, 1920–2015, economist, Austrian, fled to England in 1938, to Czechoslovakia in 1945, taught at Charles University, returned to England in 1968, professor at University of East Anglia.

88. ERICA TIETZE-CONRAT, 1883–1958, from Vienna, art historian, student of Riegl, worked with her husband, fled to the United States in 1938, lecturer at Columbia.

89. LUCIE VARGA (Rosa Stern), 1904–41, Austrian historian, student of Dopsch, married Borkenau and left for Paris in 1933, worked with Febvre as his assistant 1934–37.

90. EDITH WEIGERT (née Vowinckel), 1894–1982, from Dusseldorf, psychoanalyst, studied in Berlin, fled with husband Oscar to Ankara, then in 1938 to the United States.

91. JOSEFA WEITZMANN (née Fiedler), 1904–2000, art

historian, married Kurt Weitzmann in Germany and went with him to Princeton in 1935.

92. HERTA WESCHER (née Kauert), 1899–1971, from Krefeld, art historian, studied with Wölfflin in Munich, moved to Paris in 1933, journalist, moved to Switzerland in 1942, worked as a freelance writer and critic and became an expert on collage.

93. DOROTHEE WESTPHAL, 1902–68, art historian, studied with Wölfflin and Schlosser, wrote on Venetian painting of the Renaissance, moved to England, worked in conservation.

94. HELENE WIERUSZOWSKI, 1893–1978, from Elberfeld, historian, studied with Levison and Meinecke, librarian at the University of Bonn, dismissed in 1934, conducted research in Spain and Italy, moved to the United States 1940, held part-time posts, finally a professor at CUNY.

95. RAHEL WISCHNITZER (née Bernstein), 1885–1989, from Minsk, art historian, Jewish, studied and lived in Germany, worked on Jewish encyclopedia and at Jewish Museum in Berlin, moved to France in 1938, to the United States in 1940, taught at Yeshiva College in New York, published on Jewish art and architecture.

96. MARGOT WITTKOWER (née Holzmann), 1902–95, from Berlin, designer and art historian, married Rudolf, fled to London in 1933 and later to the United States, published books jointly with her husband.

97. ALMA WITTLIN (née Frischauer), 1899–1990, from Lv'iv, art historian, studied in Vienna with Strzygowski, fled to England in 1937, worked at Museum of Archaeology and Anthropology at the University of Cambridge, moved to the United States in 1952, museum director in Santa Fe.

98. KÄTHE MARIA WOLF, 1907–57, from Vienna, child psychologist, assistant to the Bühlers, moved to Switzerland in 1939, to the United States in 1941, worked at Yale and CUNY.

99. ALICE WOLFE (Wolf, née Frisch), 1905–83, from Hungary, art historian, studied in Vienna, fled to England in 1939 and then to the United States, worked at Yale University Art Gallery until moving to Idaho with her husband.

100. MARIA ZAMBRANO, 1904–91, philosopher, student of Ortega, moved to Cuba, Puerto Rico, Italy, France, Switzerland, and in 1984 returned to Spain.

NOTES

INTRODUCTION

1 Frederick Jackson Turner, "The Significance of History" (1891: repr. in Fulmer Mood [ed.], *The Early Writings of Frederick Jackson Turner*, Madison: University of Wisconsin Press, 1938), 47–48.

2 Karl Mannheim, "The Problem of a Sociology of Knowledge," trans. in his *Essays in the Sociology of Knowledge* (London: Routledge, 1952) 134–90; Peter Burke, *A Social History of Knowledge from Gutenberg to Diderot* (Cambridge: Polity Press, 2000); Burke, *A Social History of Knowledge from the Encyclopédie to Wikipedia* (Cambridge: Polity Press, 2012).

3 Yitzhak Baer, *Galut* (1936: English trans., New York: Schocken, 1947).

4 José Gaos, "La adaptación de un español a la sociedad hispanoamericana," *Revista de Occidente* 14 (1966): 168–78, at 178; Adolfo Sánchez Vázquez, *Del exilio en Mexico* (Mexico City: Grijalbo, 1991), 34 and passim. On Gaos, Aurelia Valero Pie, "Metáforas del exilio: José Gaos y su experiencia del 'transtierro,'" *Revista de Hispanismo Filosófico* 18 (2013), 71–78, at 72–73.

5 Fernando Ortiz, *Contrapunteo cubano* (Havana: Montero, 1940). The word *transculturación* occurs in the book's subtitle.

6 Antoon de Baets, "Exile and Acculturation: Refugee Historians Since the Second World War," *International History Review* 28 (2006): 316–35, at 329.

7 On the English terms, see the *Oxford English Dictionary* (2nd ed., Oxford: Oxford University Press, 1993); on the French, Henri Basnage, *Dictionnaire*, qtd. by David van der Linden, *Experiencing Exile: Huguenot Refugees in the Dutch Republic, 1680–1700* (Farnham: Ashgate, 2015), 11.

8 Jan Lucassen and Leo Lucassen (eds.), *Migration, Migration History, History: Old Paradigms and New Perspectives* (Bern: Peter Lang, 1997), 11.

9 Hannah Arendt, "We Refugees," in Ron H. Feldman (ed.), *The Jew as Pariah: Hannah Arendt* (New York: Grove Press, 1978), 55–66, at 55; Ariel Dorfman qtd. in Mario Sznajder and Luis Roniger, *The Politics of Exile in Latin America* (Cambridge: Cambridge University Press,

2009), 28. On Herz, Peter Stirk, "International Law, Émigrés and the Foundation of International Relations," in Felix Rösch (ed.), *Émigré Scholars and the Genesis of International Relations* (Basingstoke: Palgrave Macmillan, 2014), 61–80, at 75.

10 On denial, Nina Rubinstein, *Die französische Emigration nach 1789: Ein Beitrag zur Soziologie der politischen Emigration* (Graz: Nausner and Nausner, 2000), 93, 176. Cf. an interview with Rubinstein in 1987, qtd. in David Kettler, Colin Loader, and Völker Meja, *Karl Mannheim and the Legacy of Max Weber* (Aldershot: Ashgate, 2008), 148–49. On Jurieu and the Huguenots, Elisabeth Labrousse, *Pierre Bayle*, vol. 1 (2 vols., The Hague: Nijhoff, 1963–64), 203, 209. On Pevsner, Susie Harries, *Nikolaus Pevsner: The Life* (London: Chatto and Windus, 2011), 190.

11 Michel S. Laguerre, "The Transglobal Network Nation: Diaspora, Homeland and Hostland," in Eliezer Ben-Rafael and Yitzhak Sternberg (eds.), *Transnationalism: Diasporas and the Advent of a New (Dis) Order* (Leiden: Brill, 2009), 195–210. In German the term *Gastland*, in the sense of hostland, is older: Rubinstein, *Die französische Emigration*, 92 (written in 1933).

12 I heard Andreski say this in the 1960s, when he was visiting the University of Sussex.

13 Friedrich K. Stadler, "Transfer and Transformation of Logical Empiricism," in Gary L. Hardcastle and Alan W. Richardson (eds.), *Logical Empiricism in North America* (Minneapolis: University of Minnesota Press, 2003), 216–33, at 222. Cf. Diederick Raven and Wolfgang Krohn, "Edgar Zilsel: His Life and Work," in Zilsel, *The Social Origins of Modern Science* (Dordrecht: Kluwer, 2000), xix–lix.

14 Leonardo Olschki to Karl Vossler, Feb. 9, 1947, qtd. in Hans Helmut Christmann and Frank-Rutger Hausmann (eds.), *Deutsche und österreichische Romanisten als Verfolgte des National Sozialismus* (Tübingen: Stauffenburg, 1989), 255.

15 Colin Eisler, "*Kunstgeschichte* American Style: A Study in Migration," in Donald Fleming and Bernard Bailyn (eds.), *The Intellectual Migration: Europe and America, 1930–1960* (Cambridge, MA: Harvard University Press, 1968), 544–629, at 578; Erwin Panofsky, letter to Abraham Flexner, 1938, qtd. in Karen Michels, *Transplantierte Wissenschaft: Der Wandel einer Disziplin als Folge der Emigration deutschspra-*

chiger Kunsthistoriker in die USA (Berlin: Akademie Verlag, 1999), 119; Pevsner qtd. ibid., 123.

16 Theodor Adorno, *Minima Moralia* (Frankfurt: Suhrkampf, 1951), 13.

17 Casaubon qtd. in John P. Considine, *Dictionaries in Early Modern Europe* (Cambridge: Cambridge University Press, 2008), 98; Zweig qtd. in George Prochnik, *The Impossible Exile: Stefan Zweig at the End of the World* (New York: Other Press, 2014), 40; Edward W. Said, *Out of Place: A Memoir* (London: Granta, 2000).

18 Lee Congdon, *Exile and Social Thought: Hungarian Intellectuals in Germany and Austria, 1919–1933* (Princeton: Princeton University Press, 1991); Leo Szilard, "Reminiscences," in Fleming and Bailyn, *The Intellectual Migration*, 94–151, at 95.

19 Maria Lúcia G. Pallares-Burke, *O triunfo do fracasso: Rudiger Bilden, o amigo esquecido de Gilberto Freyre* (São Paulo: UNESP, 2012).

20 Catherine Epstein, "*Schicksalsgeschichte*: Refugee Historians in the United States," in Hartmut Lehmann and James Sheehan (eds.), *An Interrupted Past: German-Speaking Refugee Historians in the United States after 1933* (Washington, DC: German Historical Institute, 1991), 116–35.

21 Qtd. in Stephen Games, *Pevsner: The Early Life* (London: Continuum, 2010), 202.

22 Paul K. Hoch and Jennifer Platt, "Migration and the Denationalization of Science," in Elizabeth Crawford et al. (eds.), *Denationalizing Science* (Dordrecht and Boston: Kluwer, 1993), 133–52, at 143.

23 Anton Blok, *The Blessings of Adversity* (Cambridge: Polity Press, 2016).

24 Epstein, "*Schicksalsgeschichte*," 135.

25 Franz Neumann, "The Social Sciences," in Neumann (ed.), *The Cultural Migration: The European Scholar in America* (Philadelphia: University of Pennsylvania Press, 1953), 4–26.

26 Rubinstein, *Die französische Emigration.*

27 George Weidenfeld, *Remembering My Good Friends* (London: HarperCollins, 1994), 94.

28 On the arts, Jarrell J. Jackman and Carla M. Borden (eds.), *The Muses Flee Hitler* (Washington, DC: Smithsonian Press, 1983); Daniel Snowman, *The Hitler Emigrés: The Cultural Impact on Britain of Refugees from Nazism* (London: Chatto and Windus, 2002).

29 Both passages qtd. in her obituary in *The Independent*, Apr. 4, 2013.

30 Laura Fermi, *Illustrious Immigrants: The Intellectual Migration from Europe, 1930–41* (Chicago: University of Chicago Press, 1968).

31 Robert K. Merton, "The Matthew Effect in Science," *Science* 159 (1968): 56–63.

1. THE VIEW FROM THE EDGE

1 Christhard Hoffmann, "The Contribution of German-speaking Jewish Immigrants to British Historiography," in Werner E. Mosse (ed.), *Second Chance: Two Centuries of German-Speaking Jews in the United Kingdom* (Tübingen: Mohr, 1991), 153–76, at 154.

2 Mitchell Ash, "Forced Migration and Scientific Change," in Roberto Scazzieri and Raffaella Simili (eds.), *The Migration of Ideas* (Sagamore Beach, MA: Science History Publications, 2008), 161–78, at 162, 166.

3 Gilberto Freyre, *Ingleses* (Rio de Janeiro: Olympio, 1942), 115; Darcy Ribeiro, "Gilberto Freyre: Uma introdução a Casa Grande e Senzala," repr. in Freyre, *Casa Grande e Senzala: Edição crítica*, ed. Guillermo Giucci, Enrique Larreta, and Edson Nery de Fonseca (Nanterre: Allca XX, 2002), 1026–37, at 1031. Cf. Peter Burke and Maria Lúcia Pallares-Burke, *Gilberto Freyre: Social Theory in the Tropics* (Oxford: Peter Lang, 2008), ch. 2.

4 Paul Tillich, "The Conquest of Theological Provincialism," in Franz Neumann (ed.), *The Cultural Migration: The European Scholar in America* (Philadelphia: University of Pennsylvania Press, 1953), 138–56, at 138; Edit Fél and Tamás Hofer, *Proper Peasants: Traditional Life in a Hungarian Village* (Chicago: Aldine, 1969), 17.

5 W. G. Sumner, *Folkways* (Boston: Ginn, 1906), 13.

6 Qtd. by Otto P. Pflanze, "The Americanization of Hajo Holborn," in Lehmann and Sheehan, *An Interrupted Past*, 170–79, at 176.

7 Sznajder and Roniger, *The Politics of Exile*, 288; G. K. Chesterton, *Tremendous Trifles* (London: Methuen, 1909), 204; Richard Graham, "An Interview with Sergio Buarque de Holanda," *Hispanic American Historical Review* 62 (1982): 3–18, at 5.

8 Kantorowicz to Bernard Flexner, 1941, qtd. in Karen J. Greenberg, "Refugee Historians and American Academe," in Lehmann and Sheehan, *An Interrupted Past*, 94–101, at 98.

9 Karl Mannheim, "The Function of the Refugee," *New English Weekly*, Apr. 19, 1945.

10 Peter Hennock, "Myself as Historian," in Peter Alter (ed.), *Out of the Third Reich: Refugee Historians in Post-War Britain* (London: I. B. Tauris, 1998), 73–98, at 85.

11 Bruno Latour, *Science in Action* (Cambridge, MA: Harvard University Press, 1987).

12 On astronomy, Kircher received reports from the Czech Jesuit Valentin Stansel in Bahia, the Italian Nicolò Mascardi in Chile, and the Fleming Jean Raymond Coninck in Peru: Andrés I. Prieto, *Missionary Scientists: Jesuit Science in Spanish South America, 1570–1810* (Nashville: Vanderbilt University Press, 2011), 130–31.

13 Alexis de Tocqueville, *De la démocratie en Amérique* (1835–40: ed. Eduardo Nolla, vol. 1, Paris: Vrin, 1990), 310; August Schlözer, *Weltgeschichte* (1792), qtd. and trans. in Ernst Breisach, *Historiography: Ancient, Medieval And Modern* (Chicago: University of Chicago Press, 1983), 318. Important studies of cultural distance and distanciation include David Lowenthal, *The Past Is a Foreign Country* (1985: rev. ed., Cambridge: Cambridge University Press, 2015); Carlo Ginzburg, *Wooden Eyes: Nine Reflections on Distance* (1998: English trans., London: Verso, 2002); Mark S. Phillips, *On Historical Distance* (New Haven: Yale University Press, 2013).

14 Fernando Nicolazzi, *Um estilo de história* (São Paulo: UNESP, 2015), 50.

15 Erich Auerbach, *Mimesis: The Representation of Reality in Western Literature* (1947: English trans., Princeton: Princeton University Press, 1953); Américo Castro, *The Structure of Spanish History* (Princeton: Princeton University Press, 1954).

16 Fernand Braudel, "Histoire et sciences sociales: la longue durée" (1958: repr. in *Les ambitions de l'histoire*, Paris: Fallois, 1997, 149–79), at 162; Braudel, *La Méditerranée et le monde méditerranéen à l'époque de Philippe II* (1949: 2nd ed., Paris: Armand Colin, 1966), 17. Cf. John Marino, "The Exile and His Kingdom: The Reception of Braudel's *Mediterranean*," *Journal of Modern History* 75 (2004): 622–52.

17 Simmel, "The Stranger"; Karl Mannheim, *Ideology and Utopia* (1929: English trans., London: Routledge, 1936), 253.

18 Pierre Bayle, *Critique générale de l'histoire du calvinisme* (1682), qtd. in Arnaldo Momigliano, "Ancient History and the Antiquarian" (1950: repr. in *Studies in Historiography*, London: Weidenfeld and Nicolson, 1966), 1–39, at 10.

19 Lewis Namier, *The Structure of Politics at the Accession of George III* (London: Macmillan, 1929). Cf. Linda Colley, *Lewis Namier* (London: Weidenfeld and Nicolson, 1989), especially 6–20; Herbert Butterfield, *George III and the Historians* (rev. ed., New York: Macmillan, 1959), 206, 297.

20 Lewis Namier, "The Biography of Ordinary Men" (1928: repr. in *Crossroads of Power*, London: Hamish Hamilton, 1961), 1–6. Cf. Matthias Gelzer, *Die Nobilität der römanischen Republik* (Leipzig and Berlin: Teubner, 1912). For criticism, Butterfield, *George III*, 296.

21 Eric J. Hobsbawm, *Interesting Times: A Twentieth-Century Life* (London: Weidenfeld and Nicolson, 2002), 103; Hobsbawm, "The Historians' Group of the Communist Party," in Maurice Cornforth (ed.), *Rebels and Their Causes: Essays in Honour of A. L. Morton* (London: Lawrence and Wishart, 1978), 21–48, at 23.

22 Ernest Gellner, *Words and Things* (London: Gollancz, 1959), 237–39; John A. Hall, *Ernest Gellner* (London: Verso, 2010), 104.

23 Claude Lévi-Strauss, *Le regard éloigné* (Paris: Plon, 1983).

24 Examples include Meyer Fortes, Max Gluckman, Isaac Schapera, Adam Kuper, and John Comaroff.

25 Jeremy Adelman, *Worldly Philosopher: The Odyssey of Alberto O. Hirschman* (Princeton: Princeton University Press, 2013), 4, 88, 186, 383, 401, 452.

26 Helmut Koenigsberger, "Fragments of an Unwritten Biography," in Peter Alter (ed.), *Out of the Third Reich: Refugee Historians in Post-war Britain* (London: I. B. Tauris, 1998), 99–118, at 104, 109, 111.

27 Martin Jay, *Permanent Exiles: Essays on the Intellectual Migration from Germany to America* (New York: Columbia University Press, 1986), 152.

28 Mannheim, *Ideology*, 137–38.

29 Norbert Elias, "Problems of Involvement and Detachment," *British Journal of Sociology* 7 (1956): 226–52.

30 Norbert Elias and John Scotson, *The Established and the Outsiders* (London: Cass, 1965).

31 Arnold Thackray and Robert Merton, "On Discipline Building: The Paradoxes of George Sarton," *Isis* 63 (1972): 472–95.

32 Robert E. Park, "Human Migration and the Marginal Man," *American Journal of Sociology* 33 (1928): 881–93, at 888, 892. Cf. Thorstein

Veblen, "The Intellectual Pre-Eminence of Jews in Modern Europe," *Political Science Quarterly* 34 (1919): 33–42.

33 Jay, *Permanent Exiles*, 137.

34 Paul Hartig qtd. in Klaus G. Kracht, *Zwischen Berlin und Paris: Bernhard Groethuysen (1880–1946)* (Tübingen: Niemeyer, 2002), 196.

35 Fritz Stern, *Five Germanies I Have Known* (Wassenaar: NIAS, 1998), 14; Yehudah Elkanah, *Leben in Contexten* (Berlin: Wissenschaftskolleg, 2015), 76.

36 Qtd. in Robert Boyers (ed.), *The Legacy of the German Refugee Intellectuals* (New York: Schocken, 1972), 33.

37 Harald Fischer-Tiné, *Pidgin-Knowledge: Wissen und Kolonialismus* (Zurich and Berlin: Diaphanes, 2013).

38 Scott Page, *The Difference: How the Power of Diversity Creates Better Groups, Firms, Schools and Societies* (Princeton: Princeton University Press, 2007).

39 Michael Polanyi, *Personal Knowledge* (London: Routledge, 1958); John M. Ziman, *Ideas Move Around Inside People* (London: Birkbeck College, 1974).

40 Gunnar Törnqvist, "Creativity and the Renewal of Regional Life," in Anne Buttimer (ed.), *Creativity and Context* (Lund: University of Lund, 1983), 91–112, at 96; cf. Carlo Cipolla, "The Diffusion of Innovations in Early Modern Europe," *Comparative Studies in Society and History* 14 (1972): 46–52; Ziman, *Ideas*.

41 Donald A. Schön, *Displacement of Concepts* (London: Tavistock, 1963); Michael Mulkay, "Conceptual Displacement and Migration in Science," *Science Studies* 4 (1974): 205–34; Paul K. Hoch, "Institutional versus Intellectual Migrations in the Nucleation of New Scientific Specialities," *Studies in the History and Philosophy of Science* 18 (1987): 481–500; Paul B. Paulus and Bernard A. Nijstad (eds.), *Group Creativity: Innovation through Collaboration* (Oxford: Oxford University Press, 2003); Page, *The Difference*.

42 Georg Simmel, "The Stranger," in Charles Lemert (ed.), *Social Theory* (Boulder, CO: Westview Press, 1999), 184–89; cf. Zygmunt Bauman, *Modernity and the Holocaust* (Cambridge: Polity Press, 1989), 53.

43 Park, "Human Migration and the Marginal Man."

44 Leszek Kołakowski, "In Praise of Exile" (1985: repr. in his *Modernity on Endless Trial*, Chicago: University of Chicago Press, 1990), 55–59.

45 Zygmunt Bauman interviewed by Maria Lúcia Pallares-Burke: *Tempo Social* 16 (2004): 301–25, at 312–13 (my translation from the interviewer's Portuguese translation of Bauman's English).

46 Edward Said, "Reflections on Exile" (1984: repr. in his *Reflections on Exile*, London: Granta, 2001), 173–86; Said, *Representations of the Intellectual* (London: Vintage, 1994), 35–48.

47 Erwin Panofsky, *Meaning in the Visual Arts* (New York: Doubleday, 1955), 332; Marie Jahoda, "The Migration of Psychoanalysis," in Fleming and Bailyn, *The Intellectual Migration*, 371–419, at 421, 445.

2. A GLOBAL TOPIC

1 Plutarch, "On Exile," in his *Moralia*, vol. 7 (London: Heinemann, 1959), 519–71.

2 George Sarton, *Galen of Pergamon* (Lawrence: University of Kansas Press, 1954).

3 Frank W. Walbank, *Polybius* (Berkeley: University of California Press, 1972), 3, 21.

4 Erich S. Gruen, *Diaspora: Jews amidst Greeks and Romans* (Cambridge, MA: Harvard University Press, 2002), vii; Gruen, "Polybius and Josephus on Rome," in Bruce Gibson and Thomas Harrison (eds.), *Polybius and His World* (Oxford: Oxford University Press, 2013), 255–65.

5 Jérôme Labourt, *Le christianisme dans l'empire perse* (Paris: Lecoffre, 1904); Richard N. Frye, *The Golden Age of Persia* (London: Weidenfeld and Nicolson, 1975), 163–65; Seyyed Hossein Nasr, "Life Sciences, Alchemy and Medicine," in Richard N. Frye (ed.), *The Cambridge History of Iran*, vol. 4 (Cambridge: Cambridge University Press, 1975), 396–418; Dimitri Gutas, *Greek Thought, Arabic Culture: The Graeco-Arabic Translation Movement in Baghdad and Early Abbasid Society* (London: Routledge, 1998).

6 Martin Colcutt, *Five Mountains* (Cambridge, MA: Harvard University Press, 1981); Jiang Wu, "The Taikun's Zen Master from China," *East Asian History* 38 (2014): 75–96.

7 Donald M. Reid, *The Odyssey of Farah Antun* (Minneapolis and Chicago: Bibliotheca Islamica, 1975), 42–62; Sylvia G. Haim (ed.), *Arab Nationalism* (Berkeley: University of California Press, 1962), 19–25.

3. EARLY MODERN EXILES

1 Heinz Schilling, "Innovation through Migration: The Settlements of Calvinistic Netherlanders in Sixteenth- and Seventeenth-Century Central and Western Europe," *Histoire Sociale—Social History* 16 (1983): 7–34, at 32; Nicholas Terpstra, *Religious Refugees in the Early Modern World* (Cambridge: Cambridge University Press, 2015), 4.

2 Deno J. Geanakoplos, *Greek Scholars in Venice* (Cambridge, MA: Harvard University Press, 1962), 77.

3 Peter Burke, "The Myth of 1453: Notes and Reflections," in Michael Erbe et al. (eds.), *Querdenken: Dissens und Toleranz im Wandel der Geschichte: Festschrift Hans Guggisberg* (Mannheim: Palatium, 1996), 23–30, at 24, 27–28.

4 Jonathan Ray, *After Expulsion: 1492 and the Making of Sephardic Jewry* (New York: New York University Press, 2013), 8, 18–23.

5 On Isaac Abravanel, Baer, *Galut*, 60–68; Benzion Netanyahu, *Don Isaac Abravanel, Statesman and Philosopher* (1953: 2nd ed., Philadelphia: Jewish Publication Society of America, 1968), 53–60.

6 Henry Kamen, "The Mediterranean and the Expulsion of the Spanish Jews in 1492," *Past and Present* 119 (1988): 30–55; Kamen, *The Disinherited: The Exiles Who Created Spanish Culture* (London: Allen Lane, 2007), 1–52; Haim Beinart, *The Expulsion of the Jews from Spain* (English trans., Oxford: Littman Library, 2002); François Soyer, *The Persecution of the Jews and Muslims of Portugal* (Leiden: Brill, 2007), 241–81.

7 On Caro, R. J. Zwi Werblowsky, *Joseph Caro, Lawyer and Mystic* (1962: 2nd ed., Philadelphia: Jewish Publication Society of America, 1977).

8 Avigdor Levy, *The Sephardim in the Ottoman Empire* (Princeton: Darwin Press, 1992), 37.

9 Netanyahu, *Abravanel*, 130–49; Yosef H. Yerushalmi, *Zakhor: Jewish History and Jewish Memory* (Seattle: University of Washington Press, 1982), 57–76, at 58–59; Ray, *After Expulsion*, 145–55; Jacqueline Genot-Bismuth, "L'argument de l'histoire dans la tradition espagnole de polémique judéo-chrétienne," in Yedida K. Stillman and Norman A. Stillman (eds.), *From Iberia to Diaspora* (Leiden: Brill, 1999), 197–213.

10 Yosef Kaplan, "La Jérusalem du Nord," in Henry Méchoulan (ed.), *Les juifs d'Espagne: Histoire d'une diaspora, 1492–1992* (Paris: Lévi, 1992), 191–209.

11 Mark Mazower, *Salonica, City of Ghosts: Christians, Muslims and Jews, 1430–1950* (London: HarperCollins, 2004), 48.

12 Marvin J. Heller, *The Seventeenth-Century Hebrew Book* (2 vols., Leiden: Brill, 2011) vol. 1, xxix.

13 David W. Davies, *The World of the Elseviers, 1580–1712* (The Hague: Nijhoff, 1954), 129; Renata G. Fuks-Mansfield, "The Hebrew Book Trade in Amsterdam in the 17th Century," in Christiane Berkvens-Stevelinck et al. (eds.), *Le magasin de l'univers: The Dutch Republic as the Centre of the European Book Trade* (Leiden: Brill, 1992), 155–68.

14 Joseph Penso de la Vega, *Confusión de Confusiones* (1688: facsimile repr., Madrid: Sociedad de Estudios y Publicaciones, 1958), 82, 156 and passim. On its context, Jonathan Israel, "Jews and the Stock Exchange" (1990), rev. version in Israel, *Diasporas within a Diaspora* (Leiden: Brill, 2002), 449–88, at 472–74, 483–85.

15 Yosef Kaplan, "The Portuguese Community in Seventeenth-Century Amsterdam and the Ashkenazi World," in Jozeph Michman (ed.), *Dutch Jewish History*, vol. 2 (Jerusalem: Hebrew University, 1989), 23–45.

16 Lajb Fuks and Renata G. Fuks-Mansfeld, *Hebrew Typography in the Northern Netherlands, 1585–1815* (Leiden: Brill, 1984), 233–47, 340–41.

17 I should like to thank Yosef Kaplan most warmly for this information.

18 Dejanirah Couto, "The Role of Interpreters, or *Linguas*, in the Portuguese Empire in the Sixteenth Century," www.brown.edu/Departments/Portuguese_Brazilian_Studies/ejph/html/issue2/html.

19 Kapil Raj, "Beyond Postcolonialism," *Isis* 104 (2013): 337–47.

20 António Júlio de Andrade and Maria Fernanda Guimarães, *Jacob de Carlos Sarmento* (Lisbon: Vega, 2010).

21 Bernard Vincent, *1492: L'année admirable* (Paris: Aubier, 1991), 118–20; Soyer, *Persecution*, 241–81; Kamen, *The Disinherited*, 53–93.

22 Oumelbanine Zhiri, *L'Afrique au miroir de l'Europe: Fortunes de Jean-Léon l'Africain à la Renaissance* (Geneva: Droz, 1991); Natalie Z. Davis, *Trickster Travels: A Sixteenth-Century Muslim between Worlds* (London: Faber, 2007).

23 Javier Burriez Sánchez, "Los misioneros de la restauración católica: La formación en los colegios ingleses," in Charlotte de Castelnau-L'Estoile (ed.), *Missions d'évangélisation et circulation des savoirs: XVIe–XVIIIe siècle* (Madrid: Casa de Velázquez, 2011), 87–110.

24 *Oxford Dictionary of National Biography*, "Lassels, Richard."

25 Geert H. Janssen, "The Counter-Reformation of the Refugee," *Journal of Ecclesiastical History* 63 (2012): 671–92.

26 Colm Lennon, *Richard Stanihurst the Dubliner, 1547–1618* (Dublin: Irish Academic Press, 1981).

27 Vittorio Cian, *L'immigrazione dei gesuiti spagnuoli letterati in Italia* (Turin: Clausen, 1895); Miquel Batllori, *La cultura hispano-italiana de los jesuitas expulsos* (Madrid: Gredos, 1966); Manfred Tietz and Dietrich Briesemeister (eds.), *Los jesuitas españoles expulsos* (Frankfurt: Vervuert, 2001); Niccolò Guasti, "The Exile of the Spanish Jesuits in Italy," in Jeffrey D. Burston and Jonathan Wright (eds.), *The Jesuit Suppression in Global Context* (Cambridge: Cambridge University Press, 2015), 248–61.

28 Lorenzo Hervás y Panduro, *Catalogo delle lingue conosciute* (Cesena: Biasini, 1784); Marisa González Montero, *Lorenzo Hervás y Panduro, el gran olvidado de la Ilustración española* (Madrid: Iberediciones, 1994); Gerda Hassler, "Teoría lingüística y antropología en las obras de Lorenzo Hervás y Panduro," in Tietz and Briesemeister, *Los jesuitas*, 379–400; Klaus Zimmermann, "Los aportes de Hervás a la lingüística," ibid., 647–68.

29 Juan Andrés y Morell, *Dell'origine, progressi e stato d'ogni attuale letteratura* (Parma: Stamperia Reale, 1782–99); Batllori, *La cultura hispano-italiana*, 24, 84.

30 Johannes Meier, "Los jesuitas expulsados de Chile," in Tietz and Briesemeister, *Los jesuitas*, 423–41; cf. Prieto, *Missionary Scientists*, 223–27.

31 Antonello Gerbi, *La disputa del nuovo mondo: Storia di una polemica (1750–1900)* (2nd ed., Milan: Adelphi, 2000); David Brading, *The First America: The Spanish Monarchy, Creole Patriots and the Liberal State, 1492–1866* (Cambridge: Cambridge University Press, 1991), 447–64.

32 Javier Pinedo, "El exílio de los jesuitas latinoamericanos: un creativo dolor," in Carlos Sanhueza and Javier Pinedo (eds.), *La patria interrumpida: Latinoamericanos en ex exílio, siglos XVIII–XX* (Santiago: Universidad de Talca, 2010), 35–57, at 47.

33 Philip Benedict, *Rouen during the Wars of Religion* (Cambridge: Cambridge University Press, 1981), 170.

34 Kurt Johannesson, *The Renaissance of the Goths in Sixteenth-Century*

Sweden: Johannes and Olaus Magnus as Politicians and Historians (1982: English trans., Berkeley: University of California Press, 1991); Graham Parry, *The Trophies of Time: English Antiquarians of the Seventeenth Century* (Oxford: Oxford University Press, 1995), 49–69; Paul Arblaster, *Antwerp and the World: Richard Verstegan and the International Culture of Catholic Reformation* (Leuven: Leuven University Press, 2004), 265–67.

35 John Tedeschi, "Italian Reformers and the Diffusion of Renaissance Culture," *Sixteenth-Century Journal* 5 (1974): 79–94.

36 Delio Cantimori, *Eretici italiani del Cinquecento* (Florence: Sansoni, 1939); Joanna Kostylo, *Medicine and Dissent in Reformation Europe* (Oxford: Oxford University Press, 2015).

37 Markus Kutter, *Celio Secondo Curione* (Basel: Helbing and Lichtenhahn, 1955); Leandro Perini, *La vita e tempi di Pietro Perna* (Rome: Edizioni di Storia e Letteratura, 2002).

38 Simonetta Adorni Braccesi and Simone Ragagli, "Lando, Ortensio," in *Dizionario Biografico degli Italiani*, vol. 63 (Roma, Istituto dell'Enciclopedia Italiana, 2004), www.treccani.it/enciclopedia/ortensio-lando_(Dizionario_Biografico)/.

39 Heinz Schilling, *Niederländische Exulanten im 16. Jahrhundert* (Gütersloh: Mohn, 1972); Jonathan Israel, *The Dutch Republic: Its Rise, Greatness and Fall, 1477–1806* (Oxford: Oxford University Press, 1995), 308.

40 Schilling, "Innovation through Migration," 21.

41 Christina H. Garrett, *The Marian Exiles* (Cambridge, 1938), 26–7, 20 and passim.

42 Jack L. Davis, "Roger Williams among the Narragansett Indians," *New England Quarterly* 43 (1970): 593–604.

43 Milada Blekastad, *Comenius* (Oslo: Universitetsforlaget, 1969).

44 Hugh R. Trevor-Roper, "Three Foreigners," *Encounter* (Feb. 1960): 3–20, at 4.

45 Thomas Sprat, *History of the Royal Society*, ed. Jackson I. Cope and Harold W. Jones (London: Routledge, 1958), 67.

46 Mark Greengrass, Michael Leslie, and Timothy Raylor (eds.), *Samuel Hartlib and Universal Reformation* (Cambridge: Cambridge University Press, 1994), 2.

47 Pamela R. Barnett, *Theodore Haak FRS* (The Hague: Mouton, 1962).

48 John T. Young, *Faith, Medical Alchemy and Natural Philosophy: Johann Moriaen, Reformed Intelligencer, and the Hartlib Circle* (Aldershot: Ashgate, 1998), 83; Greengrass et al., *Samuel Hartlib*, 95.

49 Heiko Oberman, "*Europa Afflicta*: The Reformation of the Refugees," *Archiv für Reformationsgeschichte* 83 (1992): 91–111.

50 Hugh Trevor-Roper, "Mayerne," *Oxford Dictionary of National Biography* (Oxford: Oxford University Press, 2004), 581. Cf. Trevor-Roper, *Europe's Physician: The Various Life of Sir Theodore de Mayerne* (New Haven: Yale University Press, 2006).

51 Katherine R. Lambley, *The Teaching of French in England during Tudor and Stuart Times* (Manchester: Manchester University Press, 1920), 155–78.

52 Laurent Berec, *Claude de Sainliens: Un Huguenot bourbonnais au temps de Shakespeare* (Paris: Orizons, 2012); Juliet Fleming, "The French Garden: An Introduction to Women's French," *English Literary History* 56 (1989): 19–51.

53 Warren C. Scoville, *The Persecution of Huguenots and French Economic Development, 1680–1720* (Berkeley: University of California Press, 1960), 118–21; Myriam Yardeni, *Le Refuge huguenot: Assimilation et culture* (Paris: Champion, 2002), 15. The numbers of refugees to the Dutch Republic were revised downward from 50,000 to 35,000 by Hubert Nusteling, "The Netherlands and the Huguenot Émigrés," in Hans Bots and G. H. M. Posthumus Meyjes (eds.), *La Révocation de l'Édit de Nantes et les Provinces-Unies, 1685* (Amsterdam: APA-Holland University Press, 1986), 26–30.

54 Pierre Bayle, *Dictionnaire Historique et Critique* (5th ed., Amsterdam: Brunel, 1740), vol. 3, 25.

55 Jürgen Kämmerer, *Russland und die Huguenotten im 18. Jahrhundert* (Wiesbaden: Harrassowitz, 1978).

56 Catherine Swindlehurst, "'An unruly and presumptuous rabble': The Reaction of the Spitalfields Weaving Community to the Settlement of the Huguenots, 1660–90," in Randolph Vigne and Charles Littleton (eds.), *From Strangers to Citizens* (Brighton: Sussex Academic Press, 2001), 366–74; Ulrich Niggemann, *Immigrationspolitik zwischen Konflikt und Konsens: Die Huguenotten Siedlung in Deutschland und England, 1681–1697* (Cologne: Böhlau, 2008).

57 Scoville, *Persecution*, 325, 336.

58 Scoville, *Persecution*, 12–13, 17.

59 Yardeni, *Refuge huguenot*, 115–16.

60 Hans Bots, "Les pasteurs français au refuge des Provinces-Unies," in Jens Häseler and Antony McKenna (eds.), *La vie intellectuelle aux refuges protestants* (Paris: Champion, 1999), 9–18, at 9–10.

61 Yardeni, *Refuge protestant*, 62.

62 Bots, "Pasteurs," 11; Van der Linden, *Experiencing Exile*, 62–69.

63 Studies of individuals include Joseph Almagor, *Pierre Des Maizeaux* (Amsterdam: APA-Holland University Press, 1989); Christiane Berkvens-Stevelinck, *Prosper Marchand* (Leiden: Brill, 1987); Labrousse, *Pierre Bayle*; Margaret E. Rumbold, *Traducteur huguenot: Pierre Coste* (New York: Lang, 1991); Hugh R. Trevor-Roper, "A Huguenot Historian: Paul Rapin," in Irene Scouloudi (ed.), *Huguenots in Britain and Their French Background, 1550–1800* (Basingstoke: Macmillan, 1987), 3–19.

64 Lambley, *The Teaching of the French Language*, 400.

65 Stephen W. Massil, "Huguenot Librarians and Some Others," *World Library and Information Congress*, 2003, webdoc.sub.gwdg.de/ebook/aw/2003/ifla/vortraege/ . . . /058e-Massil.pdf; *Oxford Dictionary of National Biography*, "Justel."

66 Rumbold, *Traducteur huguenot*.

67 Donald F. Bond, "Armand de la Chapelle and the First French Version of *The Tatler*," in Carroll Camden (ed.), *Restoration and Eighteenth-Century Literature* (Chicago: University of Chicago Press, 1963), 161–84.

68 Erich Haase, *Einführung in der Literatur der Refuge* (Berlin: Duncker and Humblot, 1959), 401–4; Jens Häseler, "Les Huguenots traducteurs," in Jens Häseler and Antony McKenna (eds.), *La vie intellectuelle aux refuges protestants* (2 vols., Paris: Champion, 1999–2002), vol. 2, 15–25, at 16.

69 Hugh Trevor-Roper, "A Huguenot Historian."

70 Van der Linden, *Experiencing Exile*, 195.

71 Martin Mulsow, "Views of the Berlin Refuge," in Sandra Pott, Martin Mulsow, and Lutz Danneberg (eds.), *The Berlin Refuge, 1680–1780: Learning and Science in European Context* (Leiden: Brill, 2003), 25–46, at 26.

72 Jacques Basnage, *Histoire des Juifs* (6 vols., Rotterdam: Leers, 1706–7).

Quotations from the English trans., *The History of the Jews* (London: Bever and Linot, 1708), 465, 693. On allegory, Peter Burke, "History as Allegory," *Inti* 45 (1997): 337–51; on Basnage's allegory, Jonathan M. Elukin, "Jacques Basnage and the History of Jews," *Journal of the History of Ideas* 53 (1992): 603–30, at 606.

73 Haase, *Einführung*, 404–20; Myriam Yardeni, *Le refuge protestant* (Paris: Champion, 1985), 201–7; Herbert Jaumann, "Der Refuge und der Journalismus um 1700," in Pott, Mulsow, and Danneberg, *The Berlin Refuge*, 155–82, 161–63.

74 Hubert Bost, *Un intellectuel avant la lettre: Le journaliste Pierre Bayle* (Amsterdam-Maarssen: APA-Holland University Press, 1994), 143–60; cf. Bost, *Pierre Bayle historien, critique et moraliste* (Turnhout: Brepols, 2006), 43–54.

75 Edward Gibbon, *Decline and Fall of the Roman Empire*, ed. David Womersley (London: Allen Lane, 1994), vol. 3, 88; vol. 1, 456 (ch. 49 and 15).

76 Basnage, *History of the Jews*, ix, 693, 738.

77 Hubert Bost, *Ces messieurs de la R. P. R.* (Paris: Champion, 2001), 267–79.

78 Paul de Rapin-Thoyras, *Histoire de l'Angleterre* (1723: new ed., 4 vols., Basel: Brandmuller, 1740), voi. 1, 9, 14; voi. 3, 387–90: Trevor-Roper, "A Huguenot Historian."

79 Hans Bots, "Le role des périodiques néerlandais pour la diffusion du livre (1684–1747)," in Christiane Berkvens-Stevelinck (ed.), *Le magasin de l'univers: The Dutch Republic as the Centre of the European Book Trade* (Leiden: Brill, 1992), 49–70, at 51. The *Critique* is attributed to François Bruys.

80 Elisabeth Labrousse, *Bayle* (Oxford: Oxford University Press, 1983), 12, 22, 51; Labrousse, *Pierre Bayle*, vol. 2, 3–38, 99.

81 Hans Bots, "Pierre Bayle's *Dictionnaire* and a New Attitude towards Islam," in Marjet Derks et al. (eds.), *What's Left Behind: The Lieux de Mémoire of Europe beyond Europe* (Nijmegen: Vantilt, 2015), 183–89.

82 "l'objectivité lui était rendue plus facile par sa condition ambiguë de Français calviniste": Labrousse, *Pierre Bayle*, vol. 2, 24.

83 Lynn Hunt, Margaret Jacob, and Wijnand Mijnhardt, *The Book That Changed Europe: Picart and Bernard's Religious Ceremonies of the World* (Cambridge, MA: Harvard University Press, 2010).

84 Davies, *The World of the Elseviers*, 102–3.

85 Paul Hoftijzer, "Metropolis of Print: The Amsterdam Book Trade in the Seventeenth Century," in Patrick O'Brien (ed.), *Urban Achievement in Early Modern Europe* (Cambridge: Cambridge University Press), 249–65, at 251.

86 Richard Florida, *The Rise of the Creative Class* (New York: Basic Books, 2002).

87 Hoftijzer, "Metropolis of Print," 253.

88 Berkvens-Stevelinck, "L'édition française en Hollande," 325.

89 Manuela Böhm, *Sprachenwechsel: Akkulturation und Mehrsprachigkeit der Brandenburger Hugenotten vom 17. bis 19. Jahrhundert* (Berlin: De Gruyter, 2010).

90 Hunt, Jacob, and Mijnhardt, *The Book That Changed Europe*, 1, 129, 158, 179, 201 and passim.

91 Christiane Berkvens-Stevelinck, "Prosper Marchand, intermédiaire du refuge Huguenot," in Berkvens-Stevelinck, Hans Bots, and Jens Häseler (eds.), *Les grands intermédiaires de la République des Lettres* (Paris: Champion, 2005), 361–86.

92 On the Luzacs, Jean Sgard (ed.), *Dictionnaire des journalistes, 1600–1789* (Oxford: Voltaire Foundation, 1999), 663–67.

93 Jens Häseler, "J. H. S. Formey," in Berkvens-Stevelinck, Bots, and Häseler, *Les grands intermédiaires*, 413–34.

94 Scott Mandelbrote, "Pierre des Maizeaux: History, Toleration and Scholarship," in Christopher R. Ligota and J.-L. Quantin (eds.), *History of Scholarship* (Oxford: Oxford University Press, 2006), 385–98, at 387, 398.

95 Labrousse, *Pierre Bayle*, vol. 1, 168.

96 Formey qtd. in Frédéric Hartweg, "Die Huguenotten in Deutschland: Eine Minderheit zwischen zwei Kulturen," in Rudolf von Thadden and Michelle Magdelaine (eds.), *Die Huguenotten, 1685–1985* (Munich: Beck, 1985), 172–85, at 193.

97 Gerald Cerny, *Theology, Politics and Letters at the Crossroads of European Civilization: Jacques Basnage and the Baylean Huguenot Refugees in the Dutch Republic* (The Hague: Nijhoff, 1987), 257.

98 Bost, *Un intellectuel avant la lettre*, 110.

99 Yardeni, *Refuge protestant*, 69.

100 Haase, *Einführung*, 388–89.

101 Grahame Gibbs, "The Role of the Dutch Republic as the Intellectual Entrepôt of Europe in the Seventeenth and Eighteenth Centuries," *Bijdragen en Mededelingen betreffende de Geschiedenis van de Nederlanden* 86 (1971): 323–49; Hans Bots, "Les Provinces-Unies, centre d'information européenne au XVIIe siècle," *Quaderni del Seicento Francese* 5 (1983): 283–306; Woodruff D. Smith, "Amsterdam as an Information Exchange in the Seventeenth Century," *Journal of Economic History* 44 (1984): 985–1005; Harold J. Cook, "*Amsterdam*, entrepôt des savoirs au XVIIe siècle," *Revue d'Histoire Moderne et Contemporaine* 55 (2008): 19–42.

102 Folke Dahl, "Amsterdam—Earliest Newspaper Centre of Western Europe," *Het Boek* 25 (1939): 160–97.

103 Robert Darnton, *The Forbidden Best-Sellers of Pre-Revolutionary France* (New York: Norton, 1995); Elizabeth Eisenstein, *Grub Street Abroad: Aspects of the French Cosmopolitan Press from the Age of Louis XIV to the French Revolution* (Oxford: Clarendon Press, 1992).

104 Ross Hutchison, *Locke in France 1688–1734* (Oxford: Voltaire Foundation, 1991); on Bernard, Hunt, Jacob, and Mijnhardt, *The Book That Changed Europe*, 128.

4. THREE TYPES OF EXPATRIATE

1 Tito Boeri et al. (eds.), *Brain Drain and Brain Gain* (Oxford: Oxford University Press, 2012).

2 Michel Espagne and Michael Werner (eds.), *Transferts: Les relations interculturelles dans l'espace franco-allemand, XVIIIe et XIXe siècles* (Paris: Éditions Recherche sur les Civilisations, 1988).

3 Michael Gordin, *Scientific Babel: The Language of Science* (London: Profile Books, 2015), 192.

4 Ferdinand Geldner, *Die deutsche Inkunabeldrucker* (2 vols., Stuttgart: Hiersemann, 1968–70).

5 Joan Pau Rubiés, *Travel and Ethnology in the Renaissance: South India through European Eyes, 1250–1625* (Cambridge: Cambridge University Press, 2000), 204–22, at 207, 217. Cf. Ângela Barreto Xavier and Ines G. Županov, *Catholic Orientalism: Portuguese Empire, Indian Knowledge (16th–18th Centuries)* (Delhi: Oxford University Press, 2015), 31–35.

6 Mansel Dames (ed.), *The Book of Duarte Barbosa* (2 vols., London, Hakluyt Society, 1918–21), 193.

7 Armando Cortesão (ed.), *The* Suma Oriental *of Tomé Pires* (2 vols., London, Hakluyt Society, 1944), vol. 1, 175–76; vol. 2, 266.

8 Ursula Lamb, *Cosmographers and Pilots of the Spanish Maritime Empire* (Aldershot: Variorum, 1995); Alison Sandman, "Controlling Knowledge: Navigation, Cartography and Secrecy in the Early Modern Spanish Atlantic," in James Delbourgo and Nicholas Dew (eds.), *Science and Empire in the Atlantic World* (New York: Routledge, 2008), 31–51; Maria M. Portuondo, *Secret Science: Spanish Cosmography and the New World* (Chicago: University of Chicago Press, 2009), 95–100, 103–11. Ângela Barreto Xavier is involved in a project for the study of the Casa da Índia.

9 Günther Schilder, "Organization and Evolution of the Dutch East India Company's Hydrographic Office," *Imago Mundi* 28 (1976): 61–78.

10 Schilder, "Organization," 62–63.

11 Patrick van Mil (ed.), *De VOC in de kaart gekeken, 1602–1799* (The Hague: SDU, 1988); Kees Zandvliet, *Mapping for Money* (Amsterdam: Batavian Lion International, 1998), 86–163.

12 Adrian Delmas, "From Travelling to History: An Outline of the VOC Writing System during the Seventeenth Century," in Delmas and Nigel Penn (eds.), *Written Culture in a Colonial Context* (Leiden: Brill, 2012), 97–126, at 116.

13 Nils Steensgaard, "The Dutch East India Company as an Institutional Innovation," in Maurice Aymard (ed.), *Dutch Capitalism and World Capitalism* (Cambridge: Cambridge University Press, 1982), 235–57, at 238; on De Laet, Stefan Ehrenpreis, "Empiricism and Image-Building: the Creation and Dissemination of Knowledge in Dutch Brazil, 1636–1750," in Susanne Friedrich, Arndt Brendecke, and Stefan Ehrenpreis (eds.), *Transformations of Knowledge in Dutch Expansion* (Berlin: De Gruyter, 2015), 69–92, at 74–75.

14 Delmas, "From Travelling to History," 98.

15 Smith, "Amsterdam as an Information Exchange," 1001–3. Cf. Leonard Blussé and Ilonka Ooms (eds.), *Kennis en Compagnie: De VOC en de moderne Wetenschap* (Amsterdam: Balans, 2002).

16 Matthew H. Edney, *Mapping an Empire: The Geographical Construction of British India, 1765–1843* (Chicago: University of Chicago Press, 1990); Bernard S. Cohn, *Colonialism and Its Forms of Knowledge:*

The British in India (Princeton: Princeton University Press, 1996), 81–88.

17 Qtd. in Cohn, *Colonialism*, 31.

18 Rosane Rocher, *Orientalism, Poetry and the Millennium* (Delhi: Banarsidess, 1983), 48–72; Kapil Raj, *Relocating Modern Science: Circulation and the Construction of Knowledge in South Asia and Europe, 1650–1900* (Basingstoke: Ashgate, 2007), 125–38; Donald R. Davis Jr., "Law in the Mirror of Language," in Thomas R. Trautmann (ed.), *The Madras School of Orientalism* (Oxford: Oxford University Press, 2009), 288–309.

19 Qtd. in Charles Boxer, *Jan Compagnie in Japan, 1600–1817* (1936: 2nd ed., London: Oxford University Press, 1968), 141. Cf. Klaas van Berkel, "Een onwillige mecenas? De rol van de VOC bij het natuurwetenschappelijk onderzoek in de zeventiende eeuw," in J. Bethlehem and A. C. Meijer (eds.), *VOC en Cultuur* (Amsterdam: Schiphouwer and Brinkman, 1993), 59–76, at 56.

20 Roelof van Gelder, "Engelbert Kaempfer as a Scientist in the Service of the Dutch East India Company," in Detlef Haberland (ed.), *Engelbert Kaempfer: Ein Gelehrtenleben zwischen Tradition und Innovation* (Wiesbaden: Harassowitz, 2004), 211–25, at 212–13; Huib J. Zuidervaart and Rob H. Van Gent, "'A Bare Outpost of Learned European Culture on the Edge of the Jungles of Java': Johan Maurits Mohr (1716–1775) and the Emergence of Instrumental and Institutional Science in Dutch Colonial Indonesia," *Isis* 95 (2004): 1–33, at 2–3.

21 Gelder, "Engelbert Kaempfer," 217.

22 Derek Massarella, "Epilogue: Inquisitive and Intelligent Men," in Beatrice Bodart-Bailey and Derek Massarella (eds.), *The Furthest Goal: Engelbert Kaempfer's Encounter with Tokugawa Japan* (Folkestone: Japan Library, 1995), 152–64; Raj, *Relocating Modern Science*, 107–14.

23 Harold J. Cook, "Global Economies and Local Knowledge in the East Indies," in Londa Schiebinger and Claudia Swan (eds.), *Colonial Botany* (Philadelphia: University of Pennsylvania Press, 2005), 100–118; Anjana Singh, "Botanical Knowledge in Early Modern Malabar and the Netherlands," in Friedrich, Brendecke, and Ehrenpreis, *Transformations of Knowledge*, 187–208.

24 Klaas van Berkel, "The Natural Sciences in the Colonies," in Berkel, Albert van Helden, and Lodewijk Palm (eds.), *A History of Science in*

the Netherlands (Leiden: Brill, 1999), 210–28; Raj, *Relocating Modern Science*, 37–38, 44–52; Harold J. Cook, *Matters of Exchange: Commerce, Medicine and Science in the Dutch Golden Age* (New Haven: Yale University Press, 2007), 175–225, 304–77.

25 Ray Desmond, *The European Discovery of the Indian Flora* (Oxford: Oxford University Press, 1992); Richard H. Drayton, *Nature's Government* (New Haven: Yale University Press, 2000); Kapil Raj, "Dynamiques urbaines et savants à Calcutta (XVIIIe siècle)," *Revue d'Histoire Moderne et Contemporaine* 55 (2008): 70–99.

26 Christopher A. Bayly, *Empire and Information: Intelligence Gathering and Social Communication in India, 1780–1870* (Cambridge: Cambridge University Press, 1996), 264–83.

27 Michael J. Franklin, *Orientalist Jones* (Oxford: Oxford University Press, 2011), 205–50.

28 Zuidervaart and Van Gent, "'A Bare Outpost,'" 19; Bayly, *Empire and Information*, 261–64.

29 Franklin, *Orientalist Jones*, 1–42; Sylvia Murr, *L'Inde philosophique entre Bossuet et Voltaire* (2 vols., Paris: École Français d'Extrême-Orient, 1987); Xavier and Županov, *Catholic Orientalism*, 156, 206, 290. The memoir by Coeurdoux was not published in time for Jones to read it.

30 Thomas R. Trautmann, *Languages and Nations: The Dravidian Proof in Colonial Madras* (Berkeley: University of California Press, 2006).

31 Peter J. Marshall (ed.), *The British Discovery of Hinduism in the Eighteenth Century* (Cambridge: Cambridge University Press, 1970).

32 Peter Rietbergen, "VOC Travelogues," in Friedrich, Brendecke, and Ehrenpreis, *Transformations of Knowledge*, 231–49, at 235.

33 Peter Kornicki, "European Japanology at the end of the Seventeenth Century," *Bulletin of the School of Oriental and African Studies* 56 (1993): 502–24.

34 Lissa Roberts, "Re-Orienting the Transformation of Knowledge in Dutch Expansion: Nagasaki as a Centre of Accumulation and Management," in Friedrich, Brendecke, and Ehrenpreis, *Transformations of Knowledge*, 19–42.

35 Engelbert Kaempfer, *History of Japan* (London: Woodward, 1727), book 5, chapters 12, 4, 13; Detlef Haberland, *Engelbert Kaempfer, 1651–1716* (London: British Library, 1996); Brigitte Hoppe, "Kaempfer's

Forschungen über japanische Pflanzen," in Detlef Haberland (ed.), *Engelbert Kaempfer: Ein Gelehrtenleben zwischen Tradition und Innovation* (Wiesbaden: Harassowitz, 2004), 125–53; Wolfgang Muntschick, "The Plants That Carry His Name: Kaempfer's Study of the Japanese Flora," in Beatrice Bodart-Bailey and Derek Massarella (eds.), *The Furthest Goal: Engelbert Kaempfer's Encounter with Tokugawa Japan* (Folkestone: Japan Library, 1995), 71–95.

36 Bertil Nordenstam (ed.), *Carl Peter Thunberg: Linnean, resenäre, Naturforskare, 1743–1828* (Stockholm: Atlantis, 1993). On Titsingh, Boxer, *Jan Compagnie*, 135–72.

37 Michael S. Dodson, *Orientalism, Empire and National Culture: India, 1770–1880* (Basingstoke: Palgrave Macmillan, 2007), 112–14.

38 For the quotations about Rogier, Donald F. Lach and Edwin J. Van Kley, *Asia in the Making of Europe*, vol. 3 (Chicago: University of Chicago Press, 1993), 479; Haberland, *Engelbert Kaempfer*, 77.

39 Raj, *Relocating Modern Science*, 13.

40 Richard Grove, "The Transfer of Botanical Knowledge between Asia and Europe, 1498–1800," *Journal of the Japan-Netherlands Institute* 3 (1991): 160–76; Kapil Raj, "Surgeons, Fakirs, Merchants and Craftspeople," in Schiebinger and Swan, *Colonial Botany*, 252–69; Trautmann, *Madras School*, 7, 78–80.

41 Paul van der Velde, "The Interpreter Interpreted: Kaempfer's Japanese Collaborator Imamura Genemon Eisei," in Bodart-Bailey and Massarella, *The Furthest Goal*, 44–58.

42 Donald Keene, *The Japanese Discovery of Europe 1720–1830* (1952: rev. ed., Stanford: Stanford University Press, 1969); Rebekah Clements, *A Cultural History of Translation in Early Modern Japan* (Cambridge: Cambridge University Press, 2015), especially 146–50.

43 Castelnau-L'Estoile, *Missions*.

44 Jorge Klor de Alva, "Sahagún and the Birth of Modern Ethnography," in Klor de Alva, Henry B. Nicholson, and Eloise G. Keber (eds.), *The Work of Bernardino de Sahagún* (Austin: University of Texas Press, 1988), 31–52; Miguel León-Portilla, *Bernardino de Sahagún: Pionero de la antropología* (Mexico City: UNAM, 1999), 120–24, 212–13; Henry B. Nicholson, "Fray Bernardino de Sahagun," in Eloise Q. Keber (ed.), *Representing Aztec Ritual* (Boulder: University of Colorado Press, 2002), 21–39.

45 Urs App, *The Birth of Orientalism* (Philadelphia: University of Pennsylvania Press, 2010), 77–110; Rubiés, "Reassessing," 130–31.

46 Steven T. Harris, "Confession-Building, Long-Distance Networks, and the Organization of Jesuit Science," *Early Science and Medicine* 1 (1996): 287–318. On the Franciscans, Barreto and Županov, *Catholic Orientalism*, 158–201.

47 Harris, "Confession-Building," 299–300; Markus Friedrich, *Der lange Arm Roms? Globale Verwaltung und Kommunikation im Jesuitenorden, 1540–1773* (Frankfurt: Campus, 2011).

48 Prieto, *Missionary Scientists*, 117.

49 Mordechai Feingold, "Jesuits: Savants," in Feingold (ed.), *Jesuit Science and the Republic of Letters* (Cambridge, MA: MIT Press, 2003), 1–46, at 7.

50 Compare and contrast Riva Feldhay, "Knowledge and Salvation in Jesuit Culture," *Science in Context* 1 (1987): 195–213; Harris, "Confession-Building"; Antonella Romano, "Les jésuites entre apostolat missionaire et activité scientifique," *Archivum Historicum Societatis Jesu* 74 (2005): 213–36; Florence Hsia, *Sojourners in a Strange Land: Jesuits and Their Scientific Missions in Late Imperial China* (Chicago: University of Chicago Press, 2009); Prieto, *Missionary Scientists*, 154–59.

51 Aliocha Moldavsky, "The Problematic Acquisition of Indigenous Languages" in John O'Malley et al. (eds.), *The Jesuits, II: Cultures, Sciences and the Arts, 1540–1773* (Toronto: University of Toronto Press, 2006), 602–15.

52 Klor de Alva, "Sahagún," 43; Hervé Pennec, "Missionary Knowledge in Context: Geographical Knowledge of Ethiopia," in Delmas and Penn, *Writing in a Colonial Context*, 75–96, at 93.

53 Anthony Pagden, *The Fall of Natural Man: The American Indian and the Origins of Comparative Ethnology* (Cambridge: Cambridge University Press, 1982), 146–200; Prieto, *Missionary Scientists*, 146–68.

54 Pennec, "Missionary Knowledge."

55 Jonathan Spence, *The Memory Palace of Matteo Ricci* (London: Faber, 1985); Ronnie Po-chia Hsia, *A Jesuit in the Forbidden City* (Oxford: Oxford University Press, 2010); Mary Laven, *Mission to China: Matteo Ricci and the Encounter with the East* (London: Faber, 2011).

56 Qiong Zhang, *Making the New World Their Own: Chinese Encounters with Jesuit Science in the Age of Discovery* (Leiden: Brill, 2015).

57 Lach and Van Kley, *Asia*, 481.

58 Franco Demarchi and Riccardo Scartezzini (eds.), *Martino Martini umanista e scienziato nella Cina del secolo XVII* (Trento: Università di Trento, 1995); Henri Bernard, "Les sources mongoles et chinoises de l'Atlas Martini," in Roman Malek and Arnold Zingerle (eds.), *Martino Martini SJ und die Chinamission* (Nettetal: Institut Monumenta Serica, 2000), 223–40.

59 Lach and Van Kley, *Asia*, 368–79; Luisa Maria Paternicò, *When the Europeans Began to Study Chinese: Martino Martini's* Grammatica Linguae Sinensis (Leuven: Ferdinand Verbiest Institute, 2013).

60 Giovanni Pizzorusso, "La Congrégation De Propaganda Fide: Centre d'accumulation et de production des 'savoirs missionaires,'" in Castelnau-L'Estoile, *Missions*, 25–40.

61 Zandvliet, *Mapping for Money*, 124.

62 Hsia, *Sojourners in a Strange Land*; Catherine Jani, "The Jesuits' Negotiation of Science between France and China," in László Kontler et al. (eds.), *Negotiating Knowledge in Early Modern Empires* (Basingstoke: Palgrave Macmillan, 2014), 53–78.

63 Isabelle Landry-Deron, *La preuve par la Chine: La "description" de J.-B. Du Halde* (Paris: Éditions EHESS, 2002), 53–64, 143–75.

64 Peter Burke, "The Jesuits and the Art of Translation in Early Modern Europe," in O'Malley, *The Jesuits, II*, 24–32.

65 Luke Clossey, *Salvation and Globalization in the Early Jesuit Missions* (Cambridge: Cambridge University Press, 2008, 225–37.

66 Anthony Pagden, *The Fall of Natural Man*, 162–68.

67 Pagden, *The Fall of Natural Man*, 199; William N. Fenton and Elizabeth L. Moore, "J.-F. Lafitau (1681–1746), Precursor of Scientific Anthropology," *Southwestern Journal of Anthropology* 25 (196): 173–87.

68 Adriano Prosperi, "'Otras *Indias*': Missionari della contrarriforma tra contadini e selvaggi," in Paola Zambelli (ed.), *Scienze, credenze occulte, livelli di cultura* (Florence: Olschki, 1982), 205–34.

69 Geoffrey A. Oddie, "Constructing 'Hinduism': The Impact of the Protestant Missionary Movement on Hindu Self-Understanding," in Robert E. Frykenberg (ed.), *Christians and Missionaries in India* (London: RoutledgeCurzon, 2003), 155–82; Will Sweetman, *Mapping Hinduism: "Hinduism" and the Study of Indian Religions, 1600–1776* (Halle: Franckeschen Stiftungen, 2003); David N. Lorenzen, *Who Invented*

Hinduism? (New Delhi: Yoda Press, 2006); Barreto and Županov, *Catholic Orientalism*, 145–57.

70 On Ward, Geoffrey A. Oddie, *Imagined Hinduism: British Protestant Missionary Constructions of Hinduism, 1793–1900* (London: Sage, 2006), 159–81.

71 On Rogier, Sweetman, *Mapping Hinduism*, 89–103.

72 Joan-Pau Rubiés, *Travel and Ethnology*, 315–18; Rubiés, "The Jesuit Discovery of Hinduism," *Archiv für Religionsgeschichte* 3 (2001): 210–56; Rubiés, "Reassessing 'the Discovery of Hinduism': Jesuit Discourse on Gentile Idolatry and the European Republic of Letters," in Anand Amaladass and Ines G. Županov (eds.), *Intercultural Encounter and the Jesuit Mission in South Asia (16th–18th Centuries)* (Bangalore: ATC, 2014), 113–55.

73 Ines G. Županov, *Disputed Mission: Jesuit Experiments and Brahmanical Knowledge in Seventeenth-Century South India* (New Delhi: Oxford University Press, 1999), 52, 142, translates *maquina* as "fabrication"; I suspect that in this context, its meaning is closer to "system."

74 Rubiés, "The Jesuit Discovery"; José Wicki (ed.), *Tratado do Pe. Gonçalo Fernandez Trancoso sobre o hinduísmo* (Lisbon: Centro de Estudos Históricos Ultramarinos, 1973); Roberto de Nobili, *On Indian Customs* (Palayamkottai: St. Xavier's College, 1972), ch. 2; on his denial of a single religion, Sweetman, *Mapping Hinduism*, 62, 159.

75 Philip C. Almond, *The British Discovery of Buddhism* (Cambridge: Cambridge University Press, 1988), 4.

76 App, *The Birth of Orientalism*, 172–79.

77 Henri de Lubac, *La rencontre du Bouddhisme et de l'occident* (Paris: Aubier, 1952), especially 51–104.

78 App, *The Birth of Orientalism*, 123–25.

79 Luciano Petech (ed.), *I missionari italiani nel Tibet e nel Nepal*, pt. 6 (Rome: Istituto Poligrafico dello Stato, 1955), 115–30.

80 Leonard Zwilling (ed.), *Mission to Tibet* (Boston: Wisdom Publishers, 2010), 8.

81 Peter Burke, "The Spread of Italian Humanism," in Anthony Goodman and Angus Mackay (eds.), *The Impact of Humanism on Western Europe* (London: Longman, 1990), 1–22.

82 Denys Hay, *Polydore Vergil: Renaissance Historian and Man of Letters* (Oxford: Clarendon Press, 1952), 109, 151, 158–60, 199.

83 Ole P. Grell, Andrew Cunningham, and Jon Arrizabalaga (eds.), *Centres of Medical Excellence? Medical Travel and Education in Europe, 1500–1789* (Aldershot: Ashgate, 2010), 171.

84 Stina Hansson, *"Afsatt på Swensko": 1600-talets tryckta översättningslitteratur* (Göteborg: Litteraturvetenskapliga institutionen vid Göteborgs universitet, 1982).

85 Vladimir I. Guerrier, *Leibniz in seinen Beziehungen zu Russland und Peter den Grossen* (St. Petersburg: Akademie der Wissenschaften, 1873); Han F. Vermeulen, *Before Boas: The Genesis of Ethnography and Ethnology in the German Enlightenment* (Lincoln: University of Nebraska Press, 2015), 39–86.

86 Eduard Winter (ed.), *Die deutsch-russische Begegnung und Leonard Euler* (Berlin: Akademie Verlag, 1958); on translation, Irina Gouzévitch, "Le transfert des connaissances et les réformes de Pierre I," *Bulletin de la Sabix* 33 (2003): 74–121.

87 Gouzévitch, "Le transfert."

88 Eric Robinson, "The Transference of British Technology to Russia, 1760–1820," in Barrie M. Ratcliffe (ed.), *Great Britain and Her World* (Manchester: Manchester University Press, 1975), 1–26; Dennis Reinhartz, "In the Service of Catherine the Great: The Siberian Explorations and Map of Sir Samuel Bentham," *Terrae Incognitae* 26 (1994): 49–60.

89 Anthony Cross, *By the Banks of the Neva: Chapters from the Lives and Careers of the British in Eighteenth-Century Russia* (Cambridge: Cambridge University Press, 1997).

90 Alexander Vucinich, *Science in Russian Culture: A History to 1860* (Stanford: Stanford University Press, 1963), 75–122; James Cracraft, "Academy of Sciences," in his *The Petrine Revolution in Russian Culture* (Cambridge, MA: Harvard University Press, 2004), 240–55.

91 Leonhard Stejneger, *Georg Wilhelm Steller: The Pioneer of Alaskan Natural History* (Cambridge, MA: Harvard University Press, 1936); James R. Masterson and Helen Browe, *Bering's Successors, 1745–1780: Contributions of Peter Simon Pallas to the History of Russian Exploration toward Alaska* (Seattle: University of Washington Press, 1948).

92 On Messerschmidt, Vermeulen, *Before Boas*, 87–130.

93 Franz Babinger, *Gottlieb Siegfried Bayer* (Munich: Schön, 1915).

94 Joseph L. Black, *G.-F. Müller and the Imperial Russian Academy* (Kings-

ton and Montreal: McGill-Queen's University Press, 1986); Peter Hoffmann, *Gerhard Friedrich Müller (1705–1783): Historiker, Geograph, Archivar im Dienste Russlands* (Frankfurt: Peter Lang, 2005); Vermeulen, *Before Boas*, 131–218.

95 Martin Peters, *Altes Reich und Europa: Der Historiker, Statistiker und Publizist August Ludwig (v.) Schlözer (1735–1809)* (Münster: LIT, 2005); Vermeulen, *Before Boas*, 269–356.

96 Reinhard Lauer, "Schlözer und die Slaven," in Heinz Duchhardt and Martin Espenhorst (eds.), *August Ludwig (von) Schlözer in Europa* (Göttingen: Vandenhoeck und Rupprecht, 2012), 23–40, at 25.

97 Eduard Winter (ed.), *Lomonosov Schlözer Pallas* (Berlin: Akademie Verlag, 1962), 111; Peters, *Altes Reich*, 55–88.

98 Ludmilla Schulze, "The Russification of the St. Petersburg Academy of Sciences and Arts in the Eighteenth Century," *British Journal for the History of Science* 18 (1985): 305–35.

99 Peters, *Altes Reich*, 89–96.

100 Denis J. B. Shaw, "Geographical Practice and its Significance in Peter the Great's Russia," *Journal of Historical Geography* 22 (1996): 160–76.

101 Vermeulen, *Before Boas*, 110–11.

102 Günter Johannes Stipa, *Finnisch-Ugrische Sprachforschung von der Renaissance bis zum Neupositivismus* (Helsinki: Suomalais-Ugrilainen Seura, 1990), 167–205; Michael Branch, "The Academy of Sciences in St Petersburg as a Centre of Finno-Ugrian Studies, 1725–1860" (1994), ajsjogren.weebly.com/ . . . /m_branch_academy_in_st_petersburg_part_1.pdf.

103 Johannes Fabian, *Out of Our Minds: Reason and Madness in the Exploration of Central Africa* (Berkeley: University of California Press, 2000).

104 Peters, *Altes Reich*, 101–6.

105 On these and other Russians, Vermeulen, *Before Boas*, 196–97.

106 Qtd. in Alexander Etkind, *Internal Colonization: Russia's Imperial Experience* (Cambridge: Polity Press, 2011), 52.

107 Nikolai Riasanovsky, "The Norman Theory of the Origin of the Russian State," *Russian Review* 7 (1947): 96–110, at n. 96, 98; Lauer, "Schlözer und die Slaven," 32.

108 Günther Mühlpfordt, "Schlözer als Begründer der kritisch-ethnischen Geschichtsforschung," *Jahrbuch für Geschichte* 25 (1982): 23–72; Jus-

tin Stagl, *A History of Curiosity* (London: Routledge, 1995), 233–68; Gudrun Bucher, *"Von Beschreibung der Sitten und Gebräuche der Völker": Die Instruktionen Gerhard Friedrich Müllers und ihre Bedeutung für die Geschichte der Ethnologie und der Geschichtswissenschaft* (Wiesbaden: Harrassowitz, 2002); Han F. Vermeulen, "The German Invention of *Völkerkunde*," in Sara Eigen and Mark Larrimore (eds.), *The German Invention of Race* (Albany: State University of New York Press, 2006), 123–46; Vermeulen, "Von der Empirie zur Theorie: Deutschsprachige Ethnographie und Ethnologie, 1740–1881," *Zeitschrift für Ethnologie* 134 (2009): 253–66; Vermeulen, *Before Boas*, 269–70, 276–83, 437–58.

109 Kader Konuk, "Jewish-German Philologists in Turkish Exile: Leo Spitzer and Erich Auerbach," in Alexander Stephan (ed.), *Exile and Otherness: New Approaches to the Experience of the Nazi Refugees* (Oxford: Oxford University Press, 2005), 31–47.

110 Fermi, *Illustrious Immigrants*, 66–70; Horst Widmann, *Exil und Bildungshilfe: Die deutsch-sprachige akademische Emigration in der Türkei nach 1933* (Bern: Lang, 1973); Kemal Bozay, *Exil Türkei: Ein Forschungsbeitrag zur deutschsprachigen Emigration in der Türkei (1933–1945)* (Münster: LIT, 2001); Konuk, "Jewish-German Philologists"; Emily Apter, "Global *Translatio*: The 'Invention' of Comparative Literature, Istanbul 1933," *Critical Inquiry* 29 (2003): 253–81; Lâle Aka Burk, "An Open Door: German Refugee Scholars in Turkey," in Peter I. Rose (ed.), *The Dispossessed* (Amherst: University of Massachusetts Press, 2005), 235–56; Regine Erichsen, "Das Turkische Exil als Geschichte von Frauen," *Berichte zur Wissenschaftsgeschichte* 28 (2005): 337–53.

111 Hildegard Müller, "German Librarians in Exile in Turkey," *Libraries and Culture* 33 (1998): 294–305.

112 Jean-Paul Lefebvre, "Les professeurs français des missions universitaires au Brésil (1934–44)," *Cahiers du Brésil Contemporain* 12 (1990): 1–10, www.revues.msh-paris.fr/ . . . /8-J.P%20Lefebvre.pdf.

113 Claude Lévi-Strauss, *Tristes tropiques* (Paris: Plon, 1955), 37–38.

114 Thomas Skidmore, "Lévi-Strauss, Braudel and Brazil: A Case of Mutual Influence," *Bulletin of Latin American Research* 22 (2003): 340–49.

115 Peter Burke, *The French Historical Revolution: The Annales School, 1929–2014* (1990: rev. and enl., Cambridge: Polity Press, 2015), 37;

Erato Paris, *La genèse intellectuelle de l'oeuvre de Fernand Braudel* (Athens: Institut de Recherches Néo-Helléniques, 1999), 224–58.

116 Paul Arbousse-Bastide, "O que o Brasil me ensinou," *Revista da Faculdade de Educação* 10 (1984): 331–44.

117 Roberto Motta, "L'apport brésilien dans l'oeuvre de Roger Bastide," in Philippe Laburthe-Tolra (ed.), *Roger Bastide ou le réjouissement de l'abîme* (Paris: L'Harmattan, 1994), 169–78; Astrid Reuter, *Das wilde Heilige: Roger Bastide (1898–1974) und die Religionswissenschaft seiner Zeit* (Frankfurt: Campus, 2000); Fernand Braudel, "A travers un continent d'histoire: Le Brésil et l'oeuvre de Gilberto Freyre," *Mélanges d'Histoire Sociale* 4 (1943): 3–20; Braudel, "Introduzione" to Gilberto Freyre, *I padroni e i servi* (Turin: Einaudi, 1958), ix–xi.

118 Graham, "An Interview with Sergio Buarque," 6. Cf. Luiz Felipe de Alencastro, "Henri Hauser et le Brésil," in Séverine-Antigone Marin and Georges-Henri Soutou (eds.), *Henri Hauser* (Paris: Presses de l'Université Paris-Sorbonne, 2006), 281–96; and Marieta de Moraes Ferreira, "Les professeurs français et l'enseignement de l'histoire à Rio de Janeiro pendant les années 1930," in François Crouzet, Philippe Bonichon, and Denis Rolland (eds.), *Pour l'histoire du Brésil* (Paris: L'Harmattan, 2000), 123–40.

119 Maria Isaura Pereira de Queiroz, "La recherche géographique au Brésil," in Hervé Théry and Martine Droulers (eds.), *Pierre Monbeig* (Paris: Institut des hautes études de l'Amérique latine, 1991), 59–64.

5. THE GREAT EXODUS

1 Fernand Baldensperger, *Le mouvement des idées dans l'émigration française, 1789–1815* (2 vols., Paris: Plon, 1924), 46. Cf. Rubinstein, *Französische Emigration*; Kirsty Carpenter, *Refugees of the French Revolution: Émigrés in London, 1789–1802* (Basingstoke: Macmillan, 1999).

2 Lloyd S. Kramer, *Threshold of a New World: Intellectuals and the Exile Experience in Paris, 1830–1848* (Ithaca: Cornell University Press, 1988), 232; John D. Stanley, "Joachim Lelewel," in Peter Brock et al. (eds.), *Nation and History* (Toronto: University of Toronto Press, 2006), 52–84. For a survey of nineteenth-century European refugees, see Michael Marrus, *The Unwanted: European Refugees in the 20th Century* (New York: Oxford University Press, 1985), 14–50.

3 Marrus, *The Unwanted*, 15.

4 Rosemary Ashton, *Little Germany: Exile and Asylum in Victorian England* (Oxford: Oxford University Press, 1986); Heléna Tóth, *An Exiled Generation: German and Hungarian Refugees of Revolution, 1848–1871* (Cambridge: Cambridge University Press, 2014).

5 Edward Miller, *Prince of Librarians: The Life and Times of Antonio Panizzi of the British Museum* (London: Deutsch, 1967).

6 Kramer, *Threshold of a New World*, 175.

7 Fernando Murillo Rubiera, *Andrés Bello* (Caracas: la Casa de Bello, 1986); *Oxford Dictionary of National Biography*, "Rudolf Ackermann."

8 José Luis Renique, qtd. in Sznajder and Roniger, *The Politics of Exile*, 79.

9 Fermi, *Illustrious Immigrants*, 3.

10 Cathérine Gousseff, *L'exil russe: La fabrique du réfugié apatride* (Paris: CNRS, 2008), 54–56.

11 Robert C. Williams, *Culture in Exile: Russian Émigrés in Germany, 1881–1941* (Ithaca: Cornell University Press, 1972), 5. Cf. Marc Raeff, *Russia Abroad: A Cultural History of the Russian Emigration* (New York: Oxford University Press, 1990).

12 Gousseff, *L'exil russe*, 132–35.

13 Michel Heller, "L'histoire de l'expulsion des personnalités culturelles hors de l'Union Soviétique en 1922," *Cahiers du Monde Russe et Soviétique* 20 (1979): 131–72, at 164; Tomáš Hermann and Karel Kleisner, "The Five 'Homes' of Mikhail M. Novikov," *Jahrbuch für Europäische Wissenschaftskultur* 1 (2005): 87–130, at 96.

14 Zdeněk Sládek, "Prag: Das 'russische Oxford,'" in Karl Schlögel (ed.), *Der Grosse Exodus* (Munich: Beck, 1994), 218–33; Catherine Andreyev and Ivan Savický, *Russia Abroad: Prague and the Russian Diaspora, 1919–38* (New Haven: Yale University Press, 2004).

15 Marinus A. Wes, *Michael Rostovtzeff, Historian in Exile* (Stuttgart: Steiner, 1990), 52, 75.

16 Hermann and Kleisner, "The Five 'Homes' of Mikhail M. Novikov," 103.

17 Robert H. Johnston, *"New Mecca, New Babylon": Paris and the Russian Exiles, 1920–1945* (Kingston and Montreal: Magill University Press, 1988), 5, 28.

18 Galin Tihanov, "Russian Emigré Literary Criticism and Theory between the World Wars," in Evgeny Dobrenko and Galin Tihanov

(eds.), *A History of Russian Literary Theory and Criticism* (Pittsburgh: University of Pittsburgh Press, 2011), 144–62, at 148.

19 Congdon, *Exile and Social Thought*; Tibor Frank, *Double Exile: Migrations of Jewish-Hungarian Professionals through Germany to the United States, 1919–1945* (Oxford: Oxford University Press, 2009).

20 Charles Killinger, *Gaetano Salvemini* (Westport, CT: Praeger, 2002), 203–66, at 241, 245, 247.

21 Ariane Dröscher, "Gli italiani e l'estero: Flussi di migrazione intellettuale," in Francesco Cassata and Claudio Pogliano (eds.), *Storia d'Italia, Annali* 26 (Turin: Einaudi, 2011), 807–32.

22 Christmann and Hausmann, *Romanisten*, 255; Anke Dörner, *La Vita Spezzata: Leonardo Olschki, ein jüdische Romanist zwischen Integration und Emigration* (Tübingen: Stauffenburg, 2005).

23 Michael H. Crawford, "L'insegnamento di Arnaldo Momigliano in Gran Bretagna," in Lellia Cracco Ruggini (ed.), *Omaggio ad Arnaldo Momigliano* (Como: New Press, 1989), 27–42; Peter Miller (ed.), *Momigliano and Antiquarianism: Foundations of the Modern Cultural Sciences* (Toronto: University of Toronto Press, 2007).

24 José Luis Abellán (ed.), *El exilio español de 1939*, vol. 1 (Madrid: Taurus, 1976), 16; Francisco Caudet, *El exilio republicano de 1939* (Madrid: Cátedra, 2005); Henry Kamen, *The Disinherited*, 272; Andrea Pagni (ed.), *El exilio republicano español en México y Argentina* (Madrid: Iberoamericana, 2011), 11; on medics, Rockwell Gray, "The Spanish Diaspora: A Culture in Exile," *Salmagundi* 77 (1988): 53–83, at 72.

25 María Fernanda Mancebo, *La España de los exilios* (Valencia: Universitat de València, 2008), 255–97, at 259.

26 Gabriel Jackson, *Juan Negrín* (Eastbourne: Sussex Academic Press, 2010), 297–98.

27 Caudet, *El exilio republicano*, 127–66; José María López Sánchez, "El exilio científico republicano en México," in Luis Enrique Otero Carvajal (ed.), *La destrucción de la ciencia en España* (Madrid: Complutense, 2006), 177–239.

28 Jackson, *Juan Negrín*, 294, 309.

29 Luis Enrique Otero (ed.), *La destrucción de la ciencia en España* (Madrid: Complutense, 2006).

30 Qtd. in Kamen, *The Disinherited*, 273.

31 José Gaos, "La adaptación de un español a la sociedad hispanoamericana," *Revista de Occidente* (1966): 170–72; Angel del Río, *The Clash and Attraction of Two Cultures* (English trans., Baton Rouge: Louisiana State University Press, 1965), xii.

32 José Gaos, *En torno a la filosofía Mexicana* (Mexico: Alianza, 1980); Adolfo Sánchez Vázquez, *Rousseau en México* (Mexico City: Grijalbo, 1967).

33 Gaos, *En torno a la filosofía Mexicana*, 137–41, 159–63.

34 Adeline Rucquoi, "Spanish Medieval History and the *Annales*," in Miri Rubin (ed.), *The Work of Jacques Le Goff* (Woodbridge: Boydell Press, 1997), 123–41, at 125.

35 Fernando Larraz Elorriaga, "Los exiliados y las colecciones editoriales en Argentina, 1938–54," in Pagni, *El exilio republican español en México y Argentina*, 129–44.

36 Herbert A. Strauss, "Wissenschaftsemigration als Forschungsproblem," in Strauss et al. (eds.), *Die Emigration der Wissenschaften nach 1933* (Munich: Saur, 1991), 7–24; H. Stuart Hughes, *Sea Change: The Migration of Social Thought, 1930–1965* (New York: Harper, 1975), 18.

37 Charles Weiner, "The Refugees and American Physics," in Fleming and Bailyn, *The Intellectual Migration*, 190–228, at 228; Paul K. Hoch, "The Reception of Central European Refugee Physicists," *Annals of Science* 40 (1983): 217–46; Hoch, "Some Contributions to Physics by German-Jewish Emigrés in Britain and Elsewhere," in Mosse, *Second Chance*, 229–42, at 232–33.

38 Epstein, "*Schicksalsgeschichte*," 120.

39 Marion Berghahn, "Women Emigrés in England," in Sybille Quack (ed.), *Between Sorrow and Strength: Women Refugees in Nazi Germany* (Cambridge: Cambridge University Press, 1995), 69–80; Andrea Hammel, "Gender and Migration," in Edward Timms and Jon Hughes (eds.), *Intellectual Migration and Cultural Transformation* (Vienna and New York: Springer, 2003), 207–18.

40 Catherine Epstein, "Woman, Refugee, Historian: The Life and Career of Helene Wieruszowski," in Axel Fair-Schulz and Mario Kessler (eds.), *German Scholars in Exile* (Lanham, MD: Lexington Books, 2011), 85–92.

41 Catherine Epstein, "Fashioning Fortuna's Whim: German-Speaking

Women Emigrant Historians in the United States," in Sybille Quack (ed.), *Between Sorrow and Strength: Women Refugees in Nazi Germany* (Cambridge: Cambridge University Press, 1995), 301–23, at 306, 322.

42 E. Stina Lyon, "Karl Mannheim and Viola Klein," in Shula Marks, Paul Weindling, and Laura Wintour (eds.), *In Defence of Learning: The Plight, Persecution and Placement of Academic Refugees, 1933–1980s* (Oxford: Oxford University Press, 2011), 177–90, at 181–87.

43 Ulrike Wendland (ed.), *Biographisches Handbuch deutschsprachiger Kunsthistoriker in Exil* (Munich: Saur, 1999), "Gova," "Falk," and "Orienter."

44 Alfons Söllner, "In Transit to America: Political Scientists from Germany in Great Britain," in Mosse, *Second Chance*, 121–36.

45 Jonas Hansson and Svante Nordin, *Ernst Cassirer: The Swedish Years* (Bern: Peter Lang, 2006); Harries, *Nikolaus Pevsner*.

46 Geoffrey R. Elton, *The English* (Oxford: Blackwell, 1992), preface. Mikuláš Teich tells me that Elton's accent was that of a "Prague German."

47 Geoffrey R. Elton, *Return to Essentials* (Cambridge: Cambridge University Press, 1991), 91, 124.

48 Elton, *Return to Essentials*, 54.

49 Geoffrey R. Elton, *The Practice of History* (1967: 2nd ed., Oxford: Blackwell, 2002), 56–57.

50 Francis Carsten, "From Revolutionary Socialism to German History," in Peter Alter (ed.), *Out of the Third Reich: Refugee Historians in Post-War Britain* (London: I. B. Tauris, 1998), 25–40, at 34; John Grenville, "From Gardener to Professor," ibid., 55–72, at 70.

51 Geoffrey R. Elton, *The Tudor Revolution in Government* (Cambridge: Cambridge University Press, 1953).

52 Wolfgang Rogge (ed.), *Theodor W. Adorno und Ernst Krenek, Briefwechsel* (Frankfurt: Suhrkampf, 1974), 44.

53 Theodor Adorno, "Scientific Experiences of a European Scholar in America," in Donald Fleming and Bernard Bailyn, *The Intellectual Migration: Europe and America, 1930–1960* (Cambridge, MA: Harvard University Press, 1968), 33–70, at 38; Paul Lazarsfeld, "An Episode in the History of Social Research," ibid., 270–334, at 301.

54 Dieter Wuttke, "Die Emigration der Kulturwissenschaftlichen Bibliothek Warburg und die Anfänge des Universitätsfaches Kunstgeschichte in Grossbritannien," *Artibus et Historiae* 5 (1984): 133–46;

Dorothea McEwan, "Mapping the Trade Routes of the Mind: The Warburg Institute," in Timms and Hughes, *Intellectual Migration*, 37–50.

55 Nicholas Mann, "*Translatio Studii*: Warburgian *Kunstwissenschaft* in London, 1933–45," in Roberto Scazzieri and Raffaella Simili (eds.), *The Migration of Ideas* (Sagamore Beach, MA: Science History Publications, 2008), 151–60.

56 Jay, *Permanent Exiles*, 41, 43; David Kettler, "Negotiating Exile: Franz L. Neumann as Political Scientist," in Caroline Arni (ed.), *Der Eigensinn des Materials* (Frankfurt: Stroemfeld, 2007), 205–24; Thomas Wheatland, *The Frankfurt School in Exile* (Minneapolis: University of Minnesota Press, 2009), 66, 73, 76–77, 205–7.

57 Gordin, *Scientific Babel*, 204.

58 Lewis A. Coser, *Refugee Scholars in America: Their Impact and Their Experiences* (New Haven: Yale University Press, 1984), 12, 106.

59 Erwin Panofsky, "The History of Art," in Franz Neumann (ed.), *The Cultural Migration: The European Scholar in America* (Philadelphia: University of Pennsylvania Press, 1953), 82–111; Eisler, "*Kunstgeschichte* American Style"; Wuttke, "Die Emigration der Kunstwissenschaftlichen Bibliothek Warburg"; Michels, *Transplantierte Kunstwissenschaft*; Johannes Feichtinger, "The Significance of Austrian Emigré Art Historians for English Art Scholarship," in Timms and Hughes, *Intellectual Migration*, 51–70.

60 Kenneth Clark, *Another Part of the Wood* (London: Murray, 1974).

61 Qtd. in Mann, "*Translatio Studii*," 158.

62 Kenneth Clark, "A Lecture That Changed My Life," in Stephan Füssell (ed.), *Mnemosyne* (Göttingen: Gratia-Verlag, 1979), 47–48.

63 Coser, *Refugee Scholars in America*, 85; Michels, *Transplantierte Kunstwissenschaft*, 15.

64 Eisler, "*Kunstgeschichte* American Style," 559; Coser, *Refugee Scholars*, 255–60; Michels, *Transplantierte Kunstwissenschaft*.

65 Uwe Westphal, "German, Czech and Austrian Jews in English Publishing," in Mosse, *Second Chance*, 195–208; Nigel Spivey, *Phaidon, 1923–98* (London: Phaidon, 1999).

66 My thanks to Professor Simon Franklin of the University of Cambridge for this clarification.

67 Craig Calhoun (ed.), *Sociology in America: A History* (Chicago: Uni-

versity of Chicago Press, 2007), a collective work that lacks a chapter on the contribution of the émigrés.

68 Jean Floud, qtd. in David Kettler and Volker Meja, *Karl Mannheim and the Crisis of Liberalism* (New Brunswick, NJ: Rutgers University Press, 1995, 295; cf. her "Karl Mannheim," *New Society* Dec. 29 1966, 971).

69 Young qtd. in Colin Loader, *The Intellectual Development of Karl Mannheim* (Cambridge: Cambridge University Press, 1985), 127; Karl Mannheim, *Essays on Sociology and Social Psychology* (London: Routledge, 1953), 225.

70 Karl Mannheim, *Correspondence*, ed. Éva Gábor (Lewiston, NY: Edwin Mellen Press, 2003), 202; Loader, *The Intellectual Development of Karl Mannheim*, 127; Mannheim, "Function"; Kettler and Meja, *Karl Mannheim*, 281; Norbert Elias, "Sociology and Psychiatry," in Siegmund H. Foulkes and G. Stewart Prince (eds.), *Psychiatry in a Changing Society* (London: Tavistock, 1969), 117–44.

71 Qtd. in Dorothea McEwan, "Mapping the Trade Routes of the Mind," 42.

72 Tim Mowl, *Stylistic Cold Wars: Betjeman versus Pevsner* (London: John Murray, 2000).

73 Perry Anderson, "Components of the National Culture," *New Left Review* 50 (1968): 3–58, at 51. Wellek was born in Vienna, but of Czech descent.

74 Hobsbawm, "The Historians' Group of the Communist Party," 23.

75 Games, *Pevsner*, 2.

76 Cynthia Freeland, *Art Theory: A Very Short Introduction* (Oxford: Oxford University Press, 2003); Robert Williams, *Art Theory: An Historical Introduction* (Oxford: Blackwell, 2004).

77 Wheatland, *Frankfurt School*, 171, 178, 306–7; Mannheim, *Selected Correspondence*, 113.

78 Peter Laslett, "Karl Mannheim in 1939: A Student's Recollection," *Revue Européenne des Sciences Sociales et Cahiers Vilfredo Pareto* 17 (1979): 223–26.

79 Stephen Mennell, *Norbert Elias* (Oxford: Blackwell, 1989).

80 Carsten, "From Revolutionary Socialism," 30.

81 Rodney Livingstone, "The Contribution of German-Speaking Jew-

ish Refugees to German Studies in Britain," in Mosse, *Second Chance,* 137–52, at 147.

82 William E. Scheuerman, "Professor Kelsen's Amazing Disappearing Act," in Felix Rösch (ed.), *Émigré Scholars and the Genesis of International Relations* (Basingstoke: Ashgate, 2014), 81–102.

83 Alfons Söllner, "Von Staatsrecht zur 'political science' — die Emigration deutscher Wissenschaftler nach 1933, ihr Einfluss auf die Transformation einer Disziplin," in Herbert A. Strauss et al. (eds.), *Die Emigration der Wissenschaften nach 1933* (Munich: Saur, 1991), 137–64; Rösch, *Émigré Scholars;* Gerhard Loewenberg, "The Influence of European Émigré Scholars on Comparative Politics, 1925–1965," *American Political Science Review* 100 (2006): 597–604.

84 Herbert Feigl, "The *Wiener Kreis* in America," in Fleming and Bailyn, *The Intellectual Migration,* 630–73; Coser, *Refugee Scholars,* 202–7, 298–306; Eugene R. Sheppard, *Leo Strauss and the Politics of Exile: The Making of a Political Philosopher* (Hanover, NH: University Press of New England, 2006).

85 Fermi, *Illustrious Immigrants,* 139–73; Jean M. Mandler and George Mandler, "The Diaspora of Experimental Psychology," in Fleming and Bailyn, *The Intellectual Migration,* 371–419; Jahoda, "The Migration of Psychoanalysis"; Mitchell G. Ash, "Disziplinentwicklung und Wissenschaftstransfer — deutschsprachige Psychologen in der Emigration," *Berichte zur Wissenschaftsgeschichte* 7 (1984), 207–26; Coser, *Refugee Scholars,* 19, 22–27.

86 Mannheim, "The Function of the Refugee."

87 Hughes, *Sea Change,* 114; Lazarsfeld, "An Episode," 271, 302.

88 Walter Kaufmann, "The Reception of Existentialism in the United States," in Boyers, *The Legacy,* 69–96, at 79–80; David Pickus, "At Home with Nietzsche, at War with Germany: Walter Kaufmann and the Struggles of Nietzsche Interpretation," in Richard Bodek and Simon Lewis (eds.), *The Fruits of Exile* (Columbia: University of South Carolina Press, 2010), 156–76; Peter Breiner, "Translating Max Weber," in Rösch, *Émigré Scholars,* 40–58.

89 Jay, *Permanent Exiles,* 142.

90 Kenneth D. Barkin, "Émigré Historians in America, 1950–1980," in Lehmann and Sheehan, *An Interrupted Past,* 149–69, at 153.

91 Carsten, "From Revolutionary Socialism," 36.

92 Auerbach, *Mimesis*, 557. Spitzer too complained that "there were almost no books" at the University of Istanbul (qtd. in Konuk, "Jewish-German Philologists," 43) and so did Liselotte Dieckmann (Erichsen, "Türkische Exil," 345).

93 Yosef Kaplan, "Between Yitzhak Baer and Claudio Sánchez Albornoz: The Rift That Never Healed," in Richard I. Cohen et al. (eds.), *Jewish Culture in Early Modern Europe* (Pittsburgh: University of Pittsburgh Press, 2014), 356–68. For examples of antisemitism in the writings of Sánchez-Albornoz, see Peter Russell, "The Nessus-Shirt of Spanish History," *Bulletin of Hispanic Studies* 36 (1959): 219–25, at 223; and Peter Linehan, *History and the Historians of Medieval Spain* (Oxford: Clarendon Press, 1993), 51.

94 Erwin Panofsky, "In Defense of the Ivory Tower," *Centennial Review* 1 (1957): 111–12; Jan Białostocki, "Erwin Panofsky: Thinker, Historian, Human Being," *Simiolus* 4 (1970): 68–89, at 70.

95 H. Stuart Hughes, "Franz Neumann," in Fleming and Bailyn, *The Intellectual Migration*, 446–62, at 449, 462.

96 Lucie Varga, "La genèse du national-socialisme: Notes d'analyse sociale," *Annales d'Histoire Économique et Sociale* 9 (1937): 529–46; Norbert Elias, "Problems of Involvement and Detachment," *British Journal of Sociology* 7 (1956): 226–52.

97 Hobsbawm, *Interesting Times*, 98.

98 Eric J. Hobsbawm, *Nations and Nationalism since 1780* (Cambridge: Cambridge University Press, 1990), 1, 130, 168; Ernest Gellner, *Nations and Nationalism* (Oxford: Blackwell, 1983).

99 Hans Baron, *The Crisis of the Early Italian Renaissance* (2 vols., Princeton: Princeton University Press, 1955), vol. 1, x, xii, 8, 10; vol. 2, 389; Anthony Molho, "Hans Baron's Crisis," in David S. Peterson and Daniel E. Bornstein (eds.), *Florence and Beyond* (Toronto: University of Toronto Press, 2008), 61–90.

100 Rubinstein, *Die französische Emigration*.

101 Anderson, *Components*, 19.

102 Panofsky, *Meaning in the Visual Arts*, 329.

103 Weidenfeld, *Remembering My Good Friends*, 115.

104 Jennifer Platt, "Some Issues in Intellectual Method and Approach," in Timms and Hughes, *Intellectual Migration*, 7–20, at 14.

105 Reuben Abel, "Felix Kaufmann," in Boyers, *The Legacy*, 288–91. Cf. Feigl, "The *Wiener Kreis* in America."

106 Coser, *Refugee Scholars*, 211–12; cf. Alfons Söllner, "From International Law to International Relations: Émigré Scholars in American Political Science and International Relations," in Rösch, *Émigré Scholars*, 197–211, at 204.

107 Edward Shils, "The Calling of Sociology," in Talcott Parsons et al. (eds.), *Theories of Society* (New York: Free Press, 1961), 1405–50, at 1407.

108 Adorno, "Scientific Experiences," 340; Jay, *Permanent Exiles*, 107–37, at 123–24.

109 McIver qtd. in John Higham and Paul Conkin (eds.), *New Directions in American Intellectual History* (Baltimore: Johns Hopkins University Press, 1979), 8; Adorno, "Scientific Experiences," 343.

110 Lazarsfeld, "An Episode," 322.

111 On Horkheimer, James Schmidt, "*The Eclipse of Reason* and the End of the Frankfurt School in America," in Bodek and Lewis, *The Fruits of Exile*, 1–28, at 7; on Kelsen, Jeremy Telman, "Selective Affinities," ibid., 40–58, at 43–45; and Scheuerman, "Professor Kelsen's Amazing Disappearing Act."

112 Jay, *Permanent Exiles*, 35, 107.

113 Shils, "The Calling of Sociology," 1407.

114 Wheatland, *Frankfurt School*, 128, 131.

115 Theodor Adorno, Else Frenkel-Brunswik, Daniel J. Levinson, and Nevitt Sanford, *The Authoritarian Personality* (New York: Norton, 1950).

116 Adorno et al., *The Authoritarian Personality*; Hughes, *Sea Change*, 3, 150, 152–53.

117 Jahoda, "Migration of Psychoanalysis," 421.

118 Nicolai Rubinstein, "Germany, Italy and England," in Peter Alter (ed.), *Out of the Third Reich: Refugee Historians in Post-war Britain* (London: I. B. Tauris, 1998), 237–46, at 242.

119 Regina Weber, "Zur Remigration des Germanisten Richard Alewyn," in Herbert A. Strauss et al. (eds.), *Die Emigration der Wissenschaften nach 1933* (Munich: Saur, 1991), 235–56.

120 Hoch and Platt, "Migration," 139.

121 Tillich, "The Conquest," 155.

122 Neumann, "Social Sciences," 24; Neumann, memorandum to a conference on social sciences in Chicago in 1939, qtd. in Thomas Wheatland, "Frank L. Neumann: Negotiating Political Exile," *German Historical Institute Bulletin*, suppl. 10 (2014): 111–38, at 119–20.

123 Norbert Elias, "The Retreat of Sociologists into the Present," *Theory, Culture and Society* 4 (1987): 223–47.

124 Leonard Bloomfield, "Language or Ideas?" *Language* 12 (1936–38): 89–95; Leo Spitzer, "Answer to Mr. Bloomfield," *Language* 20 (1944): 245–51.

125 Personal communication, 1990s.

126 Andrew Graham-Yoole, "The Wild Oats They Sowed: Latin American Exiles in Europe," *Third World Quarterly* 9 (1987): 246–53.

127 Eduardo P. Archetti, *Masculinities: Football, Polo and the Tango in Argentina* (Oxford: Berg, 1999); Sznajder and Roniger, *The Politics of Exile*, 214.

128 Shula Marks, "South African Refugees in the UK," in Marks, Weindling, and Wintour, *In Defence of Learning*, 257–79.

BIBLIOGRAPHY

Abel, Reuben. "Felix Kaufmann." In *The Legacy of the German Refugee Intellectuals*, edited by Robert Boyers, 288–91. New York: Schocken, 1972.

Abellán, José Luis, ed. *El exilio español de 1939*. 2 vols. Madrid: Taurus, 1976.

Adelman, Jeremy. *Worldly Philosopher: The Odyssey of Albert O. Hirschman*. Princeton: Princeton University Press, 2013.

Adorni Braccesi, Simonetta, and Simone Ragagli. "Lando, Ortensio." In *Dizionario biografico degli Italiani*, vol. 63. Rome: Istituto dell'Enciclopedia Italiana, 2004. www.treccani.it/enciclopedia/ortensio-lando_(Dizionario_Biografico)/.

Adorno, Theodor. *Minima Moralia*. Frankfurt: Suhrkampf, 1951.

———. "Scientific Experiences of a European Scholar in America." In *The Intellectual Migration: Europe and America, 1930–1960*, edited by Donald Fleming and Bernard Bailyn, 33–70. Cambridge, MA: Harvard University Press, 1968.

———, Else Frenkel-Brunswik, Daniel J. Levinson, and Nevitt Sanford. *The Authoritarian Personality*. New York: Norton, 1950.

Alencastro, Luiz Felipe de. "Henri Hauser et le Brésil." In *Henri Hauser*, edited by Séverine-Antigone Marin and Georges-Henri Soutou, 281–96. Paris: Presses de l'Université Paris-Sorbonne, 2006.

Almagor, Joseph. *Pierre Des Maizeaux*. Amsterdam: APA-Holland University Press, 1989.

Anderson, Perry. "Components of the National Culture." *New Left Review* 50 (1968): 3–58.

Andrade, António Júlio de, and Maria Fernanda Guimarães, *Jacob de Carlos Sarmento*. Lisbon: Vega, 2010.

Andrés y Morell, Juan. *Dell'origine, progressi e stato d'ogni attuale letteratura*. Parma: Stamperia Reale, 1782–1799.

Andreyev, Catherine, and Ivan Savický. *Russia Abroad: Prague and the Russian Diaspora, 1919–38*. New Haven: Yale University Press, 2004.

App, Urs. *The Birth of Orientalism*. Philadelphia: University of Pennsylvania Press, 2010.

Apter, Emily. "Global *Translatio*: The 'Invention' of Comparative Literature, Istanbul 1933." *Critical Inquiry* 29 (2003): 253–81.

Arblaster, Paul. *Antwerp and the World: Richard Verstegan and the International Culture of Catholic Reformation*. Leuven: Leuven University Press, 2004.

Arbousse-Bastide, Paul. "O que o Brasil me ensinou." *Revista da Faculdade de Educação* 10 (1984): 331–44.

Archetti, Eduardo P. *Masculinities: Football, Polo and the Tango in Argentina*. Oxford: Berg, 1999.

Arendt, Hannah. "We Refugees." In *The Jew as Pariah: Hannah Arendt*, edited by Ron H. Feldman, 55–66. New York: Grove Press, 1978.

Ash, Mitchell G. "Disziplinentwicklung und Wissenschaftstransfer—deutschsprachige Psychologen in der Emigration." *Berichte zur Wissenschaftsgeschichte* 7 (1984): 207–26.

———. "Forced Migration and Scientific Change." In *The Migration of Ideas*, edited by Roberto Scazzieri and Raffaella Simili, 161–78. Sagamore Beach, MA: Science History Publications, 2008.

Ashton, Rosemary. *Little Germany: Exile and Asylum in Victorian England*. Oxford: Oxford University Press, 1986.

Auerbach, Erich. *Mimesis: The Representation of Reality in Western Literature* (1947). English trans. Princeton: Princeton University Press, 1953.

Babinger, Franz. *Gottlieb Siegfried Bayer*. Munich: Schön, 1915.

Baer, Yitzhak. *Galut* (1936). English trans. New York: Schocken, 1947.

Baets, Antoon de. "Exile and Acculturation: Refugee Historians since the Second World War," *International History Review* 28 (2006): 316–35.

Baldensperger, Fernand. *Le mouvement des idées dans l'émigration française, 1789–1815*. 2 vols. Paris: Plon, 1924.

Barkin, Kenneth D. "Émigré Historians in America, 1950–1980." In *An Interrupted Past: German-Speaking Refugee Historians in the United States after 1933*, edited by Hartmut Lehmann and James J. Sheehan, 149–69. Washington, DC: German Historical Institute, 1991.

Barnett, Pamela R. *Theodore Haak FRS*. The Hague: Mouton, 1962.

Baron, Hans. *The Crisis of the Early Italian Renaissance*. 2 vols. Princeton: Princeton University Press, 1955.

Barreto Xavier, Ângela, and Ines G. Županov, *Catholic Orientalism:*

Portuguese Empire, Indian Knowledge (16th–18th Centuries). Delhi: Oxford University Press, 2015.

Basnage, Jacques. *Histoire des Juifs*. 6 vols. Rotterdam: Leers, 1706–7.

Batllori, Miquel. *La cultura hispano-italiana de los jesuitas expulsos*. Madrid: Gredos, 1966.

Bauman, Zygmunt. *Modernity and the Holocaust*. Cambridge: Polity Press, 1989.

Bayle, Pierre. *Dictionnaire Historique et Critique* (1697). 5th ed. Amsterdam: Brunel, 1740.

Bayly, Christopher A. *Empire and Information: Intelligence Gathering and Social Communication in India, 1780–1870*. Cambridge: Cambridge University Press, 1996.

Beinart, Haim. *The Expulsion of the Jews from Spain*. English trans. Oxford: Littman Library, 2002.

Bellot, Jacques. *Familiar Dialogues* (1586). Facsimile repr. Menston: Scolar Press, 1969.

Benedict, Philip. *Rouen during the Wars of Religion*. Cambridge: Cambridge University Press, 1981.

Berec, Laurent. *Claude de Sainliens: Un Huguenot bourbonnais au temps de Shakespeare*. Paris: Orizons, 2012.

Berghahn, Marion. "Women Emigrés in England." In *Between Sorrow and Strength: Women Refugees of the Nazi Period*, edited by Sybille Quack, 69–80. Cambridge: Cambridge University Press, 1995.

Berkel, Klaas van. "The Natural Sciences in the Colonies." In *A History of Science in the Netherlands*, edited by Berkel, Albert van Helden, and Lodewijk Palm, 210–28. Leiden: Brill, 1999.

———. "Een onwillige mecenas? De rol van de VOC bij het natuurwetenschappelijk onderzoek in de zeventiende eeuw." In *VOC en Cultuur*, edited by J. Bethlehem and A. C. Meijer, 59–76. Amsterdam: Schiphouwer and Brinkman, 1993.

Berkvens-Stevelinck, Christiane. *Prosper Marchand*. Leiden: Brill, 1987.

———. "Prosper Marchand, intermédiaire du Refuge Huguenot." In *Les grands intermédiaires de la République des Lettres*, edited by Berkvens-Stevelinck, Hans Bots, and Jens Häseler, 361–86. Paris: Champion, 2005.

Bernard, Henri. "Les sources mongoles et chinoises de l'Atlas Martini." In *Martino Martini SJ und die Chinamission*, edited by Roman Malek and Arnold Zingerle, 223–40. Nettetal: Institut Monumenta Serica, 2000.

Białostocki, Jan. "Erwin Panofsky: Thinker, Historian, Human Being." *Simiolus* 4 (1970): 68–89.

Black, Joseph L. *G.-F. Müller and the Imperial Russian Academy*. Kingston and Montreal: McGill-Queen's University Press, 1986.

Blekastad, Milad. *Comenius*. Oslo: Universitetsforlaget, 1969.

Blok, Anton. *The Blessings of Adversity*. Cambridge: Polity Press, 2016.

Bloomfield, Leonard. "Language or Ideas?" *Language* 12 (1936–38): 89–95.

Blussé, Leonard, and Ilonka Ooms, eds. *Kennis en Compagnie: De VOC en de moderne Wetenschap*. Amsterdam: Balans, 2002.

Boeri, Tito, et al., eds. *Brain Drain and Brain Gain*. Oxford: Oxford University Press, 2012.

Bond, Donald F. "Armand de la Chapelle and the First French Version of *The Tatler*." In *Restoration and Eighteenth-Century Literature*, edited by Carroll Camden, 161–84. Chicago: University of Chicago Press, 1963.

Bost, Hubert. *Un intellectuel avant la lettre: Le journaliste Pierre Bayle*. Amsterdam-Maarssen: APA-Holland University Press, 1994.

———. *Ces Messieurs de la R. P. R.* Paris: Champion, 2001.

———. *Pierre Bayle historien, critique et moraliste*. Turnhout: Brepols, 2006.

Bots, Hans. "Les pasteurs français au refuge des Provinces-Unies." In *La vie intellectuelle aux refuges protestants*, edited by Jens Häseler and Antony McKenna, 9–18. Paris: Champion, 1999.

———. "Pierre Bayle's *Dictionnaire* and a New Attitude towards the Islam." In *What's Left Behind: The Lieux de Mémoire of Europe beyond Europe*, edited by Marjet Derks et al., 183–89. Nijmegen: Vantilt, 2015.

———. "Les Provinces-Unies, centre d'information européenne au XVIIe siècle." *Quaderni del Seicento Francese* 5 (1983): 283–306.

———. "Le role des périodiques néerlandais pour la diffusion du livre (1684–1747)." In *Le magasin de l'univers: The Dutch Republic as the Centre of the European Book Trade*, edited by Christiane Berkvens-Stevelinck, 49–70. Leiden: Brill, 1992.

Boxer, Charles R. *Jan Compagnie in Japan, 1600–1817* (1936). 2nd ed. London: Oxford University Press, 1968.

Boyers, Robert, ed. *The Legacy of the German Refugee Intellectuals*. New York: Schocken, 1972.

Bozay, Kemal. *Exil Türkei: Ein Forschungsbeitrag zur deutschsprachigen Emigration in der Türkei (1933–1945)*. Münster: LIT, 2001.

Brading, David. *The First America: The Spanish Monarchy, Creole Patriots and the Liberal State 1492–1866*. Cambridge: Cambridge University Press, 1991.

Branch, Michael. "The Academy of Sciences in St Petersburg as a Centre of Finno-Ugrian Studies, 1725–1860" (1994). ajsjogren.weebly.com /.../m_branch_academy_in_st_petersburg_part_1.pdf.

Braudel, Fernand. "Histoire et sciences sociales: La longue durée" (1958). Repr. in *Les Ambitions de l'histoire*, 149–79. Paris: Fallois, 1997.

———. *La Méditerranée et le monde méditerranéen à l'époque de Philippe II* (1949). 2nd ed. Paris: Armand Colin, 1966.

———. "A travers un continent d'histoire: Le Brésil et l'oeuvre de Gilberto Freyre." *Mélanges d'Histoire Sociale* 4 (1943): 3–20.

Breiner, Peter. "Translating Max Weber." In *Émigré Scholars and the Genesis of International Relations*, edited by Felix Rösch, 40–58. Basingstoke: Ashgate, 2014.

Bucher, Gudrun. *"Von Beschreibung der Sitten und Gebräuche der Völker": Die Instruktionen Gerhard Friedrich Müllers und ihre Bedeutung für die Geschichte der Ethnologie und der Geschichtswissenschaft*. Wiesbaden: Harrassowitz, 2002.

Burk, Lâle Aka. "An Open Door: German Refugee Scholars in Turkey." In *The Dispossessed*, edited by Peter I. Rose, 235–56. Amherst: University of Massachusetts Press, 2005.

Burke, Peter. *The French Historical Revolution: The Annales School, 1929–2014* (1990). Rev. and enl. ed. Cambridge: Polity Press, 2015.

———. "History as Allegory." *Inti* 45 (1997): 337–51.

———. "The Jesuits and the Art of Translation in Early Modern Europe." In *The Jesuits, II: Cultures, Sciences and the Arts, 1540–1773*, edited by John O'Malley et al., 24–32. Toronto: University of Toronto Press, 2006.

———. "The Myth of 1453: Notes and Reflections." In *Querdenken: Dissens und Toleranz im Wandel der Geschichte: Festschrift Hans Guggisberg*, edited by Michael Erbe et al., 23–30. Mannheim: Palatium, 1996.

———. *A Social History of Knowledge from the Encyclopédie to Wikipedia*. Cambridge: Polity Press, 2012.

———. *A Social History of Knowledge from Gutenberg to Diderot.* Cambridge: Polity Press, 2000.

———. "The Spread of Italian Humanism." In *The Impact of Humanism on Western Europe,* edited by Anthony Goodman and Angus Mackay, 1–22. London: Longman, 1990.

———, and Maria Lúcia Pallares-Burke. *Gilberto Freyre: Social Theory in the Tropics.* Oxford: Peter Lang, 2008.

Burriez Sánchez, Javier. "Los misioneros de la restauración católica: La formación en los colegios ingleses." In *Missions d'évangélisation et circulation des savoirs: XVIe-XVIIIe siècle,* edited by Charlotte de Castelnau-L'Estoile, 87–110. Madrid: Casa de Velázquez, 2011.

Butterfield, Herbert. *George III and the Historians.* Rev. ed. New York: Macmillan, 1959.

Calhoun, Craig, ed. *Sociology in America: A History.* Chicago: University of Chicago Press, 2007.

Cantimori, Delio. *Eretici italiani del Cinquecento.* Florence: Sansoni, 1939.

Carpenter, Kirsty. *Refugees of the French Revolution: Émigrés in London, 1789–1802.* Basingstoke: Macmillan, 1999.

Carsten, Francis. "From Revolutionary Socialism to German History." In *Out of the Third Reich: Refugee Historians in Post-war Britain,* edited by Peter Alter, 25–40. London: I. B. Tauris, 1998.

Castro, Américo. *The Structure of Spanish History.* Princeton: Princeton University Press, 1954.

Caudet, Francisco. *El exilio republicano de 1939.* Madrid: Cátedra, 2005.

Cerny, Gerald. *Theology, Politics and Letters at the Crossroads of European Civilization: Jacques Basnage and the Baylean Huguenot Refugees in the Dutch Republic.* The Hague: Nijhoff, 1987.

Christmann, Hans Helmut, and Frank-Rutger Hausmann, eds. *Deutsche und österreichische Romanisten als Verfolgte des National Sozialismus.* Tübingen: Stauffenburg, 1989.

Cian, Vittorio. *L'immigrazione dei gesuiti spagnuoli letterati in Italia.* Turin: Clausen, 1895.

Cipolla, Carlo. "The Diffusion of Innovations in Early Modern Europe," *Comparative Studies in Society and History* 14 (1972): 46–52.

Clark, Kenneth. *Another Part of the Wood.* London: Murray, 1974.

———. "A Lecture that Changed my Life." In *Mnemosyne,* edited by Stephan Füssell, 47–48. Göttingen: Gratia-Verlag, 1979.

Clements, Rebekah. *A Cultural History of Translation in Early Modern Japan*. Cambridge: Cambridge University Press, 2015.

Clossey, Luke. *Salvation and Globalization in the Early Jesuit Missions*. Cambridge: Cambridge University Press, 2008.

Cohn, Bernard S. *Colonialism and Its Forms of Knowledge: The British in India*. Princeton: Princeton University Press, 1996.

Colcutt, Martin. *Five Mountains*. Cambridge, MA: Harvard University Press, 1981.

Colley, Linda. *Lewis Namier*. London: Weidenfeld and Nicolson, 1989.

Congdon, Lee. *Exile and Social Thought: Hungarian Intellectuals in Germany and Austria, 1919–1933*. Princeton: Princeton University Press, 1991.

Considine, John P. *Dictionaries in Early Modern Europe*. Cambridge: Cambridge University Press, 2008.

Cook, Harold J. "Amsterdam, entrepôt des savoirs au XVIIe siècle." *Revue d' Histoire Moderne et Contemporaine* 55 (2008): 19–42.

———. "Global Economies and Local Knowledge in the East Indies." In *Colonial Botany*, edited by Londa Schiebinger and Claudia Swan, 100–118. Philadelphia: University of Pennsylvania Press, 2005.

———. *Matters of Exchange: Commerce, Medicine and Science in the Dutch Golden Age*. New Haven: Yale University Press, 2007.

Cortesão, Armando, ed. *The* Suma Oriental *of Tomé Pires*. 2 vols. London: Hakluyt Society, 1944.

Coser, Lewis A. *Refugee Scholars in America: Their Impact and Their Experiences*. New Haven: Yale University Press, 1984.

Couto, Dejanirah. "The Role of Interpreters, or *Linguas*, in the Portuguese Empire in the Sixteenth Century." c. 1998. www.brown.edu/Departments/Portuguese_Brazilian_Studies/ejph/html/issue2/html.

Cracraft, James. *The Petrine Revolution in Russian Culture*. Cambridge, MA: Harvard University Press, 2004.

Crawford, Michael H. "L'insegnamento di Arnaldo Momigliano in Gran Bretagna." In *Omaggio ad Arnaldo Momigliano*, edited by Lellia Cracco Ruggini, 27–42. Como: New Press, 1989.

Cross, Anthony. *By the Banks of the Neva: Chapters from the Lives and Careers of the British in Eighteenth-Century Russia*. Cambridge: Cambridge University Press, 1997.

Dahl, Folke. "Amsterdam—Earliest Newspaper Centre of Western Europe," *Het Boek* 25 (1939): 160–97.

Dames, Mansel, ed. *The Book of Duarte Barbosa*. 2 vols. London: Hakluyt Society, 1918–21.

Darnton, Robert. *The Forbidden Best-Sellers of Pre-Revolutionary France*. New York: Norton, 1995.

Davies, David W. *The World of the Elseviers, 1580–1712*. The Hague: Nijhoff, 1954.

Davis Jr., Donald R. "Law in the Mirror of Language." In *The Madras School of Orientalism*, edited by Thomas R. Trautmann, 288–309. Oxford: Oxford University Press, 2009.

Davis, Jack L. "Roger Williams among the Narragansett Indians." *New England Quarterly* 43 (1970): 593–604.

Davis, Natalie Z. *Trickster Travels: A Sixteenth-Century Muslim between Worlds*. London: Faber, 2007.

Delmas, Adrian. "From Travelling to History: An Outline of the VOC Writing System during the Seventeenth Century." In *Written Culture in a Colonial Context*, edited by Delmas and Nigel Penn, 97–126. Leiden: Brill, 2012.

Demarchi, Franco, and Riccardo Scartezzini, eds. *Martino Martini umanista e scienziato nella Cina del secolo XVII*. Trento: Università di Trento, 1995.

Desmond, Ray. *The European Discovery of the Indian Flora*. Oxford: Oxford University Press, 1992.

Dodson, Michael S. *Orientalism, Empire and National Culture: India, 1770–1880*. Basingstoke: Palgrave Macmillan, 2007.

Dörner, Anke. *La Vita Spezzata: Leonardo Olschki, ein jüdische Romanist zwischen Integration und Emigration*. Tübingen: Stauffenburg, 2005.

Drayton, Richard H. *Nature's Government*. New Haven: Yale University Press, 2000.

Dröscher, Ariane. "Gli italiani e l'estero: Flussi di migrazione intellettuale." In *Storia d'Italia, Annali* 26, edited by Francesco Cassata and Claudio Pogliano, 807–32. Turin: Einaudi, 2011.

Edney, Matthew H. *Mapping an Empire: The Geographical Construction of British India, 1765–1843*. Chicago: University of Chicago Press, 1990.

Ehrenpreis, Stefan. "Empiricism and Image-Building: The Creation and Dissemination of Knowledge in Dutch Brazil, 1636–1750." In

Transformations of Knowledge in Dutch Expansion, edited by Susanne Friedrich, Arndt Brendecke, and Stefan Ehrenpreis, 69–92. Berlin: De Gruyter, 2015.

Eisenstein, Elizabeth. *Grub Street Abroad: Aspects of the French Cosmopolitan Press from the Age of Louis XIV to the French Revolution.* Oxford: Clarendon Press, 1992.

Eisler, Colin. "*Kunstgeschichte* American Style: A Study in Migration." In *The Intellectual Migration: Europe and America, 1930–1960*, edited by Donald Fleming and Bernard Bailyn, 544–629. Cambridge, MA: Harvard University Press, 1968.

Elias, Norbert. "Problems of Involvement and Detachment." *British Journal of Sociology* 7 (1956): 226–52.

———. "The Retreat of Sociologists into the Present." *Theory, Culture and Society* 4 (1987): 223–47.

———. "Sociology and Psychiatry." In *Psychiatry in a Changing Society*, edited by Siegmund H. Foulkes and G. Stewart Prince, 117–44. London: Tavistock, 1969.

———, and John Scotson. *The Established and the Outsiders.* London: Cass, 1965.

Elkanah, Yehudah. *Leben in Contexten.* Berlin: Wissenschaftskolleg, 2015.

Elton, Geoffrey R. *The English.* Oxford: Blackwell, 1992.

———. *The Practice of History* (1967). 2nd ed. Oxford: Blackwell, 2002.

———. *Return to Essentials.* Cambridge: Cambridge University Press, 1991.

———. *The Tudor Revolution in Government.* Cambridge: Cambridge University Press, 1953.

Elukin, Jonathan M. "Jacques Basnage and the History of Jews." *Journal of the History of Ideas* 53 (1992): 603–30.

Epstein, Catherine. "Fashioning Fortuna's Whim: German-Speaking Women Emigrant Historians in the United States." In *Between Sorrow and Strength: Women Refugees in Nazi Germany*, edited by Sybille Quack, 301–23. Cambridge: Cambridge University Press, 1995.

———. "*Schicksalsgeschichte*: Refugee Historians in the United States." In *An Interrupted Past: German-Speaking Refugee Historians in the United States after 1933*, edited by Hartmut Lehmann and James Sheehan, 116–35. Washington, DC: German Historical Institute, 1991.

———. "Woman, Refugee, Historian: The Life and Career of Helene

Wieruszowski." In *German Scholars in Exile*, edited by Axel Fair-Schulz and Mario Kessler, 85–92. Lanham, MD: Lexington Books, 2011.

Erichsen, Regine. "Das Turkische Exil als Geschichte von Frauen." *Berichte zur Wissenschaftsgeschichte* 28 (2005): 337–53.

Espagne, Michel, and Michael Werner, eds. *Transferts: Les relations interculturelles dans l'espace franco-allemand, XVIIIe et XIXe siècles*. Paris: Éditions Recherche sur les Civilisations, 1988.

Etkind, Alexander. *Internal Colonization: Russia's Imperial Experience*. Cambridge: Polity Press, 2011.

Fabian, Johannes. *Out of Our Minds: Reason and Madness in the Exploration of Central Africa*. Berkeley: University of California Press, 2000.

Feichtinger, Johannes. "The Significance of Austrian Emigré Art Historians for English Art Scholarship." In *Intellectual Migration and Cultural Transformation*, edited by Edward Timms and Jon Hughes, 51–70. Vienna and New York: Springer, 2003.

Feigl, Herbert. "The *Wiener Kreis* in America." In *The Intellectual Migration: Europe and America, 1930–1960*, edited by Donald Fleming and Bernard Bailyn, 630–73. Cambridge, MA: Harvard University Press, 1968.

Feingold, Mordechai. "Jesuits: Savants." In *Jesuit Science and the Republic of Letters*, edited by Feingold, 1–46. Cambridge, MA: MIT Press, 2003.

Fél, Edit, and Tamás Hofer. *Proper Peasants: Traditional Life in a Hungarian Village*. Chicago: Aldine, 1969.

Feldhay, Rivka. "Knowledge and Salvation in Jesuit Culture." *Science in Context* 1 (1987): 195–213.

Fenton, William N., and Elizabeth L. Moore, "J.-F. Lafitau (1681–1746), Precursor of Scientific Anthropology." *Southwestern Journal of Anthropology* 25 (196): 173–87.

Fermi, Laura. *Illustrious Immigrants: The Intellectual Migration from Europe 1930–41*. Chicago: University of Chicago Press, 1968.

Fischer-Tiné, Harald. *Pidgin-Knowledge: Wissen und Kolonialismus*. Zurich and Berlin: Diaphanes, 2013.

Fleming, Donald, and Bernard Bailyn, eds. *The Intellectual Migration: Europe and America, 1930–1960*. Cambridge, MA: Harvard University Press, 1969.

Fleming, Juliet. "The French Garden: An Introduction to Women's French." *English Literary History* 56 (1989): 19–51.

Floud, Jean. "Karl Mannheim." *New Society* 29 (Dec. 1966): 971.

Frank, Tibor. *Double Exile: Migrations of Jewish-Hungarian Professionals through Germany to the United States, 1919–1945*. Oxford: Oxford University Press, 2009.

Franklin, Michael J. *Orientalist Jones*. Oxford: Oxford University Press, 2011.

Freeland, Cynthia. *Art Theory: A Very Short Introduction*. Oxford: Oxford University Press, 2003.

Freyre, Gilberto. *Ingleses*. Rio de Janeiro: Olympio, 1942.

Friedrich, Markus. *Der lange Arm Roms? Globale Verwaltung und Kommunikation im Jesuitenorden, 1540–1773*. Frankfurt: Campus, 2011.

Frye, Richard N. *The Golden Age of Persia*. London: Weidenfeld and Nicolson, 1975.

Fuks, Lajb, and Renata G. Fuks-Mansfeld, *Hebrew Typography in the Northern Netherlands, 1585–1815*. Leiden: Brill, 1984.

Fuks-Mansfield, Renata G. "The Hebrew Book Trade in Amsterdam in the 17th Century." In *Le magasin de l'univers: The Dutch Republic as the Centre of the European Book Trade*, edited by Christiane Berkvens-Stevelinck et al., 155–68. Leiden: Brill, 1992.

Games, Stephen. *Pevsner: The Early Life*. London: Continuum, 2010.

Gaos, José. "La adaptación de un español a la sociedad hispano-americana." *Revista de Occidente* 14 (1966): 168–78.

———. *En torno a la filosofía Mexicana*. Mexico: Alianza, 1980.

Garrett, Christina H. *The Marian Exiles*. Cambridge, 1938.

Geanakoplos, Deno J. *Greek Scholars in Venice*. Cambridge, MA: Harvard University Press, 1962.

Gelder, Roelof van. "Engelbert Kaempfer as a Scientist in the Service of the Dutch East India Company." In *Engelbert Kaempfer: Ein Gelehrtenleben zwischen Tradition und Innovation*, edited by Detlef Haberland, 211–25. Wiesbaden: Harassowitz, 2004.

Geldner, Ferdinand. *Die deutsche Inkunabeldrucker*. 2 vols. Stuttgart: Hiersemann, 1968–70.

Gellner, Ernest. *Words and Things*. London: Gollancz, 1959.

Gelzer, Matthias. *Die Nobilität der römanischen Republik*. Leipzig and Berlin: Teubner, 1912.

Genot-Bismuth, Jacqueline. "L'argument de l'histoire dans la tradition espagnole de polémique judéo-chrétienne." In *From Iberia to Diaspora*, edited by Yedida K. Stillman and Norman A. Stillman, 197–213. Leiden: Brill, 1999.

Gerbi, Antonello. *La disputa del nuovo mondo: Storia di una polemica (1750–1900)*. 2nd ed. Milan: Adelphi, 2000.

Gibbon, Edward. *Decline and Fall of the Roman Empire*, edited by David Womersley. London: Allen Lane, 1994.

Gibbs, Grahame C. "The Role of the Dutch Republic as the Intellectual Entrepôt of Europe in the Seventeenth and Eighteenth Centuries." *Bijdragen en Mededelingen betreffende de Geschiedenis van de Nederlanden* 86 (1971): 323–49.

———. "Some Intellectual and Political Influences of the Huguenot Emigrés in the United Provinces." *Bijdragen en Mededelingen betreffende de Geschiedenis der Nederlanden* 90 (1975): 264–87.

Ginzburg, Carlo. *Wooden Eyes: Nine Reflections on Distance* (1998). English trans. London: Verso, 2002.

González Montero, Marisa. *Lorenzo Hervás y Panduro, el gran olvidado de la Ilustración Española*. Madrid: Iberediciones, 1994.

Gordin, Michael. *Scientific Babel: The Language of Science*. London: Profile Books, 2015.

Gousseff, Cathérine. *L'exil russe: La fabrique du réfugié apatride*. Paris: CNRS, 2008.

Gouzévitch, Irina. "Le transfert des connaissances et les réformes de Pierre I." *Bulletin de la Sabix* 33 (2003): 74–121.

Graham, Richard. "An Interview with Sergio Buarque de Holanda." *Hispanic American Historical Review* 62 (1982): 3–18.

Graham-Yoole, Andrew. "The Wild Oats They Sowed: Latin American Exiles in Europe." *Third World Quarterly* 9 (1987): 246–53.

Gray, Rockwell. "The Spanish Diaspora: A Culture in Exile." *Salmagundi* 77 (1988): 53–83.

Greenberg, Karen J. "Refugee Historians and American Academe." In *An Interrupted Past: German-Speaking Refugee Historians in the United States after 1933*, edited by Hartmut Lehmann and James Sheehan, 94–101.Washington, DC: German Historical Institute, 1991.

Greengrass, Mark, Michael Leslie, and Timothy Raylor, eds. *Samuel*

Hartlib and Universal Reformation. Cambridge: Cambridge University Press, 1994.

Grell, Ole P., Andrew Cunningham, and Jon Arrizabalaga, eds. *Centres of Medical Excellence? Medical Travel and Education in Europe, 1500–1789*. Aldershot: Ashgate, 2010.

Grenville, John. "From Gardener to Professor." In *Out of the Third Reich: Refugee Historians in Post-war Britain*, edited by Peter Alter, 55–72. London: I. B. Tauris, 1998.

Grove, Richard. "The Transfer of Botanical Knowledge between Asia and Europe, 1498–1800." *Journal of the Japan-Netherlands Institute* 3 (1991): 160–76.

Gruen, Erich S. *Diaspora: Jews amidst Greeks and Romans*. Cambridge, MA: Harvard University Press, 2002.

———. "Polybius and Josephus on Rome." In *Polybius and his World*, edited by Bruce Gibson and Thomas Harrison, 255–65. Oxford: Oxford University Press, 2013.

Guasti, Niccolò. "The Exile of the Spanish Jesuits in Italy." In *The Jesuit Suppression in Global Context*, edited by Jeffrey D. Burston and Jonathan Wright, 248–61. Cambridge: Cambridge University Press, 2015.

Guerrier, Vladimir I. *Leibniz in seinen Beziehungen zu Russland und Peter den Grossen*. St. Petersburg: Akademie der Wissenschaften, 1873.

Gutas, Dimitri. *Greek Thought, Arabic Culture: The Graeco-Arabic Translation Movement in Baghdad and Early Abbasid Society*. London: Routledge, 1998.

Haase, Erich. *Einführung in der Literatur der Refuge*. Berlin: Duncker and Humblot, 1959.

Haberland, Detlef. *Engelbert Kaempfer, 1651–1716*. London: British Library, 1996.

Haim, Sylvia G., ed. *Arab Nationalism*. Berkeley: University of California Press, 1962.

Hall, John A. *Ernest Gellner*. London: Verso, 2010.

Hammel, Andrea. "Gender and Migration." In *Intellectual Migration and Cultural Transformation*, edited by Edward Timms and Jon Hughes, 207–18. Vienna and New York: Springer, 2003.

Hansson, Jonas, and Svante Nordin, *Ernst Cassirer: The Swedish Years*. Bern: Peter Lang, 2006.

Hansson, Stina. *"Afsatt på Swensko": 1600-talets tryckta översättningslitteratur*. Göteborg: Litteraturvetenskapliga institutionen vid Göteborgs universitet, 1982.

Harries, Susie. *Nikolaus Pevsner: The Life*. London: Chatto and Windus, 2011.

Harris, Steven T. "Confession-Building, Long-Distance Networks, and the Organization of Jesuit Science." *Early Science and Medicine* 1 (1996): 287–318.

Hartweg, Frédéric. "Die Huguenotten in Deutschland: Eine Minderheit zwischen zwei Kulturen." In *Die Huguenotten, 1685–1985*, edited by Rudolf von Thadden and Michelle Magdelaine, 172–85. Munich: Beck, 1985.

Häseler, Jens. "Les Huguenots traducteurs." In *La vie intellectuelle aux refuges protestants*, edited by Jens Häseler and Antony McKenna, vol. 2, 15–25. 2 vols. Paris: Champion, 1999–2002.

———. "J. H. S. Formey." In *Les grands intermédiaires de la République des Lettres*, edited by Christiane Berkvens-Stevelinck, Hans Bots, and Jens Häseler, 413–34. Paris: Champion, 2005.

Hassler, Gerda. "Teoría lingüística y antropología en las obras de Lorenzo Hervás y Panduro." In *Los jesuitas españoles expulsos*, edited by Manfred Tietz and Dietrich Briesemeister, 379–400. Frankfurt: Vervuert, 2001.

Hay, Denys. *Polydore Vergil: Renaissance Historian and Man of Letters*. Oxford: Clarendon Press, 1952.

Heller, Marvin J. *The Seventeenth-Century Hebrew Book*. 2 vols. Leiden: Brill, 2011.

Heller, Michel. "L'histoire de l'expulsion des personnalités culturelles hors de l'Union Soviétique en 1922." *Cahiers du Monde Russe et Soviétique* 20 (1979): 131–72.

Hennock, Peter. "Myself as Historian." In *Out of the Third Reich: Refugee Historians in Post-war Britain*, edited by Peter Alter, 73–98. London: I. B. Tauris, 1998.

Hermann, Tomáš, and Karel Kleisner. "The Five 'Homes' of Mikhail M. Novikov." *Jahrbuch für Europäische Wissenschaftskultur* 1 (2005): 87–130.

Hervás y Panduro, Lorenzo. *Catalogo delle lingue conosciute*. Cesena: Biasini, 1784.

Higham, John, and Paul Conkin, eds. *New Directions in American Intellectual History*. Baltimore: Johns Hopkins University Press, 1979.

Hobsbawm, Eric J. "The Historians' Group of the Communist Party." In *Rebels and Their Causes: Essays in Honour of A. L. Morton*, edited by Maurice Cornforth, 21–48. London: Lawrence and Wishart, 1978.

———. *Interesting Times: A Twentieth-Century Life*. London: Weidenfeld and Nicolson, 2002.

———. *Nations and Nationalism since 1780*. Cambridge: Cambridge UP, 1990.

Hoch, Paul K. "Institutional versus Intellectual Migrations in the Nucleation of New Scientific Specialities." *Studies in the History and Philosophy of Science* 18 (1987): 481–500.

———. "The Reception of Central European Refugee Physicists." *Annals of Science* 40 (1983): 217–46.

———. "Some Contributions to Physics by German-Jewish Emigrés in Britain and Elsewhere." In *Second Chance: Two Centuries of German-Speaking Jews in the United Kingdom*, edited by Werner E. Mosse, 229–42. Tübingen: Mohr, 1991.

———, and Jennifer Platt. "Migration and the Denationalization of Science." In *Denationalizing Science*, edited by Elizabeth Crawford et al., 133–52. Dordrecht and Boston: Kluwer, 1993.

Hoffmann, Christhard. "The Contribution of German-speaking Jewish Immigrants to British Historiography." In *Second Chance: Two Centuries of German-Speaking Jews in the United Kingdom*, edited by Werner E. Mosse, 153–76. Tübingen: Mohr, 1991.

Hoffmann, Peter. *Gerhard Friedrich Müller (1705–1783): Historiker, Geograph, Archivar im Dienste Russlands*. Frankfurt: Peter Lang, 2005.

Hoftijzer, Paul. "Metropolis of Print: The Amsterdam Book Trade in the Seventeenth Century." In *Urban Achievement in Early Modern Europe*, edited by Patrick O'Brien, 249–65. Cambridge: Cambridge University Press.

Hoppe, Brigitte. "Kaempfer's Forschungen über japanische Pflanzen." In *Engelbert Kaempfer: Ein Gelehrtenleben zwischen Tradition und Innovation*, edited by Detlef Haberland, 125–53. Wiesbaden: Harassowitz, 2004.

Hsia, Florence. *Sojourners in a Strange Land: Jesuits and Their Scientific*

Missions in Late Imperial China. Chicago: University of Chicago Press, 2009.

Hsia, Ronnie Po-chia. *A Jesuit in the Forbidden City*. Oxford: Oxford University Press, 2010.

Hughes, H. Stuart. "Franz Neumann." In *The Intellectual Migration: Europe and America, 1930–1960*, edited by Donald Fleming and Bernard Bailyn, 446–62. Cambridge, MA: Harvard University Press, 1968.

———. *Sea Change: The Migration of Social Thought, 1930–1965*. New York: Harper, 1975.

Hunt, Lynn, Margaret Jacob, and Wijnand Mijnhardt. *The Book That Changed Europe: Picart and Bernard's Religious Ceremonies of the World*. Cambridge, MA: Harvard University Press, 2010.

Hutchison, Ross. *Locke in France, 1688–1734*. Oxford: Voltaire Foundation, 1991.

Israel, Jonathan. *The Dutch Republic: Its Rise, Greatness and Fall, 1477–1806*. Oxford: Oxford University Press, 1995.

———. "Jews and the Stock Exchange" (1990). Rev. version in his *Diasporas within a Diaspora*, 449–88. Leiden: Brill, 2002.

Jackman, Jarrell J., and Carla M. Borden, eds. *The Muses Flee Hitler*. Washington, DC: Smithsonian Press, 1983.

Jackson, Gabriel. *Juan Negrín*. Eastbourne: Sussex Academic Press, 2010.

Jahoda, Marie. "The Migration of Psychoanalysis." In *The Intellectual Migration: Europe and America, 1930–1960*, edited by Donald Fleming and Bernard Bailyn, 371–419. Cambridge, MA: Harvard University Press, 1968.

Jani, Catherine. "The Jesuits' Negotiation of Science between France and China." In *Negotiating Knowledge in Early Modern Empires*, edited by László Kontler et al., 53–78. Basingstoke: Palgrave Macmillan, 2014.

Janssen, Geert H. "The Counter-Reformation of the Refugee." *Journal of Ecclesiastical History* 63 (2012): 671–92.

Jaumann, Herbert. "Der Refuge und der Journalismus um 1700." In *The Berlin Refuge, 1680–1780: Learning and Science in European Context*, edited by Sandra Pott, Martin Mulsow, and Lutz Danneberg, 155–82. Leiden: Brill, 2003.

Jay, Martin. *Permanent Exiles: Essays on the Intellectual Migration from Germany to America*. New York: Columbia University Press, 1986.

Johannesson, Kurt. *The Renaissance of the Goths in Sixteenth-Century Sweden: Johannes and Olaus Magnus as Politicians and Historians* (1982). English trans. Berkeley: University of California Press, 1991.

Johnston, Robert H. *"New Mecca, New Babylon": Paris and the Russian Exiles, 1920–1945*. Kingston and Montreal: Magill University Press, 1988.

Kaempfer, Engelbert. *History of Japan*. London: Woodward, 1727.

Kamen, Henry. *The Disinherited: The Exiles Who Created Spanish Culture.* London: Allen Lane, 2007.

———. "The Mediterranean and the Expulsion of the Spanish Jews in 1492." *Past and Present* 119 (1988): 30–55.

Kämmerer, Jürgen. *Russland und die Huguenotten im 18. Jahrhundert.* Wiesbaden: Harrassowitz, 1978.

Kaplan, Yosef. "Between Yitzhak Baer and Claudio Sánchez Albornoz: The Rift That Never Healed." In *Jewish Culture in Early Modern Europe*, edited by Richard I. Cohen et al., 356–68. Pittsburgh: University of Pittsburgh Press, 2014.

———. "La Jérusalem du Nord." In *Les Juifs d'Espagne: Histoire d'une disaspora, 1492–1992*, edited by Henry Méchoulan, 191–209. Paris: Lévi, 1992.

———. "The Portuguese Community in Seventeenth-Century Amsterdam and the Ashkenazi World." In *Dutch Jewish History*, edited by Jozeph Michman, vol. 2, 23–45. Jerusalem: Hebrew University, 1989.

Kaufmann, Walter. "The Reception of Existentialism in the United States." In *The Legacy of the German Refugee Intellectuals*, edited by Robert Boyers, 69–96. New York: Schocken, 1972.

Keene, Donald. *The Japanese Discovery of Europe, 1720–1830* (1952). Rev. ed. Stanford: Stanford University Press, 1969.

Kettler, David. "Negotiating Exile: Franz L. Neumann as Political Scientist." In *Der Eigensinn des Materials*, edited by Caroline Arni, 205–24. Frankfurt: Stroemfeld, 2007.

———, Colin Loader, and Völker Meja. *Karl Mannheim and the Legacy of Max Weber*. Aldershot: Ashgate, 2008.

———, and Volker Meja. *Karl Mannheim and the Crisis of Liberalism.* New Brunswick: Rutgers University Press, 1995.

Killinger, Charles. *Gaetano Salvemini*. Westport, CT: Praeger, 2002.

Klor de Alva, Jorge. "Sahagún and the Birth of Modern Ethnography." In *The Work of Bernardino de Sahagún*, edited by Klor de Alva, Henry B. Nicholson, and Eloise G. Keber, 31–52. Austin: University of Texas Press, 1988.

Koenigsberger, Helmut. "Fragments of an Unwritten Biography." In *Out of the Third Reich: Refugee Historians in Post-war Britain*, edited by Peter Alter, 99–118. London: I. B. Tauris, 1998.

Kołakowski, Leszek. "In Praise of Exile" (1985). Repr. in his *Modernity on Endless Trial*, 55–59. Chicago: University of Chicago Press, 1990.

Konuk, Kader. "Jewish-German Philologists in Turkish Exile: Leo Spitzer and Erich Auerbach." In *Exile and Otherness: New Approaches to the Experience of the Nazi Refugees*, edited by Alexander Stephan, 31–47. Oxford: Oxford University Press, 2005.

Kornicki, Peter. "European Japanology at the End of the Seventeenth Century." *Bulletin of the School of Oriental and African Studies* 56 (1993): 502–24.

Kostylo, Joanna. *Medicine and Dissent in Reformation Europe*. Oxford: Oxford University Press, 2015.

Kracht, Klaus G. *Zwischen Berlin und Paris: Bernhard Groethuysen (1880–1946)*. Tübingen: Niemeyer, 2002.

Kramer, Lloyd S. *Threshold of a New World: Intellectuals and the Exile Experience in Paris, 1830–1848*. Ithaca: Cornell University Press, 1988.

Kutter, Markus. *Celio Secondo Curione*. Basel: Helbing and Lichtenhahn, 1955.

Labourt, Jérôme. *Le christianisme dans l'empire perse*. Paris: Lecoffre, 1904.

Labrousse, Elisabeth. *Bayle*. Oxford: Oxford University Press, 1983.

———. *Pierre Bayle*. 2 vols. The Hague: Nijhoff, 1963–64.

Lach, Donald F., and Edwin J. Van Kley. *Asia in the Making of Europe*, vol. 3. Chicago: University of Chicago Press, 1993.

Laguerre, Michel S. "The Tranglobal Network Nation: Diaspora, Homeland and Hostland." In *Transnationalism: Diasporas and the Advent of A New (Dis)Order*, edited by Eliezer Ben-Rafael and Yitzhak Sternberg, 195–210. Leiden: Brill, 2009.

Lamb, Ursula. *Cosmographers and Pilots of the Spanish Maritime Empire*. Aldershot: Variorum, 1995.

Lambley, Katherine R. *The Teaching of French in England during Tudor and Stuart Times*. Manchester: Manchester University Press, 1920.

Landry-Deron, Isabelle. *La preuve par la Chine: La "description" de J.-B. Du Halde*. Paris: éditions EHESS, 2002.

Larraz Elorriaga, Fernando. "Los exiliados y las colecciones editorials en Argentina, 1938–54." In *El exilio republican español en México y Argentina*, edited by Andrea Pagni, 129–44. Madrid: Iberoamericana, 2011.

Laslett, Peter. "Karl Mannheim in 1939: A Student's Recollection." *Revue Européenne des Sciences Sociales et Cahiers Vilfredo Pareto* 17 (1979): 223–26.

Latour, Bruno. *Science in Action*. Cambridge, MA: Harvard University Press, 1987.

Lauer, Reinhard. "Schlözer und die Slaven." In *August Ludwig (von) Schlözer in Europa*, edited by Heinz Duchhardt and Martin Espenhorst, 23–40. Göttingen: Vandenhoeck und Rupprecht, 2012.

Laven, Mary. *Mission to China: Matteo Ricci and the Encounter with the East*. London: Faber, 2011.

Lazarsfeld, Paul. "An Episode in the History of Social Research." In *The Intellectual Migration: Europe and America, 1930–1960*, edited by Donald Fleming and Bernard Bailyn, 270–334. Cambridge, MA: Harvard University Press, 1968.

Lefebvre, Jean-Paul. "Les professeurs français des missions universitaires au Brésil (1934–44)." *Cahiers du Brésil Contemporain* 12 (1990): 1–10. www.revues.msh-paris.fr/ . . . /8-J.P%20Lefebvre.pdf.

Lennon, Colm. *Richard Stanihurst the Dubliner, 1547–1618*. Dublin: Irish Academic Press, 1981.

León-Portilla, Miguel. *Bernardino de Sahagún: Pionero de la antropología*. Mexico City: UNAM, 1999.

Lévi-Strauss, Claude. *Le regard éloigné*. Paris: Plon, 1983.

———. *Tristes Tropiques*. Paris: Plon, 1955.

Levy, Avigdor. *The Sephardim in the Ottoman Empire*. Princeton: Darwin Press, 1992.

Linden, David van der. *Experiencing Exile: Huguenot Refugees in the Dutch Republic, 1680–1700*. Farnham: Ashgate, 2015.

Linehan, Peter. *History and the Historians of Medieval Spain*. Oxford: Clarendon Press, 1993.

Livingstone, Rodney. "The Contribution of German-Speaking Jewish Refugees to German Studies in Britain." In *Second Chance: Two*

Centuries of German-Speaking Jews in the United Kingdom, edited by Werner E. Mosse, 137–52. Tübingen: Mohr, 1991.

Loader, Colin. *The Intellectual Development of Karl Mannheim*. Cambridge: Cambridge University Press, 1985.

Loewenberg, Gerhard. "The Influence of European Émigré Scholars on Comparative Politics, 1925–1965." *American Political Science Review* 100 (2006): 597–604.

López Sánchez, José María. "El exilio científico republicano en México." In *La destrucción de la ciencia en España*, edited by Luis Enrique Otero Carvajal, 177–239. Madrid: Complutense, 2006.

Lorenzen, David N. *Who Invented Hinduism?* New Delhi: Yoda Press, 2006.

Lowenthal, David. *The Past is a Foreign Country* (1985). Rev. ed. Cambridge: Cambridge University Press, 2015.

Lubac, Henri de. *La rencontre du Bouddhisme et de l'occident*. Paris: Aubier, 1952.

Lucassen, Jan, and Leo Lucassen, eds. *Migration, Migration History, History: Old Paradigms and New Perspectives*. Bern: Peter Lang, 1997.

Lyon, E. Stina. "Karl Mannheim and Viola Klein." In *In Defence of Learning: The Plight, Persecution and Placement of Academic Refugees, 1933–1980s*, edited by Shula Marks, Paul Weindling, and Laura Wintour, 177–90. Oxford: Oxford University Press, 2011.

Mancebo, María Fernanda. *La España de los exilios*. Valencia: Universitat de València, 2008.

Mandelbrote, Scott. "Pierre des Maizeaux: History, Toleration and Scholarship." In *History of Scholarship*, edited by Christopher R. Ligota and J.-L. Quantin, 385–98. Oxford: Oxford University Press, 2006.

Mandler, Jean M., and George Mandler, "The Diaspora of Experimental Psychology." In *The Intellectual Migration: Europe and America, 1930–1960*, edited by Donald Fleming and Bernard Bailyn, 371–419. Cambridge, MA: Harvard University Press, 1968.

Mann, Nicholas. "*Translatio Studii*: Warburgian *Kunstwissenschaft* in London, 1933–45." In *The Migration of Ideas*, edited by Roberto Scazzieri and Raffaella Simili, 151–60. Sagamore Beach, MA: Science History Publications, 2008.

Mannheim, Karl. *Correspondence*, edited by Éva Gábor. Lewiston, NY: Edwin Mellen Press, 2003.

———. *Essays on Sociology and Social Psychology*. London: Routledge, 1953.

———. "The Function of the Refugee." *New English Weekly*, 19 April 1945.

———. *Ideology and Utopia* (1929). English trans. London: Routledge, 1936.

———. "The Problem of a Sociology of Knowledge." Trans. in his *Essays in the Sociology of Knowledge*, 134–90. London: Routledge, 1952.

Marino, John. "The Exile and His Kingdom: The Reception of Braudel's *Mediterranean*." *Journal of Modern History* 75 (2004): 622–52.

Marks, Shula. "South African Refugees in the UK." In *In Defence of Learning: The Plight, Persecution and Placement of Academic Refugees, 1933–1980s*, edited by Shula Marks, Paul Weindling, and Laura Wintour, 257–79. Oxford: Oxford University Press, 2011.

Marrus, Michael. *The Unwanted: European Refugees in the 20th Century*. New York: Oxford University Press, 1985.

Marshall, Peter J., ed. *The British Discovery of Hinduism in the Eighteenth Century*. Cambridge: Cambridge University Press, 1970.

Massarella, Derek. "Epilogue: Inquisitive and Intelligent Men." In *The Furthest Goal: Engelbert Kaempfer's Encounter with Tokugawa Japan*, edited by Beatrice Bodart-Bailey and Derek Massarella, 152–64. Folkestone: Japan Library, 1995.

Massil, Stephen W. "Huguenot Librarians and Some Others." *World Library and Information Congress*, 2003. webdoc.sub.gwdg.de/ebook/aw/2003/ifla/vortraege/ . . . /058e-Massil.pdf.

Masterson, James R., and Helen Browe, *Bering's Successors, 1745–1780: Contributions of Peter Simon Pallas to the History of Russian Exploration toward Alaska*. Seattle: University of Washington Press, 1948.

Mazower, Mark. *Salonica, City of Ghosts: Christians, Muslims and Jews, 1430–1950*. London: HarperCollins, 2004.

McEwan, Dorothea. "Mapping the Trade Routes of the Mind: the Warburg Institute." In *Intellectual Migration and Cultural Transformation*, edited by Edward Timms and Jon Hughes, 37–50. Vienna and New York: Springer, 2003.

Meier, Johannes. "Los jesuitas expulsados de Chile." In *Los jesuitas españoles expulsos*, edited by Manfred Tietz and Dietrich Briesemeister, 423–41. Frankfurt: Vervuert, 2001.

Mennell, Stephen. *Norbert Elias*. Oxford: Blackwell, 1989.

Merton, Robert K. "The Matthew Effect in Science." *Science* 159 (1968): 56–63.

Michels, Karen. *Transplantierte Wisssenschaft: Der Wandel einer Disziplin als Folge der Emigration deutschsprachiger Kunsthistoriker in die USA*. Berlin: Akademie Verlag, 1999.

Mil, Patrick van, ed. *De VOC in de kaart gekeken, 1602–1799*. The Hague: SDU, 1988.

Miller, Edward. *Prince of Librarians: The Life and Times of Antonio Panizzi of the British Museum*. London: Deutsch, 1967.

Miller, Peter, ed. *Momigliano and Antiquarianism: Foundations of the Modern Cultural Sciences*. Toronto: University of Toronto Press, 2007.

Moldavsky, Aliocha. "The Problematic Acquisition of Indigenous Languages." In *The Jesuits, II: Cultures, Sciences and the Arts, 1540–1773*, edited by John O'Malley et al., 602–15. Toronto: University of Toronto Press, 2006.

Molho, Anthony. "Hans Baron's Crisis." In *Florence and Beyond*, edited by David S. Peterson and Daniel E. Bornstein, 61–90. Toronto: University of Toronto Press, 2008.

Momigliano, Arnaldo. "Ancient History and the Antiquarian" (1950). Repr. in *Studies in Historiography*, 1–39. London: Weidenfeld and Nicolson, 1966.

Moraes Ferreira, Marieta de. "Les professeurs français et l'enseignement de l'histoire à Rio de Janeiro pendant les années 1930." In *Pour l'histoire du Brésil*, edited by François Crouzet, Philippe Bonichon, and Denis Rolland, 123–40. Paris: L'Harmattan, 2000.

Mosse, Werner E., ed. *Second Chance: Two Centuries of German-Speaking Jews in the United Kingdom*. Tübingen: Mohr, 1991.

Motta, Roberto. "L'apport brésilien dans l'oeuvre de Roger Bastide." In *Roger Bastide ou le réjouissement de l'abîme*, edited by Philippe Laburthe-Tolra, 169–78. Paris: L'Harmattan, 1994.

Mowl, Tim. *Stylistic Cold Wars: Betjeman versus Pevsner*. London: John Murray, 2000.

Mühlpfordt, Günther. "Schlözer als Begründer der kritisch-ethnischen Geschichtsforschung." *Jahrbuch für Geschichte* 25 (1982): 23–72.

Mulkay, Michael. "Conceptual Displacement and Migration in Science." *Science Studies* 4 (1974): 205–34.

Müller, Hildegard. "German Librarians in Exile in Turkey." *Libraries and Culture* 33 (1998): 294–305.

Mulsow, Martin. "Views of the Berlin Refuge." In *The Berlin Refuge, 1680–1780: Learning and Science in European Context*, edited by Sandra Pott, Martin Mulsow, and Lutz Danneberg, 25–46. Leiden: Brill, 2003.

Muntschick, Wolfgang. "The Plants That Carry His Name: Kaempfer's Study of the Japanese Flora." In *The Furthest Goal: Engelbert Kaempfer's Encounter with Tokugawa Japan*, edited by Beatrice Bodart-Bailey and Derek Massarella, 71–95. Folkestone: Japan Library, 1995.

Murillo Rubiera, Fernando. *Andrés Bello*. Caracas: la Casa de Bello, 1986.

Murr, Sylvia. *L'Inde philosophique entre Bossuet et Voltaire*. 2 vols. Paris: École Français d'Extrême-Orient, 1987.

Namier, Lewis. "The Biography of Ordinary Men," (1928). Repr. in *Crossroads of Power*, 1–6. London: Hamish Hamilton, 1961.

———. *The Structure of Politics at the Accession of George III*. London: Macmillan, 1929.

Nasr, Seyyed Hossein. "Life Sciences, Alchemy and Medicine." In *The Cambridge History of Iran*, vol. 4, edited by Richard N. Frye, 396–418. Cambridge: Cambridge University Press, 1975.

Netanyahu, Benzion. *Don Isaac Abravanel, Statesman and Philosopher* (1953). 2nd ed. Philadelphia: Jewish Publication Society of America, 1968.

Neumann, Franz. "The Social Sciences." In *The Cultural Migration: The European Scholar in America*, edited by Franz Neumann, 4–26. Philadelphia: University of Pennsylvania Press, 1953.

Nicholson, Henry B. "Fray Bernardino de Sahagun." In *Representing Aztec Ritual*, edited by Eloise Q. Keber, 21–39. Boulder: University of Colorado Press, 2002.

Nicolazzi, Fernando. *Um estilo de história*. São Paulo: UNESP, 2015.

Niggemann, Ulrich. *Immigrationspolitik zwischen Konflikt und Konsens: Die Huguenotten Siedlung in Deutschland und England, 1681–1697*. Cologne: Böhlau, 2008.

Nordenstam, Bertil, ed. *Carl Peter Thunberg: Linnean, resenäre, Naturforskare, 1743–1828*. Stockholm: Atlantis, 1993.

Nusteling, Hubert. "The Netherlands and the Huguenot Émigrés." In *La Révocation de l'Édit de Nantes et les Provinces-Unies, 1685*, edited by Hans Bots and G. H. M. Posthumus Meyjes, 26–30. Amsterdam: APA-Holland University Press, 1986.

Oberman, Heiko. "*Europa Afflicta*: the Reformation of the Refugees." *Archiv für Reformationsgeschichte* 83 (1992): 91–111.

Oddie, Geoffrey A. "Constructing 'Hinduism': The Impact of the Protestant Missionary Movement on Hindu Self-Understanding." In *Christians and Missionaries in India*, edited by Robert E. Frykenberg, 155–82. London: RoutledgeCurzon, 2003.

———. *Imagined Hinduism: British Protestant Missionary Constructions of Hinduism, 1793–1900*. London: Sage, 2006.

Ortiz, Fernando. *Contrapunteo Cubano*. Havana: Montero, 1940.

Otero, Luis Enrique, ed. *La destrucción de la ciencia en España*. Madrid: Complutense, 2006.

Pagden, Anthony. *The Fall of Natural Man: The American Indian and the Origins of Comparative Ethnology*. Cambridge: Cambridge University Press, 1982.

Page, Scott. *The Difference: How the Power of Diversity Creates Better Groups, Firms, Schools and Societies*. Princeton: Princeton University Press, 2007.

Pagni, Andrea, ed. *El exilio republicano español en México y Argentina*. Madrid: Iberoamericana, 2011.

Pallares-Burke, Maria Lúcia G. Interview with Zygmunt Bauman. *Tempo Social* 16 (2004): 301–25.

———. *O triunfo do fracasso: Rudiger Bilden, o amigo esquecido de Gilberto Freyre*. São Paulo: UNESP, 2012.

Panofsky, Erwin. "In Defense of the Ivory Tower." *Centennial Review* 1 (1957): 111–12.

———. "The History of Art." In *The Cultural Migration: The European Scholar in America*, edited by Franz Neumann, 82–111. Philadelphia: University of Pennsylvania Press, 1953.

———. *Meaning in the Visual Arts*. New York: Doubleday, 1955.

Paris, Erato. *La genèse intellectuelle de l'oeuvre de Fernand Braudel*. Athens: Institut de Recherches Néo-Helléniques, 1999.

Park, Robert E. "Human Migration and the Marginal Man." *American Journal of Sociology* 33 (1928): 881–93.

Parry, Graham. *The Trophies of Time: English Antiquarians of the Seventeenth Century*. Oxford: Oxford University Press, 1995.

Paternicò, Luisa Maria. *When the Europeans Began to Study Chinese: Martino Martini's Grammatica Linguae Sinensis*. Leuven: Ferdinand Verbiest Institute, 2013.

Paulus, Paul B., and Bernard A. Nijstad, eds. *Group Creativity: Innovation through Collaboration*. Oxford: Oxford University Press, 2003.

Pennec, Hervé. "Missionary Knowledge in Context: Geographical Knowledge of Ethiopia." In *Written Culture in a Colonial Context*, edited by Adrian Delmas and Nigel Penn, 75–96. Leiden: Brill, 2012.

Pereira de Queiroz, Maria Isaura. "La recherche géographique au Brésil." In *Pierre Monbeig*, edited by Hervé Théry and Martine Droulers, 59–64. Paris: Institut des hautes études de l'Amérique latine, 1991.

Perini, Leandro. *La vita e tempi di Pietro Perna*. Rome: Edizioni di Storia e Letteratura, 2002.

Petech, Luciano, ed. *I missionari italiani nel Tibet e nel Nepal*, part 6. Rome: Istituto Poligrafico dello Stato, 1955.

Peters, Martin. *Altes Reich und Europa: Der Historiker, Statistiker und Publizist August Ludwig (v.) Schlözer (1735–1809)*. Münster: LIT, 2005.

Pflanze, Otto P. "The Americanization of Hajo Holborn." In *An Interrupted Past: German-Speaking Refugee Historians in the United States after 1933*, edited by Hartmut Lehmann and James Sheehan, 170–79. Washington, DC: German Historical Institute, 1991.

Phillips, Mark S. *On Historical Distance*. New Haven: Yale University Press, 2013.

Pickus, David. "At Home with Nietzsche, at War with Germany: Walter Kaufmann and the Struggles of Nietzsche Interpretation." In *The Fruits of Exile*, edited by Richard Bodek and Simon Lewis, 156–76. Columbia: University of South Carolina Press, 2010.

Pinedo, Javier. "El exílio de los jesuitas latinoamericanos: un creativo dolor." In *La patria interrumpida: Latinoamericanos en ex exílio. Siglos XVIII-XX*, edited by Carlos Sanhueza and Javier Pinedo, 35–57. Santiago: Universidad de Talca, 2010.

Pizzorusso, Giovanni. "La Congrégation De Propaganda Fide: Centre d'accumulation et de production des 'savoirs missionaires.'" In *Missions d'évangélisation et circulation des savoirs: XVIe-XVIIIe siècle*, edited by Charlotte de Castelnau-L'Estoile, 25–40. Madrid: Casa de Velázquez, 2011.

Platt, Jennifer. "Some Issues in Intellectual Method and Approach." In

Intellectual Migration and Cultural Transformation, edited by Edward Timms and Jon Hughes, 7–20. Vienna and New York: Springer, 2003.

Plutarch. "On Exile." In his *Moralia*, vol. 7, 519–71. London: Heinemann, 1959.

Polanyi, Michael. *Personal Knowledge*. London: Routledge, 1958.

Portuondo, Maria M. *Secret Science: Spanish Cosmography and the New World*. Chicago: University of Chicago Press, 2009.

Prieto, Andrés I. *Missionary Scientists: Jesuit Science in Spanish South America, 1570–1810*. Nashville: Vanderbilt University Press, 2011.

Prochnik, George. *The Impossible Exile: Stefan Zweig at the End of the World*. New York: Other Press, 2014.

Prosperi, Adriano. "'Otras *Indias*': Missionari della contrarriforma tra contadini e selvaggi." In *Scienze, credenze occulte, livelli di cultura*, edited by Paola Zambelli, 205–34. Florence: Olschki, 1982.

Raeff, Marc. *Russia Abroad: A Cultural History of the Russian Emigration*. New York: Oxford University Press, 1990.

Raj, Kapil. "Beyond Postcolonialism." *Isis* 104 (2013): 337–47.

———. "Dynamiques urbaines et savants à Calcutta (XVIIIe siècle)." *Revue d'Histoire Moderne et Contemporaine* 55 (2008): 70–99.

———. *Relocating Modern Science: Circulation and the Construction of Knowledge in South Asia and Europe, 1650–1900*. Basingstoke: Ashgate, 2007.

———. "Surgeons, Fakirs, Merchants and Craftspeople." In *Colonial Botany*, edited by Londa Schiebinger and Claudia Swan, 252–69. Philadelphia: University of Pennsylvania Press, 2005.

Rapin-Thoyras, Paul de. *Histoire de l'Angleterre* (1723). New ed., 4 vols. Basel: Brandmuller, 1740.

Raven, Diederick, and Wolfgang Krohn, "Edgar Zilsel: His Life and Work." Introduction to Zilsel, *The Social Origins of Modern Science*. Dordrecht: Kluwer, 2000.

Ray, Jonathan. *After Expulsion: 1492 and the Making of Sephardic Jewry*. New York: New York University Press, 2013.

Reid, Donald M. *The Odyssey of Farah Antun*. Minneapolis and Chicago: Bibliotheca Islamica, 1975.

Reinhartz, Dennis. "In the Service of Catherine the Great: The Siberian Explorations and Map of Sir Samuel Bentham." *Terrae Incognitae* 26 (1994): 49–60.

Reuter, Astrid. *Das Wilde Heilige: Roger Bastide (1898–1974) und die Religionswissenschaft seiner Zeit*. Frankfurt: Campus, 2000.

Riasanovsky, Nikolai. "The Norman Theory of the Origin of the Russian State." *Russian Review* 7 (1947): 96–110.

Ribeiro, Darcy. "Gilberto Freyre: uma introdução a *Casa Grande e Senzala*" (1977). Repr. in *Casa Grande e Senzala: Edição Crítica*, edited by Guillermo Giucci, Enrique Larreta, and Edson Nery de Fonseca, 1026–37. Nanterre: Allca XX, 2002.

Rietbergen, Peter. "VOC Travelogues." In *Transformations of Knowledge in Dutch Expansion*, edited by Susanne Friedrich, Arndt Brendecke, and Stefan Ehrenpreis, 231–49. Berlin: De Gruyter, 2015.

Río, Angel del. *The Clash and Attraction of Two Cultures*. English trans. Baton Rouge: Louisiana State University Press, 1965.

Roberts, Lissa. "Re-Orienting the Transformation of Knowledge in Dutch Expansion: Nagasaki as a Centre of Accumulation and Management." In *Transformations of Knowledge in Dutch Expansion*, edited by Susanne Friedrich, Arndt Brendecke, and Stefan Ehrenpreis, 19–42. Berlin: De Gruyter, 2015.

Robinson, Eric. "The Transference of British Technology to Russia, 1760–1820." In *Great Britain and Her World*, edited by Barrie M. Ratcliffe, 1–26. Manchester: Manchester University Press, 1975.

Rocher, Rosane. *Orientalism, Poetry and the Millennium*. Delhi: Banarsidess, 1983.

Rogge, Wolfgang, ed. *Theodor W. Adorno und Ernst Krenek, Briefwechsel*. Frankfurt: Suhrkampf, 1974.

Romano, Antonella. "Les jésuites entre apostolat missionaire et activité scientifique." *Archivum Historicum Societatis Jesu* 74 (2005): 213–36.

Rubiés, Joan Pau. "The Jesuit Discovery of Hinduism." *Archiv für Religionsgeschichte* 3 (2001): 210–56.

———. "Reassessing 'the Discovery of Hinduism': Jesuit Discourse on Gentile Idolatry and the European Republic of Letters." In *Intercultural Encounter and the Jesuit Mission in South Asia (16th–18th Centuries)*, edited by Anand Amaladass and Ines G. Županov, 113–55. Bangalore: ATC, 2014.

———. *Travel and Ethnology in the Renaissance: South India through European Eyes, 1250–1625*. Cambridge: Cambridge University Press, 2000.

Rubinstein, Nicolai. "Germany, Italy and England." In *Out of the Third Reich: Refugee Historians in Post-War Britain*, edited by Peter Alter, 237–46. London: I. B. Tauris, 1998.

Rubinstein, Nina. *Die französische Emigration nach 1789: Ein Beitrag zur Soziologie der politischen Emigration*. Graz: Nausner and Nausner, 2000.

Rucquoi, Adeline. "Spanish Medieval History and the *Annales*." In *The Work of Jacques Le Goff*, edited by Miri Rubin, 123–41. Woodbridge: Boydell Press, 1997.

Rumbold, Margaret E. *Traducteur huguenot: Pierre Coste*. New York: Lang, 1991.

Russell, Peter. "The Nessus-Shirt of Spanish History." *Bulletin of Hispanic Studies* 36 (1959): 219–25.

Said, Edward W. *Out of Place: A Memoir*. London: Granta, 2000.

———. "Reflections on Exile" (1984). Repr. in his *Reflections on Exile*, 173–86. London: Granta, 2001.

———. *Representations of the Intellectual*. London: Vintage, 1994.

Sánchez Vázquez, Adolfo. *Del exilio en Mexico*. Mexico City: Grijalbo, 1991.

———. *Rousseau en México*. Mexico City: Grijalbo, 1967.

Sandman, Alison. "Controlling Knowledge: Navigation, Cartography and Secrecy in the Early Modern Spanish Atlantic." In *Science and Empire in the Atlantic World*, edited by James Delbourgo and Nicholas Dew, 31–51. New York: Routledge, 2008.

Sarton, George. *Galen of Pergamon*. Lawrence: University of Kansas Press, 1954.

Scheuerman, William E. "Professor Kelsen's Amazing Disappearing Act." In *Émigré Scholars and the Genesis of International Relations*, edited by Felix Rösch, 81–102. Basingstoke: Ashgate, 2014.

Schilder, Günther. "Organization and Evolution of the Dutch East India Company's Hydrographic Office," *Imago Mundi* 28 (1976): 61–78.

Schilling, Heinz. "Innovation through Migration: The Settlements of Calvinistic Netherlanders in Sixteenth- and Seventeenth-Century Central and Western Europe." *Histoire Sociale — Social History* 16 (1983): 7–34.

———. *Niederländische Exulanten im 16. Jahrhundert*. Gütersloh: Mohn, 1972.

Schmidt, James. "*The Eclipse of Reason* and the End of the Frankfurt School in America." In *The Fruits of Exile*, edited by Richard Bodek and Simon Lewis, 1–28. Columbia: University of South Carolina Press, 2010.

Schön, Donald A. *Displacement of Concepts*. London: Tavistock, 1963.

Schulze, Ludmilla. "The Russification of the St Petersburg Academy of Sciences and Arts in the Eighteenth Century." *British Journal for the History of Science* 18 (1985): 305–35.

Scoville, Warren C. *The Persecution of Huguenots and French Economic Development, 1680–1720*. Berkeley: University of California Press, 1960.

Sgard, Jean, ed. *Dictionnaire des journalistes, 1600–1789*. Oxford: Voltaire Foundation, 1999.

Shaw, Denis J. B. "Geographical Practice and its Significance in Peter the Great's Russia." *Journal of Historical Geography* 22 (1996): 160–76.

Sheppard, Eugene R. *Leo Strauss and the Politics of Exile: The Making of a Political Philosopher*. Hanover, NH: University Press of New England, 2006.

Shils, Edward. "The Calling of Sociology." In *Theories of Society*, edited by Talcott Parsons et al., 1405–50. New York: Free Press, 1961.

Simmel, Georg. "The Stranger." In *Social Theory*, edited by Charles Lemert, 184–89. Boulder, CO: Westview Press, 1999.

Singh, Anjana. "Botanical Knowledge in Early Modern Malabar and the Netherlands." In *Transformations of Knowledge in Dutch Expansion*, edited by Susanne Friedrich, Arndt Brendecke, and Stefan Ehrenpreis, 187–208. Berlin: De Gruyter, 2015.

Skidmore, Thomas. "Lévi-Strauss, Braudel and Brazil: A Case of Mutual Influence." *Bulletin of Latin American Research* 22 (2003): 340–49.

Sládek, Zdeněk. "Prag: Das 'russische Oxford.'" In *Der Grosse Exodus*, edited by Karl Schlögel, 218–33. Munich: Beck, 1994.

Smith, Woodruff D. "Amsterdam as an Information Exchange in the Seventeenth Century." *Journal of Economic History* 44 (1984): 985–1005.

Snowman, Daniel. *The Hitler Emigrés: The Cultural Impact on Britain of Refugees from Nazism*. London: Chatto and Windus, 2002.

Söllner, Alfons. "From International Law to International Relations: Émigré Scholars in American Political Science and International

Relations." In *Émigré Scholars and the Genesis of International Relations*, edited by Felix Rösch, 197–211. Basingstoke: Ashgate, 2014.

———. "In Transit to America: Political Scientists from Germany in Great Britain." In *Second Chance: Two Centuries of German-Speaking Jews in the United Kingdom*, edited by Werner Mosse, 121–36. Tübingen: Mohr, 1991.

———. "Von Staatsrecht zur 'political science' — die Emigration deutscher Wissenschaftler nach 1933, ihr Einfluss auf die Transformation einer Disziplin." In *Die Emigration der Wissenschaften nach 1933*, edited by Herbert A. Strauss et al., 137–64. Munich: Saur, 1991.

Soyer, François. *The Persecution of the Jews and Muslims of Portugal.* Leiden: Brill, 2007.

Spence, Jonathan. *The Memory Palace of Matteo Ricci*. London: Faber, 1985.

Spitzer, Leo. "Answer to Mr Bloomfield." *Language* 20 (1944): 245–51.

Spivey, Nigel. *Phaidon, 1923–98*. London: Phaidon, 1999.

Sprat, Thomas. *History of the Royal Society*, edited by Jackson I. Cope and Harold W. Jones. London: Routledge, 1958.

Stadler, Friedrich K. "Transfer and Transformation of Logical Empiricism." In *Logical Empiricism in North America*, edited by Gary L. Hardcastle and Alan W. Richardson, 216–33. Minneapolis: University of Minnesota Press, 2003.

Stagl, Justin. *A History of Curiosity*. London: Routledge, 1995.

Stanley, John D. "Joachim Lelewel." In *Nation and History*, edited by Peter Brock et al., 52–84. Toronto: University of Toronto Press, 2006.

Steensgaard, Nils. "The Dutch East India Company as an Institutional Innovation." In *Dutch Capitalism and World Capitalism*, edited by Maurice Aymard, 235–57. Cambridge: Cambridge University Press, 1982.

Stejneger, Leonhard. *Georg Wilhelm Steller: The Pioneer of Alaskan Natural History*. Cambridge, MA: Harvard University Press, 1936.

Stern, Fritz. *Five Germanies I Have Known*. Wassenaar: NIAS, 1998.

Stipa, Günter Johannes. *Finnisch-Ugrische Sprachforschung von der Renaissance bis zum Neupositivismus*. Helsinki: Suomalais-Ugrilainen Seura, 1990.

Stirk, Peter. "International Law, Émigrés and the Foundation of

International Relations." In *Émigré Scholars and the Genesis of International Relations*, edited by Felix Rösch, 61–80. Basingstoke: Palgrave Macmillan, 2014.

Strauss, Herbert A. "Wissenschaftsemigration als Forschungsproblem." In *Die Emigration der Wissenschaften nach 1933*, edited by Strauss et al., 7–24. Munich: Saur, 1991.

Strauss, Herbert A., et al., eds. *Die Emigration der Wissenschaften nach 1933*. Munich: Saur, 1991.

Sweetman, Will. *Mapping Hinduism: "Hinduism" and the Study of Indian Religions, 1600–1776*. Halle: Franckeschen Stiftungen, 2003.

Swindlehurst, Catherine. "'An unruly and presumptuous rabble': The Reaction of the Spitalfields Weaving Community to the Settlement of the Huguenots, 1660–90." In *From Strangers to Citizens*, edited by Randolph Vigne and Charles Littleton, 366–74. Brighton: Sussex Academic Press, 2001.

Szilard, Leo. "Reminiscences." In *The Intellectual Migration: Europe and America, 1930–1960*, edited by Donald Fleming and Bernard Bailyn, 94–151. Cambridge, MA: Harvard University Press, 1968.

Sznajder, Mario, and Luis Roniger. *The Politics of Exile in Latin America*. Cambridge: Cambridge University Press, 2009.

Tedeschi, John. "Italian Reformers and the Diffusion of Renaissance Culture." *Sixteenth-Century Journal* 5 (1974): 79–94.

Telman, Jeremy. "Selective Affinities." In *The Fruits of Exile*, edited by Richard Bodek and Simon Lewis, 40–58. Columbia: University of South Carolina Press, 2010.

Terpstra, Nicholas. *Religious Refugees in the Early Modern World*. Cambridge: Cambridge University Press, 2015.

Thackray, Arnold, and Robert Merton. "On Discipline Building: The Paradoxes of George Sarton." *Isis* 63 (1972): 472–95.

Tietz, Manfred, and Dietrich Briesemeister, eds. *Los jesuitas españoles expulsos*. Frankfurt: Vervuert, 2001.

Tihanov, Galin. "Russian Emigré Literary Criticism and Theory between the World Wars." In *A History of Russian Literary Theory and Criticism*, edited by Evgeny Dobrenko and Galin Tihanov, 144–62. Pittsburgh: University of Pittsburgh Press, 2011.

Tillich, Paul. "The Conquest of Theological Provincialism." In *The Cultural Migration: The European Scholar in America*, edited by Franz

Neumann, 138–56. Philadelphia: University of Pennsylvania Press, 1953.

Timms, Edward, and Jon Hughes, eds. *Intellectual Migration and Cultural Transformation: Refugees from National Socialism in the English-Speaking World.* Vienna: Springer, 2003.

Tocqueville, Alexis de. *De la démocratie en Amérique* (1835–40), edited by Eduardo Nolla, vol. 1. Paris: Vrin, 1990.

Törnqvist, Gunnar. "Creativity and the Renewal of Regional Life." In *Creativity and Context*, edited by Anne Buttimer, 91–112. Lund: University of Lund, 1983.

Tóth, Heléna. *An Exiled Generation: German and Hungarian Refugees of Revolution, 1848–1871.* Cambridge: Cambridge University Press, 2014.

Trautmann, Thomas R. *Languages and Nations: The Dravidian Proof in Colonial Madras.* Berkeley: University of California Press, 2006.

Trevor-Roper, Hugh R. *Europe's Physician: The Various Life of Sir Theodore de Mayerne.* New Haven: Yale University Press, 2006.

———. "A Huguenot Historian: Paul Rapin." In *Huguenots in Britain and their French Background, 1550–1800*, edited by Irene Scouloudi, 3–19. Basingstoke: Macmillan, 1987.

———. "Mayerne." *Oxford Dictionary of National Biography*, 581. Oxford: Oxford University Press, 2004.

———. "Three Foreigners." *Encounter*, Feb. 1960: 3–20.

Turner, Frederick Jackson. "The Significance of History." In *The Early Writings of Frederick Jackson Turner*, edited by Fulmer Mood. Madison: University of Wisconsin Press, 1938.

Valero Pie, Aurelia. "Metáforas del exilio: José Gaos y su experiencia del 'transtierro.'" *Revista de Hispanismo Filosófico* 18 (2013): 71–8.

Varga, Lucie. "La genèse du national-socialisme: Notes d'analyse sociale." *Annales d'Histoire Économique et Sociale* 9 (1937): 529–46.

Veblen, Thorstein. "The Intellectual Pre-Eminence of Jews in Modern Europe." *Political Science Quarterly* 34 (1919): 33–42.

Vega, Joseph Penso de la. *Confusión de Confusiones* (1688). Facsimile repr. Madrid: Sociedad de Estudios y Publicaciones, 1958.

Velde, Paul van der. "The Interpreter Interpreted: Kaempfer's Japanese Collaborator Imamura Genemon Eisei." In *The Furthest Goal: Engelbert Kaempfer's Encounter with Tokugawa Japan*, edited by

Beatrice Bodart-Bailey and Derek Massarella, 44–58. Folkestone: Japan Library, 1995.

Vermeulen, Han F. *Before Boas: The Genesis of Ethnography and Ethnology in the German Enlightenment.* Lincoln: University of Nebraska Press, 2015.

———. "The German Invention of *Völkerkunde.*" In *The German Invention of Race,* edited by Sara Eigen and Mark Larrimore, 123–46. Albany: State University of New York Press, 2006.

———. "Von der Empirie zur Theorie: Deutschsprachige Ethnographie und Ethnologie, 1740–1881." *Zeitschrift für Ethnologie* 134 (2009): 253–66.

Vincent, Bernard. *1492: L'année admirable.* Paris: Aubier, 1991.

Vucinich, Alexander. *Science in Russian Culture: A History to 1860.* Stanford: Stanford University Press, 1963.

Walbank, Frank W. *Polybius.* Berkeley: University of California Press, 1972.

Weber, Regina. "Zur Remigration des Germanisten Richard Alewyn." In *Die Emigration der Wissenschaften nach 1933,* edited by Herbert A. Strauss et al., 235–56. Munich: Saur, 1991.

Weidenfeld, George. *Remembering My Good Friends.* London: HarperCollins, 1994.

Weiner, Charles. "The Refugees and American Physics." In *The Intellectual Migration: Europe and America, 1930–1960,* edited by Donald Fleming and Bernard Bailyn, 190–228. Cambridge, MA: Harvard University Press, 1968.

Wendland, Ulrike, ed. *Biographisches Handbuch deutschsprachiger Kunsthistoriker in Exil.* Munich: Saur, 1999.

Werblowsky, R. J. Zwi. *Joseph Caro, Lawyer and Mystic* (1962). 2nd ed. Philadelphia: Jewish Publication Society of America, 1977.

Wes, Marinus A. *Michael Rostovtzeff, Historian in Exile.* Stuttgart: Steiner, 1990.

Westphal, Uwe. "German, Czech and Austrian Jews in English Publishing." In *Second Chance: Two Centuries of German-Speaking Jews in the United Kingdom,* edited by Werner E. Mosse, 195–208. Tübingen: Mohr, 1991.

Wheatland, Thomas. "Frank L. Neumann: Negotiating Political Exile." *German Historical Institute Bulletin,* suppl. 10 (2014): 111–38.

———. *The Frankfurt School in Exile*. Minneapolis: University of Minnesota Press, 2009.

Wicki, José, ed. *Tratado do Pe. Gonçalo Fernandez Trancoso sobre o hinduísmo*. Lisbon: Centro de Estudos Históricos Ultramarinos, 1973.

Widmann, Horst. *Exil und Bildungshilfe: Die deutsch-sprachige akademische Emigration in der Türkei nach 1933*. Bern: Lang, 1973.

Williams, Robert. *Art Theory: An Historical Introduction*. Oxford: Blackwell, 2004.

Williams, Robert C. *Culture in Exile: Russian Émigrés in Germany, 1881–1941*. Ithaca: Cornell University Press, 1972.

Winter, Eduard, ed. *Die deutsch-russische Begegnung und Leonard Euler*. Berlin: Akademie Verlag, 1958.

———. *Lomonosov Schlözer Pallas*. Berlin: Akademie Verlag, 1962.

Wu, Jiang. "The Taikun's Zen Master from China," *East Asian History* 38 (2014): 75–96.

Wuttke, Dieter. "Die Emigration der Kulturwissenschaftichen Bibliothek Warburg und die Anfänge des Universitätsfaches Kunstgeschichte in Grossbritannien." *Artibus et Historiae* 5 (1984): 133–46.

Yardeni, Myriam. *Le refuge huguenot: Assimilation et culture*. Paris: Champion, 2002.

———. *Le refuge protestant*. Paris: Champion, 1985.

Yerushalmi, Yosef H. *Zakhor: Jewish History and Jewish Memory*. Seattle: University of Washington Press, 1982.

Young, John T. *Faith, Medical Alchemy and Natural Philosophy: Johann Moriaen, Reformed Intelligencer, and the Hartlib Circle*. Aldershot: Ashgate, 1998.

Zandvliet, Kees. *Mapping for Money*. Amsterdam: Batavian Lion International, 1998.

Zhang, Qiong. *Making the New World Their Own: Chinese Encounters with Jesuit Science in the Age of Discovery*. Leiden: Brill, 2015.

Zhiri, Oumelbanine. *L'Afrique au miroir de l'Europe: Fortunes de Jean-Léon l'Africain à la Renaissance*. Geneva: Droz, 1991.

Ziman, John M. *Ideas Move Around Inside People*. London: Birkbeck College, 1974.

Zimmermann, Klaus. "Los aportes de Hervás a la lingüística." In *Los jesuitas españoles expulsos*, edited by Manfred Tietz and Dietrich Briesemeister, 647–68. Frankfurt: Vervuert, 2001.

Zuidervaart, Huib J., and Rob H. Van Gent, "'A Bare Outpost of Learned European Culture on the Edge of the Jungles of Java': Johan Maurits Mohr (1716–1775) and the Emergence of Instrumental and Institutional Science in Dutch Colonial Indonesia." *Isis* 95 (2004): 1–33.

Županov, Ines G. *Disputed Mission: Jesuit Experiments and Brahmanical Knowledge in Seventeenth-Century South India*. New Delhi: Oxford University Press, 1999.

Zwilling, Leonard, ed. *Mission to Tibet*. Boston: Wisdom Publishers, 2010.

INDEX

THE
MENAHEM STERN JERUSALEM
LECTURES
Sponsored by the HISTORICAL SOCIETY OF ISRAEL
and published for BRANDEIS UNIVERSITY PRESS
by UNIVERSITY PRESS OF NEW ENGLAND

Peter Burke, *Exiles and Expatriates in the History of Knowledge, 1500–2000*
Paul R. Katz, *Religion in China and Its Modern Fate*
Richard J. Evans, *Altered Pasts: Counterfactuals in History*
Patrick J. Geary, *Language and Power in the Early Middle Ages*
G. W. Bowersock, *Empires in Collision in Late Antiquity*
Sanjay Subrahmanyam, *Three Ways to Be Alien: Travails and Encounters in the Early Modern World*
Jürgen Kocka, *Civil Society and Dictatorship in Modern German History*
Heinz Schilling, *Early Modern European Civilization and Its Political and Cultural Dynamism*
Brian Stock, *Ethics through Literature: Ascetic and Aesthetic Reading in Western Culture*
Fergus Millar, *The Roman Republic in Political Thought*
Peter Brown, *Poverty and Leadership in the Later Roman Empire*
Anthony D. Smith, *The Nation in History: Historiographical Debates about Ethnicity and Nationalism*
Carlo Ginzburg, *History, Rhetoric, and Proof*